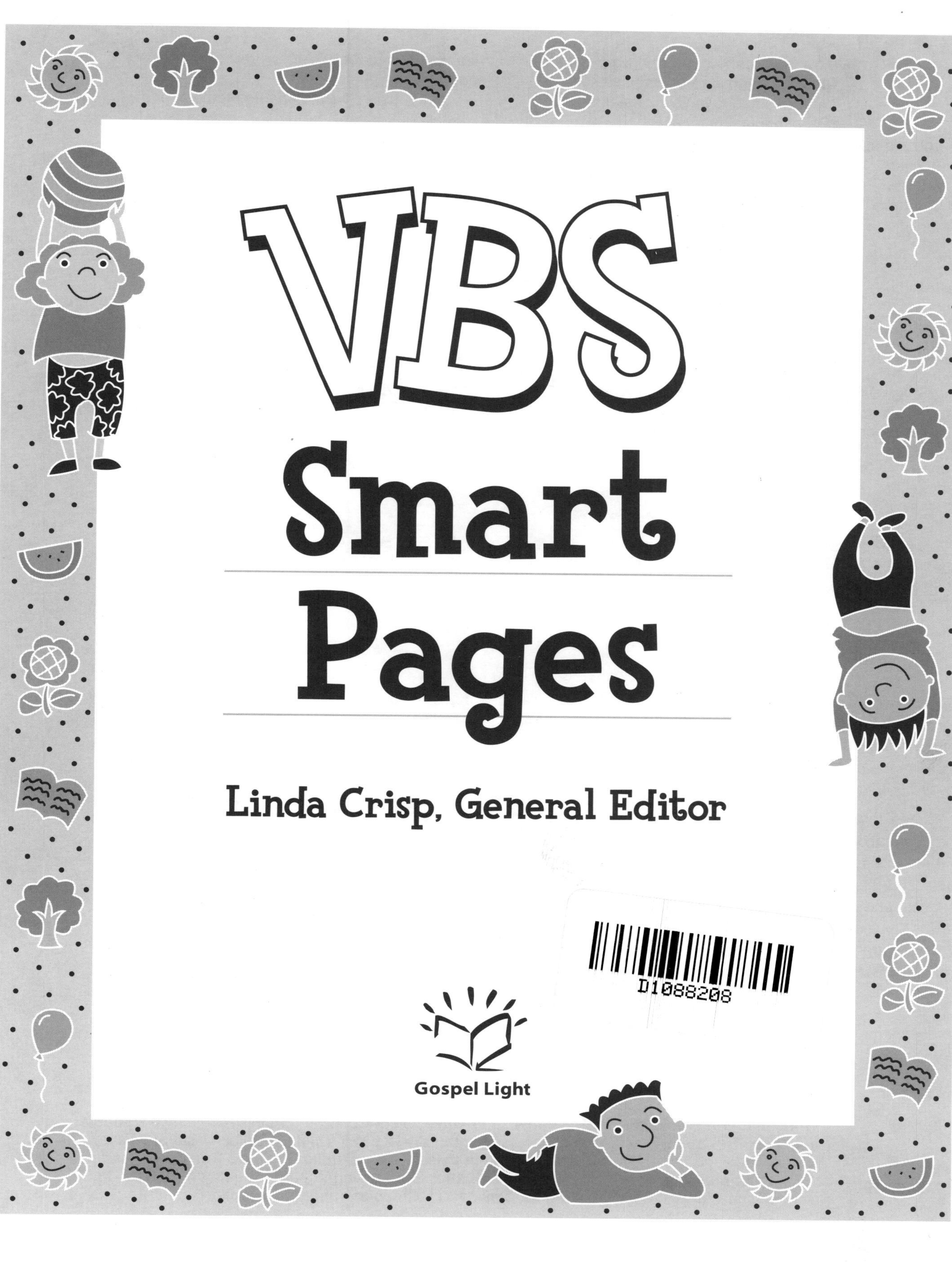

VBS Smart Pages

Linda Crisp, General Editor

Gospel Light

HOW TO MAKE CLEAN COPIES FROM THIS BOOK

Gospel Light VBS

William T. Greig, Publisher • **Dr. Elmer L. Towns,** Senior Consulting Publisher • **Billie Baptiste,** Publisher, Research, Planning and Development • **Christy Weir,** Senior Editor • **Bayard Taylor, M.Div.,** Editor, Theological and Biblical Issues • **Linda Crisp,** General Editor • **Linda Bossoletti,** Assistant Editor • **Karen Stimer,** Assistant Editor • **Margie Buster,** Contributing Writer • **Wesley Haystead, M.S.Ed.,** Contributing Writer • **Carolyn Thomas,** Designer • **Chizuko Yasuda,** Illustrator

Contents

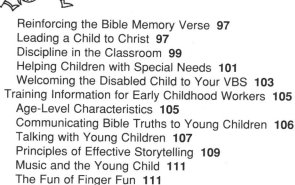

Dear VBS Director,

CONGRATULATIONS! You have been chosen (or maybe dragged, kicking and screaming) to take on the very important job of Vacation Bible School Director. For the next six to nine months you will be involved in praying, planning, purchasing, proactively recruiting, preparing, promoting, pointing, possibly panicking and definitely praising. Sounds fun, doesn't it? Actually, it is! In fact, when asked a few months after VBS is over, many first-time directors agree to direct VBS the next year.

If you are a first-time director, be assured that although planning a VBS will require your time and attention, you can do it! Remain confident that God has chosen you to be part of touching and ministering to the lives of children in your church and your community. What a privilege and an honor! That's the first key to running a successful VBS program.

The second key to having a great VBS program is planning. That's where this book comes in! We will take you through each part of planning, in ten easy-to-follow steps, so that by the time your VBS date approaches, you will be prepared for almost anything. This book was specifically written for you by people who have learned much from their successes and failures. To get the most out of this wealth of knowledge and information, we would suggest you skim over the entire book first; then carefully read each step individually.

One last word of advice: Always keep in mind the purpose of your program—leading children into a personal relationship with Jesus Christ. Don't get so caught up in the hustle and bustle of doing God's work that you forget about God's heart. Love the kids He brings your way. Yours may be the only hug they receive that day. As colaborers in Christ, we want to thank you for saying "yes" to being a part of God's work in your part of the world. May the Lord bless you in the coming months and may you have the best VBS ever!

Why Should You Have Vacation Bible School?

The term "VBS" is probably one of the most familiar acronyms found in churches across the United States today. But what exactly does it mean? To those who are unfamiliar with Vacation Bible School, it sounds like an oxymoron. How can the word "vacation," synonymous with "fun," be used to describe the word "school," synonymous with "work"? To better understand the meaning and unique value of Vacation Bible School, it is helpful to look at its history and how it has evolved over the years.

VBS Has a Rich History

Surprisingly enough, the earliest record of Vacation Bible School dates back to the 1860s. However, it wasn't until the 1890s that this outreach began to become organized. Eliza Hawes could well be called the pioneer of Vacation Bible School. In 1898, Mrs. Hawes, superintendent of the children's department at the Epiphany Baptist Church in New York City, became interested in her city's East Side slum children. She began a summer program that included worship music, Bible stories and verse memorization, nature study, games, crafts, drawing and even cooking and sewing. The program lasted six weeks each summer and was held in the only place she could find to rent—a beer parlor! She ran this program for seven years until she moved away.

Dr. Robert Boville, who worked for the Baptist Mission Society, recommended Mrs. Hawes's program to many churches and thus "officially" set in motion the VBS movement. The idea met with overwhelming success. In fact, Dr. Boville started a national and later an international Vacation Bible School association.

In those same pre-World-War-I-years, the Lutheran and Reformed churches established summer Bible and language schools primarily for Swedish immigrant children. Though eventually those schools were discontinued, it is interesting to note that by 1960 the Lutheran church documented 3,000 established VBS programs. The Lutheran church used VBS both to augment what children learned in Sunday School and to acquaint unchurched children with the gospel and with Sunday School. These two goals are still the major emphases of most VBS programs.

The Presbyterian church adopted VBS as part of its Christian Education program in 1910 and the Northern Baptist Convention did the same in 1915. A 94-year-old Baptist woman, Mrs. Nancy Hodgson, recalled teaching Vacation Bible School from 1930 to 1950. She said, "The kids loved it! There were outdoor games to play; they learned fun songs and sang in a program at the end. For several years we got students from California Bible School to come for two weeks and tell the Bible stories to the kids. They often stayed in my home. We usually had at least 50 to 60 kids at our little church. Eventually, in the 1940s, we made flannelgraph pictures to tell the stories with."

Standard Publishing company was the first independent publisher to produce VBS materials. Prior to this, nearly all churches created their own. Since then many other publishers have begun producing new VBS materials every year. Gospel Light Publications, which began in 1933, first offered a VBS curriculum in 1951 and currently supplies tens of thousands of churches with new and up-to-date materials each year.

From a program designed to reach slum children in turn-of-the-century New York City, VBS has developed into a meaningful part of the church's total Christian education ministry. In fact, a majority of churches attest that Vacation Bible School has been the single most strategic and effective outreach in leading people to Christ and bringing new families into their congregations. Using those carefree, unhurried summer months to reach children for Christ has proven to bear rich fruit for the kingdom of God. We think Mrs. Hawes would be delighted.

VBS Presents an Exciting Opportunity Today

Over the past three decades, the basic Vacation Bible School program has expanded to include a wide variety of different methods. But the purpose has remained the same—to reach people of all ages with the gospel of Jesus Christ and to help people become His disciples. What sets VBS apart from Sunday School in fulfilling that purpose is the emphasis on learning essential Bible truths in an "out-of-the-ordinary," fun way in order to attract churched and unchurched children and the continuity offered by consecutive days of teaching on a single concept or theme.

In regard to creative learning, "the sky is the limit." However, the backbone of VBS is the time of concentrated Bible study in which a Bible story, passage or concept is taught—always with an evangelism emphasis in which the gospel message is clearly presented. The extended hours of VBS also provide a unique opportunity to reinforce and bring to life important biblical concepts through various activities. Some of these activities may feature exciting games, stimulating crafts, fun music and, of course, yummy snacks!

The challenge of VBS is to relay essential Bible truths in fresh, fun ways without sacrificing content; but that is also the incredible opportunity of VBS—to pass on truths to the next generation in a time frame and a format that are unique. Christian publishers and churches have come up with a variety of different options and methods to achieve this goal. This book will help you explore the many alternatives and ways to approach Vacation Bible School to make it the life-changing adventure in Bible learning it can be.

Evaluating Your VBS Options

Shopping for ideas for your Vacation Bible School program is much like shopping for a car. There are so many wonderful models to choose from, it's almost overwhelming! Not only are there models to choose from but there are also countless lists of options upon which to decide. The key to surviving this decision-making process is to be well-informed about what's available and then find the right program for you and your church. This chapter will help you sort through and evaluate different formats, activities and curriculum options so that you can discover what kind of VBS you would like to direct.

Scheduling

The first stop on your VBS journey is your church calendar. Keep in mind the group or groups of people you will be trying to reach—the dates you choose will affect your ability to reach that target audience.

Here are some other things to consider:

- Be considerate of other church functions—look for weeks with little or no daily activities planned in the facilities you will need.
- Identify local school vacations, breaks and camps.
- Determine the normal pattern of family vacations based on past Sunday School attendance.
- If you are planning a family VBS or one that includes adults, consider holidays, weekends or weeknights.
- If you are dealing with year-round school, choose either the school break which frees the greatest number of children or the hours immediately after the school day. If your church has had VBS before, ask former directors what worked best for them in the past.
- Consider the availability of volunteers. Do the majority of families in your church have parents who both work? If so, you might opt for having Vacation Bible School in the evenings or on weekends. If you have a large pool of teenagers or college students, you may want to consider the beginning of summer, before summer jobs are found. If you are fortunate enough to have a good group of retired adults, plan your VBS around their scheduled church activities.

The important thing to remember is that there is no "right" or "wrong" when it comes to scheduling your Vacation Bible School—the personalization is what makes it *yours*. However, wise planning choices at this stage can boost your outreach potential from "better" to "best." The ideas listed below will help spark your creativity as you consider your many scheduling options. Have fun choosing the one that's right for you!

Daytime

Because Vacation Bible School is usually held during the summer, the daily schedule can vary a great deal. Daytime has been the traditional choice because children and young people tend to be most available and alert then. Mornings are good because they are generally cooler. Afternoons work just as well, however, especially where the climate is moderate or the facilities are "weather appropriate."

Evening

An evening VBS opens up greater possibilities for recruiting adult staff. However, it limits the amount of time available due to work schedules, dinner and bedtimes. Some churches start each session with a simple meal that provides children and staff a time for casual fellowship and enables an earlier start. An evening VBS works well for an intergenerational program.

Summer Sundays (Children's Church)

A VBS program can be a fun and exciting alternative to the regular Sunday School and Children's Church format. Many churches use this plan as a break for both Sunday School teachers and kids. It also tends to make the summer seem extra special by providing a change of pace from traditional church activities. Plan to use VBS lessons for a three-hour session each Sunday throughout the summer. If you have only one-hour sessions or wish to extend a five-day VBS curriculum, divide the lesson activities and review the Bible story.

Backyard Bible Schools

You can take VBS to your community through Backyard Bible Schools. These are miniature versions of VBS held in homes whose hosts serve as contacts with their neighborhoods. A Backyard Bible School is a wonderful evangelistic tool. Many children who do not attend church may feel more comfortable in the familiar surroundings of a neighbor's backyard than at the church. And hosting one is an ideal way for Christian families to minister within their own neighborhoods. If you lack a permanent facility for a VBS, this is a tremendously effective alternative.

As with the traditional Vacation Bible School, the key to a successful Backyard Bible School is planning, promoting, enlisting and then training your staff in the proper use of the material. For complete information on how to carry out a Backyard Bible School, see pages 41-42.

Mission VBS

This type of VBS takes your program "on-the-road" to minister to communities that aren't able to provide their own. Churches have gone to inner-city neighborhoods, Indian reservations, orphanages and churches in neighboring countries, translating the materials as necessary. Some do this as a follow-up to their own VBS, using the same volunteers. Others use it as an exciting mission project for high-school youth or college students, training those who serve as well as reaching the lost. Contact your church's missions department for information and coordination.

VBS Camp

A camp or retreat is a wonderful way to combine enjoyable camping activities with time for Bible learning.

 Day Camp

With some creative planning, you can use your VBS in a day camp format at your church facility or other location in your community. Extend the length of your VBS program by having children bring sack lunches. Then head out on daily field trips. Meet at a park, camp, forest preserve or farm. You can even use VBS materials to plan a complete day camp program at your church facilities.

 Resident Camp

Camping in the outdoors takes students away from familiar surroundings to the adventure of new discoveries. Adapt the theme setting and course materials to provide a variety of activities throughout the day. Use your VBS theme to plan decorations, costumes, crafts and snacks.

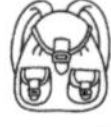 Weekend Retreat

Plan a weekend retreat at your church or rent a local camping facility or resort. Invite children or whole families to participate in an action-packed, two-day event. Alter and combine two or three normal VBS sessions for Saturday morning, afternoon (after lunch) and evening (after dinner), and one or two sessions for Sunday.

Intergenerational VBS

The families of your church and community will thoroughly enjoy participating in an intergenerational VBS. Instead of the traditional VBS which focuses separately on the different age levels, an intergenerational VBS brings family members together for parts—or even all—of your VBS activities. With the traditional VBS, parents either send their children, drop them off or go to another part of the building for "grown-up" activities. At an intergenerational VBS, parents and children have the opportunity to participate together in activities specially designed to strengthen family relationships.

In today's busy, fragmented world, few families have many opportunities to work, learn and laugh together. Even less likely for most families are times of exploring solid, practical guidance for improving the quality of daily family living. An intergenerational VBS is an effective means of attracting families to come together for fun and growth. For detailed information on how to plan this unique event and a variety of ideas on adapting your VBS materials see the *Intergenerational VBS Planning Guide* on pages 43-46.

There's More...

Terrific Tuesdays, Wacky Wednesdays, Tremendous Thursdays or Super Saturdays

Choose one day per week for a VBS program. If you have a large number of children and a limited number of volunteers, schedule a different day of the week for each age group. For example, Wednesdays could be just for preschoolers, Thursdays for younger elementary and Fridays for older elementary.

The 3-3-3 Plan

Many families take long weekends and are unavailable for the Monday or Friday of a traditional VBS. Using the 3-3-3 plan, VBS is held Tuesday, Wednesday and Thursday for three weeks. You will need to provide nine lessons.

Family Nights

One night every other week throughout the summer families gather for a special event. Use VBS lessons for your curriculum.

Split Week A.M./P.M.

Plan a two-week VBS. The first week is held in the daytime and the second week in the evening.

Split Season

Offer a traditional VBS in the summer and additional days (up to a week) for winter or spring breaks. (This is especially effective for churches who have children in a year-round school schedule.)

All Day Saturday

Plan a special Saturday event from 9:00 a.m. to 7:00 p.m. Use three Bible lessons in addition to a variety of VBS activities, including a promotion day fair. People can come and go as they wish or stay for the entire day. This idea may also be used late in August as a kickoff for your fall programming.

Just for Kids

This is an evangelistic event, usually on a Saturday morning. Once each quarter, children are urged to bring their friends to a special event. As an added treat, a special movie, magician, puppets, etc., can be brought in to entertain the children. Use VBS lessons and pass out evangelistic booklets.

And the List Goes On

Other variations on VBS include every day or evening for one or two weeks, once a week for five weeks, twice a week for five weeks, once a week for 10 weeks, younger children in the morning and older ones in the afternoon, a VBS only for preschoolers with a parenting class for moms and dads. There is no end to the possibilities! VBS materials are uniquely suited to all kinds of adaptations. Who knows where your VBS can go?

Activities

This section will help you decide the types of activities you want to include in your VBS. Much of this depends on the curriculum you choose. However, knowing which VBS activities are important to you will help you as you evaluate your curriculum options.

Bible Study

The most essential and important component of Vacation Bible School is the Bible. Teaching principles and making life applications from the Word of God are ultimately what VBS is all about. Plan the Bible study segment carefully to allow a sufficient amount of time for the different age groups. The time will vary from 15 to 20 minutes for preschoolers to 30 minutes to an hour for older children. Included in this Bible study time should be a Bible story or Bible passage and a life application. Be careful not to compromise this time for other activities. For helpful information on choosing curriculum, see pages 15-16.

Crafts

Crafts have always been a popular activity at VBS. They are another effective tool in reinforcing Bible learning, as long as they are well chosen. Make the craft time effective by using conversation that helps the pupil relate the craft to the Bible lesson. Allow students to take the crafts home each day or display them at the end of VBS. Another option is to choose one large project that the older children can work on each day, such as a diorama. The important thing to remember is that the *process* of creating, not the end product, is what counts. Make craft time an enjoyable, not stressful, learning time. For more information on planning your craft time, see *For the Craft Coordinator* on pages 72-76.

Music

Music is another important part of VBS. It is a highly effective tool in reinforcing Bible concepts and memorizing Bible verses. Providing a time of group singing is essential in creating a unified spirit and building excitement. The usual time for group singing is during an opening assembly. The assembly should also include a general greeting, announcements, prayer and the introduction (or review) of the day's lessons. Some churches also include skits, team cheers, mini-devotions, missions presentations, contests and special music during this time. You may even choose to have both an opening and a closing assembly. Many VBS programs also schedule a separate class time for learning and performing songs.

The choice of songs will depend on the curriculum. Most prepackaged VBS materials provide cassettes, CDs and music books with unique songs that reinforce the week's theme. Some also include hand motions, choreography and drama to go along with the music.

Many churches conclude their VBS with a musical program on the last evening. This is an exciting way to end VBS, especially when the parents are invited. It displays and reviews what the children have been learning, and it gives the VBS staff an opportunity to make contact with parents. For more information on planning your VBS music, see *For the Music Director* on pages 77-79.

Bible Learning Activities

The goal of Bible learning activities is simply to reinforce what the students have been learning throughout the day. Repetition is an excellent tool for helping ideas and concepts sink into the minds of both children and adults. Provide fun activities, contests and creative games that challenge students to learn Bible memory verses word for word. Plan a science or object-lesson center where children can gain hands-on experience to help them grasp Bible truths. Set up a history center where children can learn what it was like to live in Bible times. These are just a few of the learning activities that you can use to your advantage. The key is to make each one a fun learning experience!

Recreation or Free Time

It is wise to include an organized break time in the schedule for any VBS program that is two hours or longer. If not, one will probably happen anyway. Children, and adults too, need a chance to shake off their restlessness and move around. A break time also provides a nice change of pace in activities. There are countless game books to help you plan your recreation. The ideal place for recreation is outside or in a large gym. If you choose to make this a free play time, set boundaries and have plenty of supervision. Make sure that you plan enough time for the children to get their wiggles out but not so much that it is hard for them to make the transition into a sedentary activity. Many churches combine snack time and recreation time to allow children to eat and play outdoors. For more information, see *For the Recreation Coordinator*, page 84.

Snacks

Snack time is an important part of any VBS that runs three hours or longer. It serves two purposes: it refuels children's energy levels and it provides a nice social break for them to enjoy. Have parents or other volunteers in the church provide batches of homemade or store-bought goodies.

Many churches make snack time a learning time. They allow children to work together to make or assemble the snack. Children's cookbooks can give you loads of fun ideas to go along with your theme. Plus, most of the published curriculums come with their own assortment of suggested snacks for children to make. For more information on planning your snack time, see *For the Snack Coordinator* on pages 82-83.

Others

A variety of other activities can also be chosen, such as puppets, drama, working around the church building, a VBS store with prizes given for reciting memory verses or completing certain tasks, a quiet time or a journal time. Keep in mind that all these activities should fit in with your overall VBS goals.

Curriculum

Now that you have seen the range of activities available, you can make an informed decision on curriculum. There are basically two choices: purchase a packaged kit from a publisher (denominational or independent) or write your own. First we will take a brief look at the advantages and disadvantages of each. Then we will discuss some criteria to use in evaluating your curriculum choices.

Prepackaged Kits vs. Creating Your Own

If you are a first-time director, we would highly recommend that you first look into the published VBS curriculums. With all that goes into planning a VBS, writing your own curriculum will probably be overwhelming. So, unless you have a lot of time and a creative team of experienced VBS leaders who can write, and write well, stick with the "relatively easier" road of the prepackaged kit option.

Prepackaged Kits

Advantages:

* Provide a theme, all-inclusive lessons and ideas for other learning activities.
* Offer related promotional items for purchase.
* Often come with support and training options if needed.
* Are usually written by experienced people who test-market and know what works best.
* Are usually easy for volunteers to understand and carry out.

Disadvantages:

* Could be costly, depending on what is ordered.
* Are not written specifically for your church or denomination.

Creating Your Own

Advantages:

* Can be personalized to fit the needs of your unique denomination, church size and community profile.
* Will probably cost less, excluding time and effort to write it.

Disadvantages:

* Takes time to create and write.
* May be difficult for volunteers to understand.
* May be difficult to find related publicity and support items.

Evaluating Curriculum

The first step in choosing a curriculum is finding out what's available. There are many independent publishers and denominations that advertise in Christian magazines and supply Bible bookstores. Ask your local Bible bookstore to direct you to possible resources.

Most publishers allow you to examine their VBS kits for thirty days before making a decision. Use this time to skim over all the materials and listen to the music. The decision you make will be based partly on the appeal of the theme, music, crafts, etc. However, there are other, more crucial, criteria you'll need to take into consideration. Ask yourself the following questions as you sort through the endless possibilities of VBS curriculums.

Biblical Foundation

1. Are the lessons Biblically based? Do they teach the Word of God?
2. Read over the publisher's doctrinal statement. Check with church leadership on any questions or concerns.
3. Do the materials present a salvation message? Is the gospel message concise, clear and appropriately presented?
4. Does the content relate to children who have already accepted Christ and need guidance for spiritual growth?
5. Does the material provide devotions or spiritual guidance for the teachers or volunteers?

Theme Continuity

1. Examine the learning activities, crafts, music, games, etc. Do they reinforce the lesson focus and teaching aim?
2. Will the theme captivate the students' attention?

Relevance

1. Review the learning objectives and aims for all lessons. Do the aims correlate with the Bible story? Are they relevant to the age and life needs of the student?
2. Study the life-application sections at the end of the Bible story. Are the learning objectives related to the life application?
3. Is the content sensitive to a variety of real-life problems? Does it use modern-day vocabulary?
4. Are the lesson activities interactive and fun?
5. Do they provide a wide variety of learning activities to meet the different learning styles?

Teachability

1. Review one lesson from each age level. Are the lessons age-appropriate?
2. Are the lesson plans organized clearly and easy to follow?
3. Do the lessons give helpful hints for teachers?
4. Are visual aids and enhancement resources available?
5. Do the instructions include sketches and illustrations to make it user-friendly?
6. Is the material well-written and grammatically correct?

Attractiveness

1. Is the material neat and organized?
2. Are the art, layout and style up-to-date and appealing?

Once you have decided on the curriculum that you think will work best for you and your church, you should get the approval of your church leader(s). Keep the VBS catalog and publisher's phone number handy for ordering additional materials.

Small Church Tips

Most VBS curriculums are written for an average-sized attendance of 50 to 150 children. The biggest challenge for smaller churches seems to be in the area of resources—facilities, volunteers and materials. Consider the following suggestions:

Combine with other churches to provide an area-wide VBS. Choose a neutral community site or use a larger church with appropriate facilities. This kind of cooperation can be a tremendous testimony to the entire area.

Use VBS as "Summer Sundays," replacing the traditional Sunday School/Children's Church format. This can be effective if combined with an adult outreach in your church. And don't be afraid to hold this outdoors! (See p. 11.)

Be creative in adapting the materials. If you don't have enough volunteers for skits, use puppets. If you can't change rooms for different activities, mark off various areas with posters, masking tape on the floor, etc., to create room "divisions" in the space you have. Incorporate the life-skills of people within your congregation to create your own craft and game ideas. Call a Saturday "Jump-Start Day" and let the entire church family help with decorations, name tags, scenery, craft or lesson preparations that need to be made.

Hold Backyard Bible Schools, especially if your facilities are limited. This not only expands your outreach but also allows for multiple use of many of the materials. Hold the classes on consecutive weeks rather than simultaneously, especially if your pool of teachers is limited. (See pp. 41-42.)

Consider an intergenerational program involving the whole church family in an evening program. It can be done for an entire week or one night a week throughout the summer. This could be another opportunity to combine with sister churches in the area. (See pp. 43-46.)

Most of all, take advantage of the opportunities to develop one-on-one relationships with the children. The less-hurried pace of a smaller group allows for more of the interaction and nurture that are the whole purpose of VBS.

Large Church Tips

Planning

Good planning is absolutely vital in a large-church context. You will need to begin at least 24 to 32 weeks early with preliminary details such as curriculum overview, leadership recruitment and calendar deadline commitments. You will also need to establish the dates and determine the location for your VBS. Since most large churches have complex church calendars with numerous programs and ministries, you will need to inform the church staff and confirm a commitment from them for your VBS dates.

Make it a priority to establish and maintain good communication with all areas of the church affected by your plans. VBS may be one of several children's ministry options offered during the summer months and could certainly be the largest, utilizing all age groups and ministries within the church family. Cooperation and interaction are crucial.

Always keep the child in mind as you plan. One of the greatest challenges in dealing with large VBS efforts is assuring that every child walking through the door receives individualized attention to nurture the opportunity of salvation and growth in Christ. This goal frequently seems to be in conflict with managing an efficient and well-organized VBS. Commit to seeing each child and not simply the total numbers. It can be done.

Recruitment and Staff Organization

As we all know, the success of any endeavor depends greatly on its leadership. A large VBS is best managed by breaking its staff down into departments headed by good, qualified leaders. This breakdown can be specialized to fit the needs of your own program but is most effective if done by age groupings and by tasks. A large VBS attendance may require splitting age groups, which in turn will require more staffing. Recruiting one person to oversee each age department is an efficient way to handle a large staff.

Your team of department leaders will need to be assembled early, as they will need to develop their own subcommittees within their areas of responsibility. Make sure you meet with your department leaders often in order to keep the overall ministry picture and vision for the VBS effort on track.

Working with large numbers of children sometimes encourages a warehouse or assembly line approach to planning. Creativity is often squelched or not even attempted; and efficiency, rather than imagination, becomes the common denominator to planning. Allowing time for your staff to brainstorm encourages dreaming with no rules or barriers. Although dreams may eventually have to meet the reality of large numbers of children, the creative base to plan from will provide enthusiasm and cohesiveness for the program. For more complete information on recruiting staff, see *Staffing*, pages 31-36.

Facilities

Adapting Adult-Use Rooms

Facilities can pose problems for a large-effort VBS, especially when you must use the space which normally services adults and contains only adult furniture. Here are some ideas that have worked for others.

* Have children stand around adult-sized tables to do crafts and hands-on activities. Use the tables as centers.
* For teacher-directed times—students doing Bible pages or listening to teachers—fold in the table legs and place tables on the floor. This allows space so that teachers and children may sit on the floor. For the sake of comfort, a carpeted room would be most suitable.
* Remove adult chairs, especially folding chairs, from the large room needed for the Bible story presentation or missions education. Arrange beach mats, beach towels or quilts (depending on your VBS theme) on the floor; or make circles with masking tape to direct children where to sit.

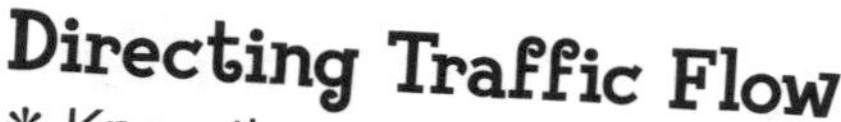

Directing Traffic Flow

* Know the capacity of each room being used. As numbers grow in registration, be sure a department is not overflowing its assigned rooms.
* Designate which doors are to be used for entering and exiting of individual rooms. This is especially true of an activity center VBS.
* Arrange traffic patterns for moving children from one classroom site to another. Walk this through to make sure it works.
* Train your entire staff in the established traffic flow pattern, the use of department maps and giving tours to disoriented students and parents.
* Post a facility directory at multiple sites around your church campus. Be sure to list room locations and ages of children. Make it clear and user-friendly to the newcomer to VBS.

Registration

Use at least two registrars to lead this area—one for actual students and one for those children of staff members outside the age groupings of VBS whether they be nursery, preschool or seventh grade.

Each registrar should recruit his or her own department secretaries. These secretaries will begin their work the month before VBS, coordinating child placement and making children's name tags. They are also responsible for attendance counts and offering totals during VBS. For more complete registration information, see pages 120-123.

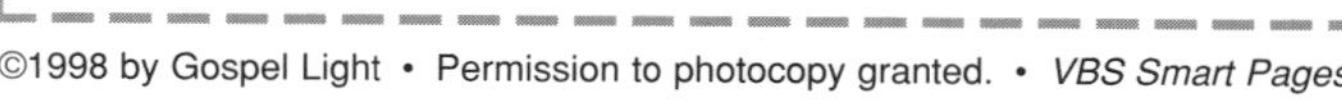

Groupings and Schedules

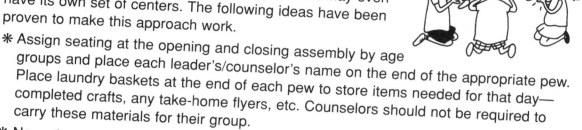

Large VBS efforts are ideally suited to the activity center approach. This approach differs from a VBS using individual classrooms only in that children move to separate sites for Bible story, missions, crafts, music, snack/recreation and Bible memory verse. In a large VBS, each department may even have its own set of centers. The following ideas have been proven to make this approach work.

- Assign seating at the opening and closing assembly by age groups and place each leader's/counselor's name on the end of the appropriate pew. Place laundry baskets at the end of each pew to store items needed for that day—completed crafts, any take-home flyers, etc. Counselors should not be required to carry these materials for their group.
- Name tags are essential for a large VBS. Each child's name tag should clearly show the child's name and his or her counselor's name. Color code name tags by department or sub-grouping.
- Use young people from your church as helpers. Some can assist children in primary grades with reading, cutting, etc. Older ones (those proven in character and spiritual maturity) are often helpful in co-counseling the 3rd and 4th grade Middler Department. For more helpful information, see *Using Teen Helpers*, pages 35-36.
- Set up a good support system. Each department should have its own secretary and superintendent to support its teachers and workers. A 20-minute staff meeting before the day begins would do much to smooth out problems and keep the team spirit high. It would also be beneficial for each department to have an office where issues could be handled by the support staff as they arose.

Special Needs and Procedures

Parking Lots

Parking lots can be a real challenge when children are being dropped off or picked up from VBS. Cone off curbing so cars must park in the proper places. If possible, have monitors in the parking lot to encourage the use of parking spaces and to discourage any dangerous dropping off and picking up of children.

Staff Lounges

Staff lounges provide wonderful break times of good refreshment and fellowship throughout the day. For a large staff, if possible, provide several lounges in various areas. All that is needed are tables and chairs and access to a kitchen sink and refrigerator. A more adult menu of breads, dip and vegetables, cut-up fruit, iced tea, and chips and salsa may be served. The most important component in providing meaningful breaks for your VBS staff is a gracious hostess.

Step 3

Preliminary Planning Tips

Once you have decided on the kind of VBS you would like to have, you will be ready—and hopefully excited—to get started. But before you dive in, make sure you have all of the life-saving equipment you'll need. This chapter will help prepare you with the not-so-obvious but essential tools you will need for your VBS journey.

The first two most valuable tools are prayer support and staff support. There are also some important preliminary steps you will need to address, so don't skip this chapter!

Establish a Prayer Base

As with any task you undertake, the most important thing you can do is pray. The responsibilities of your position are great, but so are your resources in Christ. God is "able to do immeasurably more than all we ask or imagine, according to His power that is at work within us" (Ephesians 3:20). Prayer should be a part of every decision you make and every task you perform. Without it, you won't experience all that God can do in and through your VBS. You could even be heading for trouble.

Make it a priority to establish a prayer base for your VBS. Be bold in asking others to pray. Enlist a team of people who otherwise may not be involved in VBS—perhaps seniors in your church or existing prayer groups or chains. Present this team early on as your "vanguard volunteers"—people who will go before you, committing to pray daily/weekly for the various facets of VBS from the moment planning begins until the final follow-up is completed. The group need not be large—only faithful. Two or three committed prayer warriors will make an incredible difference. Keep them informed of your goals, the names of committee members/volunteers as they are added and tasks and special needs as they arise.

Work to keep VBS before your church staff for prayer in their weekly meetings. Well-timed notes with progress reports and answers to prayer already received will do so much to build the sense that VBS is a whole-church effort, not just "something for the kids."

You shouldn't have any problem coming up with specific requests as your planning gets under way, but here are some suggestions to get you started:

* wisdom in all aspects of planning your church's VBS;
* God's guidance, wisdom and peace in your own life;
* volunteers with willing spirits to minister to the children;
* preparation of the hearts of the children who will attend your VBS;
* for many to come to know Christ.

FIRST-TIMER TIP

If you have never been to a VBS, it is a good idea to visit other programs and talk with the directors to get some good pointers.

Enlist a Dedicated VBS Committee

One important key to survival, especially for first-time directors, is don't try to do everything by yourself! Your job is to delegate responsibilities so that you are free to oversee the entire program. If you allow yourself to get involved leading any one area, you will lose the ability to coordinate the big picture.

One way to share the load is to form a VBS committee. Committee members will help oversee specific areas, contribute ideas and solutions to problems and help in recruiting. It is a good idea to begin by choosing an assistant director with whom you can work comfortably. His or her primary duty will be to assist you in all your responsibilities. Oftentimes, this person will be next year's Director. The other committee members should be the department leaders who will supervise all departmental activities and help recruit age-level staff.

To form your VBS committee, look for individuals in your church who meet the following criteria:

* is growing in his or her Christian walk;
* demonstrates gifts, talents or abilities in the area he or she may oversee;
* is dependable, able to follow through on his or her commitments;
* has experience working with children and/or volunteers;
* is flexible, open to accepting others' ideas.

While all these qualities are not necessary for every VBS volunteer, you will want people of this caliber on your leadership committee. For tips on how to go about recruiting your team, see pages 31-32.

One alternative to a VBS committee is a team of two or three codirectors. Many churches successfully run their VBS programs in this manner.

Most people would agree that being a codirector is much less demanding than being the "VBS Director." However, it is essential to divide clearly the leadership tasks among your fellow codirectors. It is also a good idea to have one codirector be the spokesperson. This individual will serve as the contact person for the church body and should always be updated on the status of your VBS planning. Codirectors will need to meet together often to ensure that responsibilities are being covered and work isn't being duplicated.

Once you have a committee of at least two or three people, plan an informal meeting at your house or your church. Invite members to review the VBS curriculum, watch the VBS preview video together (if available), suggest names of prospective volunteers, brainstorm new ideas, delegate responsibilities, review goals, pray and establish the dates of your VBS. Allow your creative juices to flow...and have fun!

FIRST-TIMER TIP

Plan ahead! Start making plans for VBS well in advance, about nine months ahead of time. This allows you more time to take care of details and will help to eliminate last-minute stress.

Take the Time to Set Goals

This is another important step in the initial planning of VBS. Clearly defined goals are absolutely essential. They provide motivation and direction for the people involved in the program and help ensure that you accomplish your intended purpose.

Sadly, some churches seem to just "drift" in their VBS programs. They may have started out with a clearly defined purpose but have somehow lost track. Not surprisingly, their results are equally unclear. Don't let this happen to you! Take time to think about your goals. If you have trouble with this, begin by envisioning the kind of VBS you want to look back on at the end of the summer. What do you want to be able to say at that closing assembly or volunteer picnic or church staff meeting that this VBS accomplished?

FIRST-TIMER TIP

If possible, meet with former VBS directors and volunteers from your church. Oftentimes there are church traditions or rules that you may not be aware of and which are not included in the curriculum. Don't expect former volunteers to approach you with this information, as many of them will assume that you know.

That simple exercise should help you define what you want to accomplish and why. These "larger goals" will serve to unite and motivate your entire team. They may include such things as:

- to help children come to know Jesus Christ;
- to reach out to the community around your church;
- to teach the Bible so that both churched and unchurched children can understand;
- to educate children about missions;
- to enrich the lives of every family represented by your VBS students.

But that is not enough. Next you need to determine how you are going to *meet* each one of those goals. These more specific goals will provide direction for individual tasks, so they need to be both realistic and measurable. Some examples of specific goals are:

- to present the gospel to ___ new families in your community;
- to increase attendance of unchurched children by ___% over last year;
- to help each child learn ___ Bible verses;
- to make a follow-up contact with each unchurched child within ___ week(s) of VBS;
- to have volunteers from every age group represented on your VBS staff.

Include your leadership team in all this. Brainstorm, dream, pray together. Keep in mind the strengths and weaknesses of your church and the needs of your community. But don't be afraid to aim high. Remember the saying, "Aim at nothing and you'll hit it every time." Ask God to show you what He wants to do in and through your VBS program.

Then you must articulate your goals. Write them down. Communicate them to the rest of your VBS staff, church leaders and the congregation. Continually look at them on your countdown to VBS. It is easy to get caught up in both the mundane details and the fun aspects of VBS and lose sight of the larger goals. In the end you will agree that determining where you are going, why you are headed in that direction and how you are going to get there is time well spent, indeed.

FIRST-TIMER TIP

Don't be afraid to launch new ideas. Remember, you are the director. Sometimes the best VBS is the one that breaks the mold. However, make sure you get the approval of your church leaders before implementing changes.

Determine the Date

Once you have determined your goals, the next step is to establish the date(s) your VBS will take place. Families today are planning their vacations six months to a year ahead of time; so, if you are planning to have your VBS in the summer, try to announce the date by the beginning of the year. If you still aren't sure about dates, reread the scheduling section on pages 10-12. Remember to look at your personal calendar as well as the church calendar. One word of caution—with the exception of your VBS committee, don't ask your VBS volunteers to vote on the "best" date. There is no way you will be able to please everyone, and, most likely, it will only create resentment.

After you have picked the date(s), clear it with the rest of the church staff. Once it has been cleared, write the date(s) on the church calendar so that other church activities can work around it. This will also help you stick to your date(s) so you won't be tempted to change it. Then, publicize the date(s) in your church bulletin, newsletter, flyer and any other appropriate place. Undoubtedly, your church family will appreciate the advance notice and schedule their vacations around your Vacation Bible School.

Order Materials Early

If you are using a prepackaged VBS curriculum, NOW is the time to order. Ordering materials well in advance is one way to prevent having to wait for backorders, which can be a nightmare. Most publishers provide a VBS kit which has all you need to get started in your planning. However, look closely at the materials and the catalog to determine additional resources you will need to purchase. At this time, you will also need to make a close estimate of how many children will be attending your VBS. This number will help you determine how many teacher and student guides are needed.

How many students can you expect to have? There is no way to know for sure, but you can do your best to come up with a close estimate. Use the following steps to determine your potential enrollment:

1. Study VBS attendance figures from previous years.
2. Add the number of new students in Sunday School to last year's VBS enrollment.
3. Divide your total number by 3. (This takes into consideration that 1/3 of your children will bring one visitor.) Add that answer to your original sum.

If you can't use this method due to a drastic change in church attendance or a lack of previous VBS attendance records, don't despair. Use your best judgment and promote VBS preregistration to help guide you. It is better to overestimate and return unused items than to find you don't have enough materials the first day of VBS.

FIRST-TIMER TIP

Although preregistration will give you a guideline for the number of children who will be attending VBS, many families wait until the first day of VBS to register. Plan on it!

Planning Your VBS Strategy

The preliminary steps of the last chapter create a good foundation for your VBS. Now you are ready to start shaping your program. What exactly do you want your VBS to look like? Do you want an indoor or outdoor setting? Will you use traditional self-contained classrooms or activity centers? How many volunteers will you need? How do you find them? This chapter should help with those questions and much more.

Budgeting Your Expenses

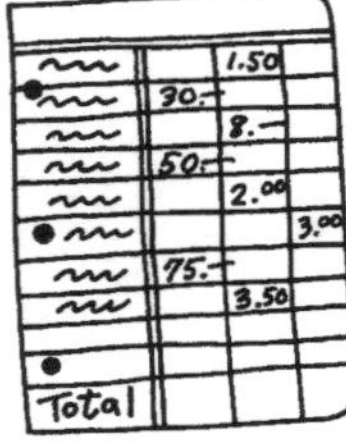

Creating a Budget

Before you purchase any materials, it's a good idea to determine the budget you will be working with. If your church has had VBS before, you will probably be given an estimated figure based on previous years. However, if you find that there are no designated funds or that VBS is part of another department's budget, such as Christian Education, you will need to come up with your own estimate of costs. Use the worksheet below to determine your needs. Then get the budget approved by church leadership. Know which areas you can cut down, if needed. It is helpful to designate a VBS financial coordinator to keep track of monies going in and out, to handle reimbursements and to make sure that you stay within your budget.

VBS BUDGET WORKSHEET

	Estimated	Actual
1. Curriculum Starter Kit	$____	$____
2. Teaching resources and additional curriculum items	$____	$____
3. Promotional materials	$____	$____
4. Craft supplies	$____	$____
5. Snack supplies	$____	$____
6. Misc. supplies	$____	$____
7. Paid child care for volunteers' children (if needed)	$____	$____
Total expenses	$____	$____

Cost-Cutting Options

What can you do if you have very little with which to work? Consider these options to help defray expenses:

* Print a list of craft and snack needs in the church bulletin/newsletter asking for donations.
* Have teachers make a list of supplies that are needed. Consolidate the lists and buy items in bulk.
* Promote VBS using local media that allow free advertising for church events.
* Check with churches in your area that may be using the same VBS. Ask in advance to borrow decorations, used curriculum or promotional supplies. If possible, offer to pay a portion of their costs for the items you use.
* Take an offering at the closing program of Vacation Bible School. To avoid making visitors feel obligated to give, simply mention that there is a donation box available for any contributions.
* Many churches now charge a registration fee for each child. Fees range from $5 to $20 (usually includes a T-shirt). Consider this option prayerfully and ask for others' opinions. Check to see if other VBS programs in your area charge. If you are conducting a VBS in a low-income area, charging admission will prohibit many from attending. However, many parents view VBS as a day camp for their children and are more than happy to pay a low registration fee. You may want to offer discounts or free registration to those who preregister or bring a new friend.

Choosing a Setting (Indoor or Outdoor)

Indoor VBS

Traditionally, VBS programs have been held in local churches. If you have a church facility available, this is one of your best options. It makes for easier planning, setup and control. It also helps by providing a familiar location for volunteers and church members.

Many churches today meet in unconventional facilities that make it almost impossible to host a VBS. With a little creativity, however, you can find a suitable place to conduct your VBS. Here are a few ideas:

* **Schools—**Public or private schools are an excellent option since most remain vacant for a large part of the summer.
* **Rented facilities—**Look in your local telephone directory for halls or facilities available for rent. Take into account the extra costs this will incur. You may also have to condense your VBS into fewer days.
* **Churches**—Consider asking a local church for use of their facilities. Offer to pay a fee or otherwise help cover their overhead costs. Make sure that you verify all plans well in advance to prevent confusion. Also, take into consideration that many visitors may associate your VBS program with the church where it is being held.
* **Double-Up**—Look for churches in your area that would be willing to combine efforts to provide a VBS program. Quite often, a church may have an excellent facility but lack leadership or volunteers to staff a VBS. By working together you may be able to establish a very successful VBS!

Outdoor VBS

Not enough room in your church? No available facilities? Then take your VBS outside—to a church courtyard, a large backyard or, better yet, a neighborhood park. Parks are excellent sites because they are usually conveniently located and have adequate space for the activities. When using a public outdoor area, make sure you reserve the space well in advance and allow for any deposits/fees in your budget.

Here are a few tips to remember when planning an outdoor VBS:

* **Weather—**Before planning an outside VBS, consider the weather conditions in your area. Always have an alternative plan in case the weather changes and your VBS must move indoors. Be sure to provide canopies, tree shade or umbrellas for areas where children may be in the sun for long periods of time.
* **Music**—Singing activities are sometimes difficult outside because the sound dissipates and children may become self-conscious about hearing their own voices. To encourage children to sing out, use a battery-operated cassette player or a guitarist who can play vigorously to generate some background music.
* **Lessons**—A Bible story area can easily be set up in a grassy place, playground or parking lot. Children can sit on the grass or on small rugs or blankets.
* **Games—**Active games are the best for outside—there is plenty of room for the children to move around. However, make sure that you set clear boundaries so children do not wander away.
* **Snacks—**Most snacks can be prepared and served outside if they do not require kitchen appliances. Even messy or juicy foods can be included because cleanup is easier. Children may sit on picnic benches or on blankets. Provide a wash basin or moist towelettes for children to wash their hands before and after eating, and make sure there are plenty of trash cans around.
* **Supplies**—Portable storage of supplies is a necessity for an outdoor VBS. Corrugated file boxes are excellent options. They are inexpensive, lightweight, readily available from stationery suppliers and easy to store. You may want to purchase large envelopes instead of file folders to organize the separate items in the boxes.

Self-Contained Classes vs. Activity Centers

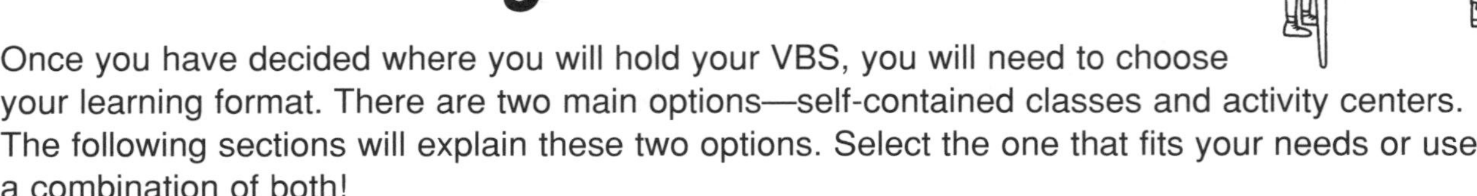

Once you have decided where you will hold your VBS, you will need to choose your learning format. There are two main options—self-contained classes and activity centers. The following sections will explain these two options. Select the one that fits your needs or use a combination of both!

Self-Contained Classes

The traditional VBS method uses self-contained classes similar to the way most elementary schools are set up. Children are divided by age or grade. Each group has a teacher who leads his or her class in all of the learning and recreational activities (with the exception of the opening and closing assemblies). Assistants are also usually needed, depending on the size of the class. For personnel needs, see pages 31-36.

When using the self-contained class setting, it is helpful to set up learning centers within the classroom. Designate centers by decorating areas appropriately. This helps in providing visual interest as children transition from one activity to another.

The greatest benefit of the self-contained classroom is that teachers are able to form meaningful relationships with the children since they remain together during the entire session. The biggest disadvantage is the difficulty in recruiting teachers who feel comfortable leading a variety of activities.

Activity Centers

The activity center plan is an exciting schedule variation. Following a junior high or high school format, the activity center plan involves groups of students rotating between a variety of activity centers. Each center is led by a teacher or coordinator who is responsible for only that activity. In other words, rather than presenting the entire lesson, each teacher is responsible for only one part. Many churches have found that this kind of specialization simplifies teacher preparation and improves teaching effectiveness. It prevents inexperienced or busy teachers from feeling overwhelmed. And teachers who don't enjoy crafts or are apprehensive about telling Bible stories can leave those tasks to others more skilled in those areas. The activity center approach makes recruiting easier when volunteers know they will only have one area of responsibility.

Students are divided into small groups, usually based on age or grade. These groups are assigned one or two counselors/guides who remain with them for the entire program, guiding them to the various centers. Groups should be no larger than is manageable for counselors to control (usually between 12 and 16 children).

Teachers or coordinators conduct their individual centers, working with each age group as it arrives. This gives children both a variety of talented, motivated teachers from whom to learn and one or two counselors with whom to develop more meaningful relationships.

The activity center plan is recommended for children in grades 1 to 6. Preschoolers need the security of a self-contained early childhood classroom. For more in-depth information on how to conduct this interesting option, see *Activity Center Planning Guide* on pages 37-40.

Class-Time Scheduling

A well-planned daily time schedule will make it possible for your VBS to accomplish its goals. Whether you decide to use self-contained classes, activity centers or a combination of both, it is a good idea to write out the time schedule for each session. If you are using a published curriculum, the time periods will most likely be spelled out for you. If you are doing your own, see pages 159-160 for schedule worksheets.

The average total time for most VBS sessions runs between 2½ and 3½ hours. However, if you are conducting an all-day VBS, evening VBS, Sunday VBS or other alternative program, you will need to adjust your times accordingly. If you find yourself in a time crunch, be careful not to reduce the Bible story and life application times. They are the most important.

If you are designing your own daily time schedule, you should include the following in your considerations:

✻ **Total time available for your use.**
This may be influenced by facility limitations and/or staff availability.

✻ **The time needed to achieve the goals for each activity.**
If you are not able to give a close estimate, conduct a practice lesson with a group of Sunday School children.

✻ **Attention span variations.**
Most activities for early childhood should be no longer than 15 minutes each, 30 minutes for elementary grades.

✻ **Traffic flow within your facilities.**
When using the activity center method, each activity will need to be given the same amount of time. Twenty-five to thirty minutes at each center works well. Consider combining two or three short activities to make up one center (e.g., snacks and recreation). Include a five-minute transition time for students to travel from one center to another.

✻ **Time for the opening and closing assemblies.**
Allow time for children to get settled, for announcements to be made and for worship to be meaningful.

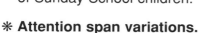

✻ **Maintaining a schedule.**
For counselors or guides who have never participated in a VBS activity center setting, keeping up the schedule may be a little confusing. Make sure they understand the rotation and give each guide an individualized group schedule (see p. 171).

✻ **Time for interaction with children.**
Give counselors/ guides a list of suggestions on ways to interact with children (see p. 172).

Ensuring Church Leadership Support

Many churches tend to view Vacation Bible School as just an extracurricular activity—something to occupy children during the summer—rather than an integral part of their total ministry. As a result, church leaders may express little interest in or offer little support for VBS. The most successful programs, however, have church leaders who understand the need and join in the effort to minister effectively to children and their families. Such understanding does not happen by accident. The following useful tips should help you keep the mission of VBS before your church leaders and gain their positive support for your VBS program.

* **Identify the key leaders in your church whose counsel and support are most crucial for a successful VBS.** It may be the senior pastor, a church board member or another staff member. Which leaders already have a good understanding of what VBS is? Which ones need to be made more aware of its goals, challenges and achievements?

* **Plan a variety of ways and times to report on the status of your VBS planning.** This includes attending regular church board meetings in addition to specifically scheduled VBS meetings. Express the importance of church leadership support by sending a short note or a letter to your senior pastor. (See pp. 180-181 for a sample.)

* **Be ready to take advantage of opportunities to communicate with staff/board while they are doing something else.** For example, at a meeting with a full agenda, simply distribute something of interest from your program—a list of volunteers, pre-enrollment status, a sample lesson, etc. Be careful not to interfere, but be graciously "available" to answer any questions about VBS.

* **Ask your pastor or other church leaders to encourage the congregation to be involved in VBS.**

* **When making a presentation in a meeting, be sure to capture interest and clearly communicate one or more of the positive elements of VBS.** For example, show a clip from the VBS preview video, play an audiocassette of a VBS song, dress up according to your theme, give everyone a chocolate kiss to express thanks for previous support, etc.

* **Look for ways to expose leaders to your VBS in action.** Create reasons to bring them into the classrooms, meeting teachers and seeing the children's excitement. If possible, ask your pastor to be a part of a special assembly or closing program. A first-hand visit by a pastor often has far more impact than any presentation you can make.

Staffing

Assessing Your Personnel Needs

One of the most valuable insights you will gain from directing a VBS is appreciating the impact it makes on not just the children but the volunteers as well. VBS is an excellent opportunity for many people to find, use and develop their special gifts. Because it's a relatively short-term commitment and offers a variety of opportunities for service, even the easily intimidated can be a part of your VBS. And the strong team spirit VBS creates carries over into the larger life of the church. Many who have never served before have found their beginning in VBS.

Begin the staffing process by assessing your needs. Make a list of all the jobs that need to be done, no matter how small. Then determine which tasks can be combined to be done by one person.

When you have identified the jobs to be done, you need to factor in the teacher-to-student ratio you want to maintain. The guidelines below will help you evaluate the number of volunteers you need.

With your list of jobs in hand and the number of volunteers in mind, you are ready to take the next step.

Teacher-Student Ratios

PRESCHOOLERS

For birth to two-year-olds:
1 adult for every 3 children

For three- to five-year-olds:
1 adult for every 8 children

ELEMENTARY

For six- to twelve-year-olds:
1 adult for every 10 to 12 children

Recruiting Staff

Recruiting personnel is one of the most difficult yet critical duties of the VBS Director. The staff you recruit will directly affect the success of your VBS. Your goal, simply put, is to match the talents of your volunteers to the tasks to be done. That will happen if you keep the following things in mind:

* **Start early** (see *Director's Master Checklist* on pp. 48-53).
* **Pray for guidance** in finding the people God wants to serve in this ministry.
* **Share the recruiting responsibilities with the VBS leaders and teachers you have already enlisted.** This helps prevent discouragement and increases the pool of people from whom to draw volunteers.
* **Regularly present to the congregation information about the benefits of and the opportunities available for working with VBS children.** Make liberal use of the printed church bulletin and the bulletin boards throughout the church buildings. If you have a preview video, show it in a church service. People do not want to make a commitment to an organization or program about which they are unfamiliar. Nor do they get excited about becoming part of a group which always seems to be making desperate appeals for somebody—anybody—to help. Try to present all personnel needs in a positive manner. Expect God's people to respond to the vision.
* **Use reproducible flyers to help you recruit staff for your program.** Put copies in your church bulletin or personally hand them to people you think might be interested. (See pp. 162-163.)

* **Make sure there is a written job description for each position on your VBS staff.** People deserve to know what they are being asked to do. See *Job Descriptions* on pp. 33-35.
* **Send a letter and a stamped response postcard to veteran VBS volunteers whom you would like to return** (see pp. 165-166). VVV's (Veteran VBS Volunteers) make a great staff because of their experience. However, avoid the trap of only looking for prospects who have had previous VBS experience.
* **Make a list of names and telephone numbers of possible prospects for your staff,** keeping in mind the goal of helping people find a chance to serve in a ministry. Consider everyone in your congregation in your discovery efforts. Use church memberships lists, new members' classes, adult class rolls, previous VBS workers and suggestions from leaders. Don't overlook singles, senior citizens, youth and collegians.
* **Prayerfully prioritize your developing prospect list.** Of all the people who could possibly be contacted, who should be approached first? Determine which job description best fits each candidate's strengths and gifts. If you feel uncomfortable or wary about a certain prospect, ask other staff members for references.
* **Personally contact the prospects.** A personal letter is a good first step, allowing the prospect time to prayerfully consider the matter without the pressure of someone eagerly looking for a response. Follow up the letter with a phone call to answer any questions or to see if the candidate has made a decision. You might want to schedule a face-to-face meeting with the person if you are unfamiliar with him or her. If you must recruit a large number of people, consider scheduling meetings with groups of prospects. Avoid the temptation to "arm-twist" lest you end up having reluctant personnel.
* Provide new volunteers with all of the needed materials, forms, helpful hints and training that would help equip them to succeed.

Screening Potential Staff

If recruiting isn't already a difficult enough task, in today's world it is wise to screen all potential volunteers who will be in contact with children. This is important for two reasons: it protects the safety of the children and it protects your church from potential false allegations.

These four safety tips will help you select responsible volunteers for your VBS program:

* **Set a tenure rule.** Never consider anyone until he or she has been a faithful member of your church for at least six months to one year. A tenure rule is helpful in providing a period of observation for detecting potential "problems."
* **Use a screening form.** First check with appropriate leaders to find out which volunteers have previously been involved in children's ministry functions and have already been screened. If a volunteer is new to your church or has never been screened, have him or her fill out an application. (See sample form on p. 167.) A completed application will give you most of the information you will need. It may also protect your church from a negligent hiring lawsuit. This may seem like a nuisance; however, if you neglect to check backgrounds and recruit a volunteer with a past criminal conviction, your church could be held liable.
* **Verify information given on screening forms.** Randomly check references by phone. Call the volunteer's former church and check with both the pastor and the person in charge of the area in which he or she served.
* **Interview prospective volunteers.** Interviews allow you to observe mannerisms and ask any questions. Make the conversation and atmosphere casual and try to make the individual feel comfortable.

If any volunteer refuses to complete any of these steps or seems "questionable," do not consider him or her. Inform your pastor or other church leader about your hesitation. Depending on the degree of unease, suggest the applicant be involved in your VBS in another way, one that does not involve contact with children.

Job Descriptions

Below is a suggested list of staff and responsibilities for your VBS program. Personnel needs will depend on your choice of self-contained classrooms or the activity center method. You will also need to adjust this list to the size of your staff and the number of children in your program. We've also included curriculum materials needed for each staff member.

VBS Director

The VBS director plans the overall organization and ministry of VBS, including decisions on the kind of VBS to be held and where, the goals to be met, the countdown schedule to be followed and the daily time schedule for the program itself. He or she recruits and coordinates all staff. The director may also conduct daily staff devotions and lead large group assembly times. Needs: entire curriculum and director's guidebook.

Assistant Director

The assistant director assists director in all responsibilities by helping with paperwork, organization, planning and recruiting. (In many churches, this person will be next year's director.) Needs: entire curriculum and director's guidebook.

Department Leaders

The department leaders supervise all departmental activities, handle the distribution of materials and help recruit age-level staff. Needs: department leader's or teacher's manual.

Publicity Coordinator

The publicity coordinator plans and carries out all promotion for your program, both before and during VBS. This involves getting the word out in the community through posters, flyers, advertisements, public events, etc. This person may also be in charge of promoting VBS within the church as well. Needs: promotional materials from curriculum. See *For the Publicity Coordinator* on pages 56-66.

Financial Coordinator

The financial coordinator is responsible for establishing and maintaining a workable budget. All purchases and receipts should be turned into him or her for recording and for reimbursements. (See sample forms on pp. 182-183). The financial coordinator will also handle all registration fees and donations. It is important that this person keep the VBS Director informed on the status of monies available in the budget to ensure that money allocated for the program is wisely spent. Needs: budget worksheet, publisher's catalog/order form.

Registration Secretary

The registration secretary coordinates and oversees preregistration activities, makes or purchases registration cards, groups children into classes, files completed registration cards and distributes class rosters. He or she also sets up the registration table each day during VBS, maintains attendance records, deposits registration fees and ensures each child knows his or her teacher or counselor.

Teachers (Self-contained Classroom)

Teachers are responsible for preparing and teaching the lesson, setting up the classrooms and leading the activities. They should attend all training sessions. Needs: teacher's manual, visual resources and student-use materials and resources.

Teacher's Assistant (Self-contained Classroom)

Assistants work closely with the lead teacher, helping with all activities as needed. Duties may include taking attendance, giving high-need students extra attention, helping with class-control and stepping in as teacher whenever the teacher is absent. Needs: teacher's manual.

Bible Story Teacher (Activity Center)

The Bible story teacher tells the Bible story to each group as it visits the Bible Story Center and leads the life application time after the story (unless this segment is led by counselors). Needs: teacher's book, visual resources and student materials.

Counselors or Guides (Activity Center)

Counselors or guides are assigned to each small group. Having one adult and one teen per group usually works well. They guide group to various activities, build rapport, maintain discipline, may lead discussion or life application segments and are prepared to lead children to Christ. Needs: teacher's manual and student guides or VBS handbook. See pages 171-172 for helpful information for guides.

Bible Learning Activity Coordinator (Activity Center)

This coordinator chooses Bible learning activities, gathers materials, recruits staff, prepares supplies and may possibly lead the activities. Needs: teacher's manual or Bible learning activity guides, if available.

Snack Coordinator

The snack coordinator selects snacks, gathers all ingredients, recruits helpers and distributes snack items. For an activity center format, the coordinator also sets up and decorates snack area and leads groups of children in the preparation of daily snacks. Needs: publisher's snack guide. See *For the Snack Coordinator* on pages 82-83 and *Snack Supplies List* on page 186.

Craft Coordinator

The craft coordinator chooses craft projects, makes a sample of each craft, gathers and distributes needed materials and recruits helpers. For the activity center method the craft coordinator also sets up and decorates the craft area and explains and supervises the crafts during each group's visit to the center. Needs: publisher's craft book. See *For the Craft Coordinator* on pages 72-76.

Recreation Coordinator

The recreation coordinator selects games, gathers all equipment, recruits assistants, explains and supervises games. Needs: recreation guide. See *For the Recreation Coordinator on page 84 and Recreation Schedule* on page 187.

Skit Director

The skit director recruits/auditions/selects actors, schedules and directs rehearsals, supervises preparation of the skit backdrop and secures needed costumes and props. Needs: skit production script and skit video, if available. See *For the Skit Director* on pages 80-81.

Music Director

The music director selects and learns songs, coordinates music activities and leads singing during the opening assembly. For activity center method, the music director also sets up and decorates music area, leads music activities in the music center and teaches children songs and motions. He or she may also prepare children to perform at the closing program. Needs: musical songbook, music cassette or CD. See *For the Music Director* on pages 77-79.

Music Accompanist

If you want to use live music during your VBS, you'll need to enlist a pianist or guitarist to help lead singing. Needs: musical songbook.

Missions Coordinator

The missions coordinator plans, gathers information and materials, and supervises missionary projects. If this person is not part of your church's missions committee, he or she will need to act as a liaison for VBS. See *For the Missions Coordinator* on pages 67-71.

Photographer/Videographer

This person will be responsible for taking posed and candid pictures for a presentation at the closing of VBS. Needs: class schedules. See worksheets on pages 159-160.

Transportation Coordinator

The transportation coordinator will oversee that all children have safe transportation to and from your VBS. This may include coordinating a bus route, organizing car pools or actually driving several children to your VBS. All drivers for your VBS activities should be screened. See *Driver Application Form*, page 168.You should also have on file signed permission slips and liability releases from each child's parent. Check with your church for the proper forms.

Child Care Coordinator

The child care coordinator is responsible for organizing, coordinating and providing child care for your VBS workers. This may include planning simple activities for young children. Child care should be provided for workers' children (four and under) during preliminary VBS staff meetings and for all workers' children not included in the VBS program. This is especially important if you expand the program to include entire families. See *Nursery and Child Care* on page 55.

Nursery Attendants

Nursery attendants are responsible for providing a safe, secure and loving environment for the children of your VBS staff. This may need to be a paid position, as it is important that the attendants be consistent and reliable.

Using Teen Helpers

Many churches find great value in using middle school and high school young people in leadership roles in Vacation Bible School. It's good for the children—they readily admire and enjoy following a young person's guidance and look forward to becoming helpers themselves. It's good for the adult staff—they benefit from the energy and enthusiasm of young assistants. And it's good for the young people—they gain valuable ministry experience and personal spiritual growth. This kind of VBS becomes a truly intergenerational experience, actively involving adults, youth and children in learning together.

The following guidelines have proven helpful in making youth leadership a positive experience for everyone involved:

1. **Far in advance of VBS, talk with the church's youth leaders about involving young people in working with the children.** Enlist their support in encouraging youth participation. If possible, seek to involve at least some of the youth leaders in various phases of VBS preparation and VBS itself.
2. **Recruit one person to coordinate the process of enlisting, training and supervising young people to serve in VBS.**
3. **Define the requirements for the young people who will serve.** How old must they be? How involved in your church's programs? What meetings must they attend? What is the process for applying and being approved? Within the framework of your church's youth programs and child safety policies, set standards that will challenge young people while being as inclusive as possible. Often young people, even those who seem to be less than ideal candidates for leadership, will blossom when given the opportunity to serve.

4. **Decide on the positions young people can fill.** The specific combination of tasks may vary depending on how you structure your VBS. Regardless of the structure, there may be some specialized roles some young people can fill: skit performers, musicians, Bible verse listeners, etc.
   * **Activity Center Plan**—Young people can serve as counselors/guides or activity aides. Counselors stay with the same group of children as they move from activity to activity, focusing on building friendships and keeping children involved. Activity aides stay in an assigned activity area (Bible story, crafts, games, snack, etc.), assisting the teacher(s) with specific functions.

* **Traditional Classroom Plan—**Young people stay in same room with the same children and staff for most activities, performing a combination of tasks.

5. **Enlist young people to serve.** At least several months in advance of VBS, begin announcing this opportunity to teens and their parents. Provide an application form (see p. 169) and printed information about what the young people will be doing. Allow teens to indicate their job preferences (age groups, functions, etc.). You may want to announce that job assignments will be made at least partly on a first-come, first-served basis to encourage young people to respond promptly.
6. **Prayerfully assign young people to specific positions.** In general, try to give the older, more experienced teens their first choice of jobs. This will pay off in subsequent years as younger people look forward to when they can get a preferred position. In most cases, it is best to have both a boy and a girl with any group of children, providing role models for both genders. (NOTE: Be careful how many young people you assign to work together. One potential problem in using teens is their tendency to focus on each other rather than on the children they are supposed to be guiding.)
7. **Promote your use of teenagers to your congregation, to children and to their parents.** Present it as a great opportunity for children to benefit from positive youth role models.
8. **Schedule one or more training sessions in advance of VBS just for the youth guides.** Make the sessions very specific in covering what you expect of the young people.

See page 170 for a sample commitment form. Provide ideas of what they should wear to fit in with your VBS theme. Also, make the training session(s) fun, perhaps playing a game or two that will be used with the children in VBS—and, of course, provide refreshments. If your publisher provides a handbook for youth aides, give one to each young person. It's a small investment that will pay big dividends.

9. **Prepare your adult staff to work with the youth guides.** Provide copies of the same instructions given to the youth guides and explain that having a young person to assist them will bring some added responsibilities along with some valuable help. Encourage adults not to limit young people to "flunky" jobs, but to be alert to assigning jobs the young person will view as meaningful. See page 173 for a sample handout to give your adult staff.
10. **Schedule at least one meeting with all staff together to help adults and teens get to know each other and to finalize plans and assignments for each person.** Emphasize the real goals of VBS, challenging the young people to make this event more than just a fun time playing with the children.
11. **During VBS, plan for ways to make sure youth guides have a good time and feel appreciated.** Ideas include:
    * Provide a special treat each day.
    * Encourage the children to thank their youth guides. (Affirmation from children is one of the biggest benefits guides will receive.)
    * During the opening or closing assembly, comment on the great job the guides are doing.
    * Have a youth leader, one who already knows the teenagers, make a point of checking in with each young person, affirming their work and seeing if there are any problems or difficulties.
    * Schedule a special event just for the youth guides, such as a pizza party, a picnic in the afternoon, a social event in the evening, etc.

Activity Center Planning Guide

The charts and sample schedules found on the following pages show how the activity center plan can work in your church. Adjust the schedule according to the number of staff and children in your program. As each child arrives, he or she will be assigned to a counselor (or guide) and a permanent small group. He or she should be given a name tag or wristband which carries all that information.

Opening Assembly

The day (or evening) begins as all children and counselors meet together for the opening assembly, which includes a welcome, songs and a skit. Children should be seated with their small groups/counselors for easy dismissal.

After the Opening Assembly

Counselors lead their small groups to move from center to center:

* **Bible Story/Application Center**
  The Bible story teacher tells the Bible story and leads his or her small group in a life application discussion. Students may work on a student guide. Counselors may be used to lead the discussion.

* **Bible Learning Activity Center**
  In a large room or outdoor area, the Bible learning activity coordinator sets up and leads activities that reinforce the Bible story, memory verse and/or life application.

* **Music Center**
  In a large room or outdoor area, the music director leads each group in a variety of music activities and teaches the VBS songs.

* **Craft Center**
  The craft coordinator leads the group in making a craft project.

* **Snack Center**
  The snack coordinator leads group in preparing and eating fun snacks.

Closing Assembly

To conclude, meet together for a closing assembly. This may be done with all children together or with smaller departmental groups. Include announcements, songs and verse review. Counselors collect name tags. As children leave, they collect take-home materials from designated tables.

Activity Center Flow Chart and Schedule

FOR 36 TO 48 ELEMENTARY-AGE CHILDREN

Place 12 to 16 children in each group. Allow five minutes transition time between centers.

Plan to set up:

* One Bible Story/Application Center
* One Craft Center
* One Bible Learning Activity Center
* One Snack Center
* One Music Center

SAMPLE THREE-HOUR SCHEDULE

	PRIMARY	MIDDLER	JUNIOR
9:00–9:15	Opening Assembly	Opening Assembly	Opening Assembly
9:20–9:45	Bible Story/Application	Craft Center	Music Center
9:50–10:15	Bible Learning Activity Center	Bible Story/ Application	Craft Center
10:20–10:45	Snack Center	Bible Learning Activity Center	Bible Story/ Application
10:50–11:15	Music Center	Snack Center	Bible Learning Activity Center
11:20–11:45	Craft Center	Music Center	Snack Center
11:50–12:00	Closing Assembly	Closing Assembly	Closing Assembly

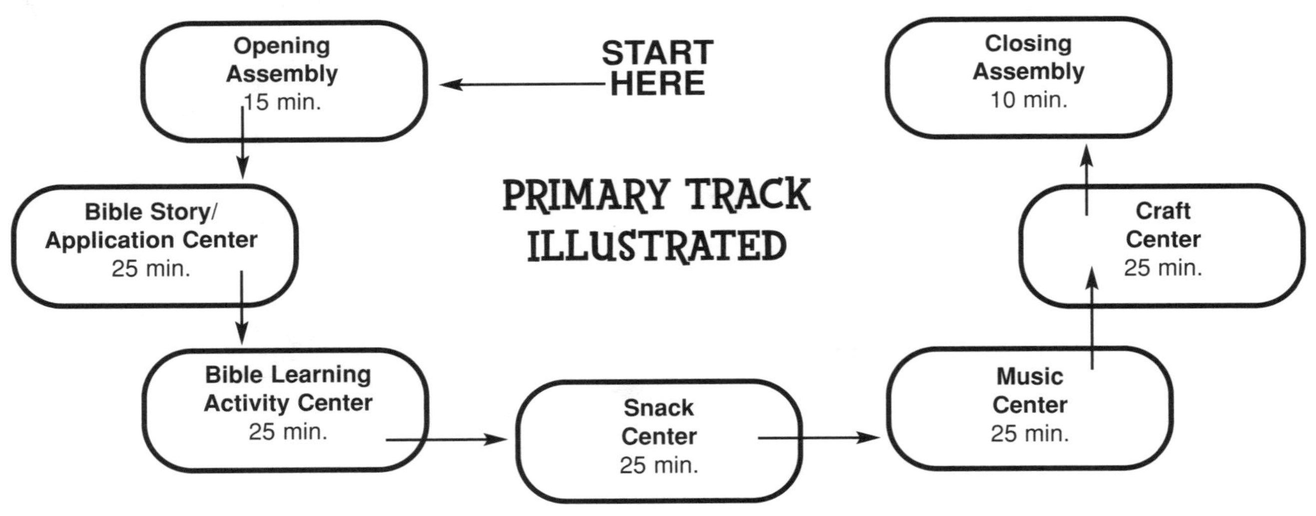

Prekindergarten Classroom	**PLAYGROUND**	Kindergarten Classroom

NOTE: Preschool and Kindergarten Departments remain in separate area. They do not rotate through elementary activity centers.

Activity Center Flow Chart and Schedule

FOR 72 TO 96 ELEMENTARY-AGE CHILDREN

Place 12 to 16 children in each group. Allow five minutes transition time between centers.

Plan to set up:

- ❋ Two Bible Story/Application Centers (A and B: one for 1st and 2nd graders; one for 3rd–6th graders)
- ❋ Two Craft Centers (A and B: one for 1st and 2nd graders; one for 3rd–6th graders)
- ❋ Two Bible Learning Activity Centers (A and B: one for 1st and 2nd graders; one for 3rd–6th graders)
- ❋ One Snack Center (3rd and 4th graders will be in this center at the same time)
- ❋ One Music Center (2nd and 3rd graders will be in this center at the same time)

SAMPLE THREE-HOUR SCHEDULE

	1ST GRADE (group a)	1ST GRADE (group b)	2ND GRADE	3RD GRADE	4TH GRADE	5TH/6TH GRADE
9:00–9:15	Opening Assembly	Opening Assembly	Opening Assembly	Opening Assembly	Opening Assembly	Opening Assembly
9:20–9:45	Bible Story/ App. A	Craft Center A	Snack Center	Bible Story/ App. B	Music Center	Craft Center B
9:50–10:15	Bible Learning Activity Center A	Bible Story/ App. A	Craft Center A	Bible Learning Activity Center B	Bible Story/ App. B	Snack Center
10:20–10:45	Snack Center	Bible Learning Activity Center A	Bible Story/ App. A	Craft Center B	Bible Learning Activity Center B	Music Center
10:50–11:15	Music Center	Music Center	Bible Learning Activity Center A	Snack Center	Snack Center	Bible Story/ App. A
11:20–11:45	Craft Center A	Snack Center	Music Center	Music Center	Craft Center B	Bible Learning Activity Center B
11:50–12:00	Closing Assembly	Closing Assembly	Closing Assembly	Closing Assembly	Closing Assembly	Closing Assembly

1ST GRADE (group a) TRACK ILLUSTRATED

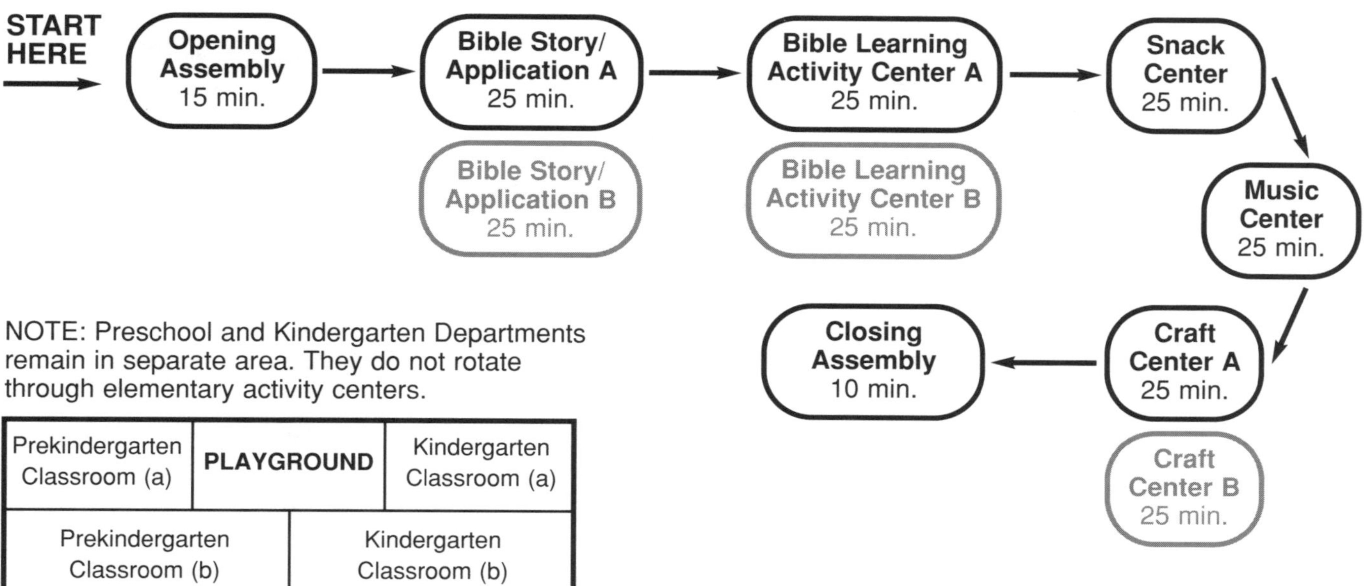

NOTE: Preschool and Kindergarten Departments remain in separate area. They do not rotate through elementary activity centers.

Prekindergarten Classroom (a)	PLAYGROUND	Kindergarten Classroom (a)
Prekindergarten Classroom (b)		Kindergarten Classroom (b)

Activity Center Terminology

Small Groups

Children are placed into small, permanent groups (12 to 16 is the best size).

Centers

One room or outside area is designated for each of the activities your program provides, such as crafts, Bible story/application, snacks, music, Bible learning activities, recreation and missions. Each group of children, along with their counselors, visits each center each day (or evening) of the program.

Teachers or Coordinators

Each teacher or coordinator takes responsibility for one center. The teacher remains at the center and instructs each small group as it visits the center. Teachers make adjustments in method and content according to the age level of the children visiting the center.

Counselors or Guides

Each small group of children has two counselors or guides who lead the group to various centers. Many churches use one adult and one teen helper to lead each group.

(NOTE: The activity center plan is recommended for children in grades 1–6. Preschoolers need the security of a single early childhood classroom.)

Helpful Hints

- Predetermine the route each group will travel, including entrances and exits. Have counselors walk their routes in advance to become familiar with all locations.
- Establish a signal for letting groups know when it's time to move to the next center.
- Provide labeled tables, bins or other areas where children may leave their belongings throughout the day.
- Set up your centers in classrooms, in tents, under awnings or under shade trees. Students can sit on blankets, beach towels or picnic benches.
- Give each group of children a team name and/or color that relates to the VBS theme.
- Color-code name tags or wristbands to identify groups and include the counselor's name on each one.
- Post a large sign to identify each center.
- Give each center a fun and interesting name that goes along with your VBS theme.

Backyard Bible School Planning Guide

A Backyard Bible School provides unique opportunities for neighborhood outreach and evangelism. Of course, you can still use a published VBS curriculum; simply adjust the activities and time schedule to meet your students' needs.

Why Does a Backyard Bible School Work?

- It provides a place close to home for children to learn about Jesus.
- It is an ideal means for Christians to minister within their own neighborhoods.
- Everyone loves it! Kids love the relaxed setting where bare feet and play clothes are the usual attire. Usually every child in the neighborhood comes, so there isn't anyone left to play with anyway. And parents are happy because their children will be busy for over two hours.

Facilities

The home in which the VBS is held need not be large, but it should have a few basics:

- A place to tell the story such as a family room, patio or shaded lawn.
- A place to do crafts that is not the same place where the story is told—a patio, garage or basement. (A table or two in this area is a good idea, but not necessary. Children can work while standing at the table or they can work on the floor.)

- A place for serving refreshments. (This can be the same area as used for crafts.)
- A place to play active games such as a front yard, backyard or a driveway. If necessary, a nearby park or common area will do.

Workers

The Hostess

The Backyard Bible School can't be done without a hostess. She is the cake to which the frosting is added. Her natural hospitality and friendliness among her neighbors will assure good attendance. If she is new in the neighborhood, this will be an opportunity to meet neighbors and establish rapport.

The specific responsibilities of a hostess are:

- to invite the other teaching team members to her home a week ahead of time to look over the facilities and make plans;
- to give out the invitations to neighborhood families;
- to have her home clean and in good order;
- to plan and serve the refreshments.

The Teacher

The teacher's spirit, knowledge of the subject matter and love for children will "make or break" the week for everyone involved. It is the teacher's job to take the reins on Monday morning as the first child steps into the home. The teacher's smile and friendly, decisive directions will help each child feel wanted, happy and cooperative.

The teacher's specific responsibilities are:

- to learn the Bible story and present it to the children;
- to delegate or lead other activities such as crafts, recreation and singing;
- to keep the schedule moving;
- to lead the planning meeting at the home of the hostess.

The Aides

In most cases two aides are needed. It is best to have no more than 20 children in one home. Aides should have a love for children and a willing spirit. Some aides may have special abilities or interests in songs, crafts or recreation.

It is important for aides to participate directly with the children. They should talk with the children when they come in and learn their names. Aides will guide children in Bible learning activities, sing with them, play games with them and enjoy the story with them. The aides may be assigned to participate in VBS skits. The general rule for aides is to follow the lead of the teacher—he or she is in charge. However, if the teacher asks an aide to be in charge of any specific activity, then the aide should do just that—be in charge.

Special Two-Hour Schedule

20–30 MINUTES	Team Devotions and Preparations
20–30 MINUTES	Interest Builders and Opening Assembly
20–30 MINUTES	Bible Story and Life Application
20–30 MINUTES	Snacks and Recreation
20–30 MINUTES	Crafts
10 MINUTES	Closing

Backyard Bible School Countdown Schedule

8 WEEKS BEFORE:

- ❑ Educate the congregation with write-ups in bulletin or newsletter.
- ❑ Order course supplies.

4 WEEKS BEFORE:

- ❑ Enlist hostess, teacher and two aides.
- ❑ Set the date, time and place of the Backyard Bible School.

3 WEEKS BEFORE:

- ❑ Make up a kit of materials and give teacher books to teacher and aides.

2 WEEKS BEFORE:

- ❑ Hostess calls the team to schedule the meeting at her home the next week.
- ❑ Teacher prepares to delegate responsibilities at the meeting.

1 WEEK BEFORE:

- ❑ Have meeting at home of hostess. Teacher delegates responsibilities.
- ❑ Team prepares for their parts.

DURING THE WEEK:

- ❑ Have a great time!

Intergenerational VBS Planning Guide

An intergenerational VBS provides a wonderful opportunity for families in your church to have fun and learn together. This section will give you ways to schedule your intergenerational VBS and ideas to productively involve families in your church and community.

There are basically three different schedule options:

* **OPTION A**—Plan the opening assembly for families and then have family members go to their age-level groups;
* **OPTION B**—Plan one or more family activities in addition to the opening assembly, with a shorter time in age-level groups;
* **OPTION C**—Keep families together for the entire session, moving them from center to center in an activity center approach.

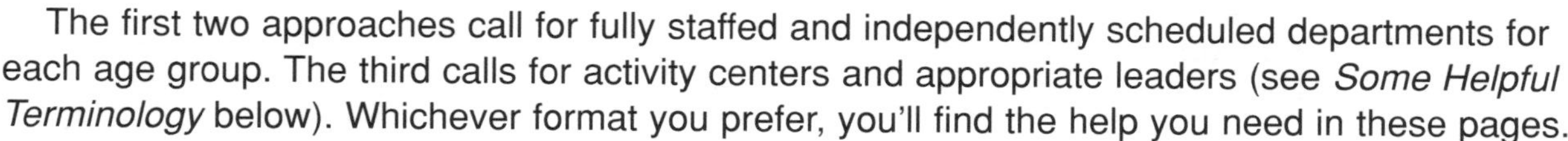

The first two approaches call for fully staffed and independently scheduled departments for each age group. The third calls for activity centers and appropriate leaders (see *Some Helpful Terminology* below). Whichever format you prefer, you'll find the help you need in these pages.

Some Helpful Terminology

Family Tour Group

Assign each family to a larger tour group with other families. The number of tour groups you form will depend on the total number of people attending, as well as the room(s) and the leaders you have available. Seek to form tour groups with four to six families or 12 to 16 people.

Tour Guide

Each tour group has one or more tour guides who lead that tour group to the appropriate family activity areas throughout the session. The tour guide also helps people in the various families to get to know each other better. The tour guide is available to assist parents in involving their children in the family activities.

Family Activity Centers

Designate at least one room or outside area for each of the family activities you will provide (crafts, snack preparation, Bible story/application, etc.). Each tour group visits each center at a designated time each day (or evening) of the program.

Family Activity Leaders

Enlist at least one person to direct each activity center. These leaders remain at one location and instruct or direct each tour group as it visits that center.

Helpful Hints

* Make sure your intergenerational VBS is all-inclusive. Provide opportunities for single-parent families, single adults, childless couples and children who come alone to participate. Make them feel welcome by pairing them with another family; or mix all family members in separate groups.
* An intergenerational VBS is recommended for children ages four and up and their families. Younger children need the security and familiarity of a program designed for their special needs. Provide child care for children under four.

How It Works

As families arrive, they are assigned to a permanent tour group and introduced to their tour guides. Everyone in a tour group wears a name tag of the same color or design. Tour group members may want to create a name for their tour group.

Opening Assembly

The day (or evening) begins as all tour groups and tour guides meet together for the opening assembly, which includes a welcome, songs and a skit. To get all ages participating right from the start:

1. Prepare two or three families in advance to help lead in teaching a new song (including any motions).
2. Assign parts of songs to different family members (dads, moms, all kids, dads and daughters, moms and sons, etc.).
3. Invite a family from each tour group to come to the front and participate in a simple stunt or contest which involves the whole family. Use a different stunt each day. For example:
   - join hands in a circle and see how long they can keep a balloon off the ground by hitting it;
   - complete an obstacle course based on your VBS theme;
   - blow the biggest bubble-gum bubble or the longest-floating soap bubble;
   - put words of the session's Bible memory verse into the correct order;
   - answer questions about the previous session's Bible story.

After the Opening Assembly

In Option A, family members separate to their own age-level groups. In Option B, families stay together for an activity and then go to their separate groups. In Option C, tour guides lead their tour groups to their assigned activity centers. Use as many of the following activity centers as your schedule and facilities allow. Tour guides rotate among the available centers as determined by your schedule.

Craft Center

Choose from a variety of theme-appropriate craft ideas, including many that easily lend themselves to being done as family projects, rather than one per individual. (You may prefer to have crafts done in age-level groups.)

Snack/Game Center

Choose an interesting and theme-appropriate snack that allows families to work together in preparing as well as eating it. The snack coordinator provides the snack supplies and instructions; then families do the preparation. If necessary, to balance the time required for the other family activities, you may lead families in playing a recreational game. (You may prefer to have snacks and games done in age-level groups.)

Bible Story/Application Center

The Bible story leader presents each day's story to tour groups. Then families explore ways that the story applies to families today. To keep the attention of the various age levels in each tour group, consider these ideas:

- Arrange seating in a wide semicircle to avoid having any of the younger children in the back. Families should sit together so parents can help their children focus on the story presentation.
- Enlist a drama team who can act out the story.
- Engage everyone in the story action. Include group participation ideas (motions, sound effects, etc.).
- Keep the story brief. With four- and five-year-olds in the group, a story should not exceed five minutes.
- Suggest ways for families to apply the Bible story in their own homes. Prepare some questions/activities for each family to work on among themselves. Also have ready a few questions to ask for responses from the whole group.

If you choose to do one or more of the above activities in age-level groups, parents may participate in an adult Bible study.

Closing Assembly

To conclude, all tour groups meet together to wrap up with singing, Bible verse review and an invitation to the next session. Tour guides collect name tags and distribute take-home materials as families leave.

Intergenerational VBS Schedule Options

See next page for Helpful Hints.

Option A: Family Opening Plus Age-Level Activities

Sample 90- to 120-Minute Schedule

	CHILDREN	PARENTS
15 MINUTES	Opening Assembly	Opening Assembly
60–90 MINUTES	Age-Level Groups for Crafts, Snacks, Games and Bible Story/Application	Adult Bible Study
15 MINUTES	Closing Assembly	Closing Assembly

Option B: Family Opening Plus Activity, Then Separate Age-Level Activities

Sample 90- to 120-Minute Schedule

	CHILDREN	PARENTS
15 MINUTES	Opening Assembly	Opening Assembly
20–30 MINUTES	Family Activity	Family Activity
40–60 MINUTES	Age-Level Groups for Snacks, Games and Bible Story/Application	Adult Bible Study
15 MINUTES	Closing Assembly	Closing Assembly

Sample 3-Hour Schedule

	TOUR GROUP 1 / CHILDREN	TOUR GROUP 1 / PARENTS	TOUR GROUP 2 / CHILDREN	TOUR GROUP 2 / PARENTS
15 MINUTES	Opening Assembly	Opening Assembly	Opening Assembly	Opening Assembly
30 MINUTES	Bible Story/Application	Bible Story/Application	Family Activity	Family Activity
30 MINUTES	Family Activity	Family Activity	Bible Story/Application	Bible Story/Application
90 MINUTES	Age-Level Groups for Snacks, Music	Adult Bible Study	Age-level groups for Snacks, Music	Adult Bible Study

Option C: All Family

Sample 90- to 120-Minute Schedule

	TOUR GROUP 1	TOUR GROUP 2	TOUR GROUP 3
15 MINUTES	Opening Assembly	Opening Assembly	Opening Assembly
20–30 MINUTES	Family Activity	Snacks/Games	Bible Story/Application
20–30 MINUTES	Snacks/Games	Bible Story/Application	Family Activity
20–30 MINUTES	Bible Story/Application	Family Activity	Snacks/Games
15 MINUTES	Closing Assembly	Closing Assembly	Closing Assembly

Sample 3-Hour Schedule

	TOUR GROUP 1	TOUR GROUP 2	TOUR GROUP 3
15 MINUTES	Opening Assembly	Opening Assembly	Opening Assembly
30 MINUTES	Bible Story/Application	Family Activity	Crafts
30 MINUTES	Snacks/Games	Bible Story/Application	Family Activity
30 MINUTES	Music	Snacks/Games	Bible Story/Application
30 MINUTES	Crafts	Music	Snacks/Games
30 MINUTES	Family Activity	Crafts	Music

Helpful Hints for Schedule Options

1. Suggested times in each block include five minutes of transition time from the previous activity.
2. Two- and three-year-olds remain in separate area, following their own program schedule.
3. If you form more tour groups than shown on these charts, two or more tour groups can be doing the same activity at the same time in different areas or rooms.
4. Except for the opening and closing assemblies, avoid grouping too many people together for any of the activities. Participation will be greatest and potential behavior problems minimized when tour groups are kept to four to six families (or 12 to 16 individuals).

Tips On Intergenerational Teaching

Most of your families and leaders are likely to have only limited experience at participating in family learning activities along with other family groups. Groups that have a wide range of age levels pose some unique challenges for those who are more familiar with groups of a narrower age range. A few helpful guidelines:

* **Use a signal to get everyone's attention before you speak.** A musical note, quickly flashing the lights or a large gesture (holding both arms straight overhead) are all effective ways to get attention without shouting. Explain your signal and practice it several times with the group. Ask the children to help their parents learn to respond to your signal.
* **Talk to all age groups.** If a leader focuses on the four-year-olds, older children and adults will tune out. If a leader focuses on the parents, the children get restless. Remember, even four-year-olds can understand over 90 percent of normal adult conversation.
* **Be brief, keep sentences short, use ample gestures and facial expressions and vary your pitch and volume.**
* **Intentionally use references to different age and grade levels, as well as specific families, in your talk.** For example, "I'm sure all the fifth graders already know that...," or "The runaway son ran a long, long way from home—further than going to your grandma's house, Jesse." When you need to say something specifically to parents, you may ask the children to cover their ears because you want to tell their parents a secret. Of course, the kids will suddenly become highly attentive!
* **Enlist parents as partners in "crowd control."** Many parents who are perfectly capable of controlling their children when *they* are in charge will abdicate that responsibility when someone else is the leader. And many leaders are reluctant to deal with a behavior problem when the parents are present. Explain to parents that in a group family-learning situation, parents and leaders must take joint responsibility for guiding children. "Because there are a lot of people and lots of activity, it is not always possible for a parent or leader to see everything. Therefore, we must help each other in giving good directions and enforcing limits so that we can all have a relaxed, enjoyable time together."
* **When families are working together, encourage parents to allow their children to do as much of the work as possible.** Because of the variance in children's age levels, some parents will need to do more "helping" than others. Remind parents that the goal is not to see which family does the best in an activity. The goal is for families to enjoy working and learning together.
* **When families are given a question to discuss, alert parents to share answers and experiences that encourage children to participate.** Lengthy explanations or stories tend to stifle children's interest, so parents should keep their comments as brief as possible.
* **Provide an opportunity for families to pray together during the session.** Instruct parents to keep the prayers very simple so that even the youngest child can participate fully. You may suggest these helpful approaches, which can also enable parents who are uncomfortable with praying aloud:
  1. Let a family member suggest one thing to pray about; then each family member offers a one-sentence prayer of agreement about that ("I'm glad Jeremy is thankful for our family.").
  2. Invite each family member to tell God one thing for which he or she is thankful or to ask Him for one thing.
  3. Each family member thanks God for the family member to his or her right.
  4. One family member volunteers to pray; then they all join in saying "amen" ("so be it" or "let it be done") at the end.

Step 5

Your VBS Master Plan

One of the most difficult aspects of planning a Vacation Bible School or, for that matter, any large event, is dealing with the details while still keeping in mind the large picture. If you're like most directors, you probably need help in one of these two areas. That is why having a master plan is so important—it helps you keep track of both the small and large tasks. And since allowing sufficient time for planning is the whole key to having a fantastic VBS, a master plan almost forces you into thinking ahead.

We have provided two sample checklists in different formats to help you with your planning (see pp. 48-53 and pp. 150-158). One sample organizes your VBS as a countdown schedule by dates; the other breaks it down into categories. Read them over and adapt them to your own needs. And don't forget to check off each item as it is completed. This will give you an encouraging sense of accomplishment and help you stay on top of all facets of your VBS.

This chapter also includes useful planning and organizational tips for specific volunteer leadership roles such as craft coordinator, music director, snack coordinator, etc. These are all reproducible so that you can give them to the appropriate volunteers. Remember, volunteers come with a variety of needs—from the completely self-sufficient, dependable worker to the nervous, completely reliant volunteer. This chapter is designed to help you help them! Use the checklists in your regular VBS meetings to gauge progress and to encourage and pray for each other.

Director's Master Checklist by Date

24 WEEKS BEFORE:

- ❑ Begin regular prayer for VBS. Ask church groups to pray for VBS from now until the program is over. (See *Establish a Prayer Base,* p. 22.)
- ❑ Determine type of VBS (mornings, evenings, camp format, Backyard Bible School, etc.). (See *Scheduling,* pp. 10-12.)

20 WEEKS BEFORE:

- ❑ If you are a first-time director, meet with former VBS directors and/or leaders to glean pertinent information and suggestions.
- ❑ Meet with church leaders to discuss your role as VBS Director. (See *Ensuring Church Leadership Support*, p. 30.)
- ❑ Decide on possible dates for VBS. (See *Determine the Date*, p. 24.)
- ❑ Compare and evaluate VBS curriculum choices. (See *Curriculum*, pp. 15-16.)

18 WEEKS BEFORE:

- ❑ Appoint VBS committee (assistant director, department leaders, publicity coordinator, etc.). (See *Enlist a Dedicated VBS Committee*, p. 22-23.)
- ❑ Set goals and determine unique needs of your VBS. (See *Take the Time to Set Goals*, pp. 23-24.)
- ❑ Choose setting and location for your VBS. Reserve area if needed. (See *Choosing a Setting*, p. 27.)
- ❑ Meet with church leaders and secure a VBS budget. (See *Budgeting Your Expenses*, p. 26.)
- ❑ Decide on a VBS curriculum and return all unused kits to publisher.
- ❑ Order basic VBS curriculum (such as a Starter Kit).
- ❑ Establish and announce VBS dates in church bulletin/newsletter.

16 WEEKS BEFORE:

- ❑ Meet with VBS committee (including all department leaders) to:
  1. Pray for VBS.
  2. Outline time schedules for both self-contained classrooms and activity centers. (See *Class-Time Scheduling*, p. 29.)
  3. Set deadline dates for all activities.
  4. Estimate VBS enrollment and determine staff needs (departmental and general). (See *Staffing*, pp. 31-36.)
  5. Compile lists of prospective workers.
  6. Schedule training workshop(s).
  7. Make a list of supplies to be purchased.
- ❑ Plan publicity with publicity coordinator. (See *For the Publicity Coordinator*, pp. 56-66.)
- ❑ Order publicity and curriculum materials.
- ❑ Send letter and response postcards to veteran VBS volunteers you want to return. (See sample postcards pp. 165-166.)
- ❑ Begin personal contacts to recruit rest of staff. (See *Recruitment Planning Worksheet*, p. 161.)
- ❑ Publish bulletin insert listing craft supply needs, refreshment donations and other materials needed. (See sample copy p. 74.)

12 WEEKS BEFORE:

- ❑ Distribute curriculum materials to department leaders.
- ❑ Publicize in the church bulletin the need for workers. Give names of department leaders as "persons to see." (See sample flyers, pp. 162-163.)
- ❑ Choose and plan missions project. (See *For the Missions Coordinator*, pp. 67-71.)

10 WEEKS BEFORE:

- ❏ Distribute second notice regarding supplies.
- ❏ Distribute supplies to department leaders.
- ❏ Meet with department leaders to work out training workshop procedures. Discuss the overall goals and aims for VBS and the individual lesson aims.
- ❏ Outline and prepare for training workshop(s). (See Step 6.)
- ❏ List all VBS staff in church bulletin, asking prayer for them and for any remaining vacancies.
- ❏ Contact all recruits, confirming preliminary assignments, notifying them of training workshop(s).
- ❏ Begin displaying banners and posters throughout church building and community.

8 WEEKS BEFORE:

- ❏ Purchase remaining craft supplies.
- ❏ Plan and prepare preregistration activities. (See *Preregistration*, pp. 120-122.)
- ❏ Make VBS flyers for church members to use for invitations.
- ❏ Publicize training workshop(s) in church bulletin. Identify any new staff additions and remaining vacancies.
- ❏ Plan dedication service for workers; secure minister's approval and help. (See *Dedicating Volunteers*, p. 124.)
- ❏ Plan closing program. (See *Preparing Your Closing Program*, pp. 137-138.)
- ❏ Plan follow-up efforts with Sunday School leaders. (See *Follow Up on Children*, p. 140.)
- ❏ Enlist qualified crew of child-care workers for volunteers' children. (See *Nursery and Child Care*, p. 55.)

6 WEEKS BEFORE:

- ❏ Meet with the leaders (missions, publicity, finance, crafts, snacks, transportation, etc.) for prayer and to determine if they are accomplishing their assignments. Use the checklists from this section for evaluations.
- ❏ Begin preregistration.
- ❏ Plan all activities for opening and closing assemblies and for any special mid-week events. (See *Conducting the Assemblies*, p. 129.)
- ❏ Plan theme-decorating ideas. This may include having backdrops painted.
- ❏ Plan for and enlist substitutes.

4 WEEKS BEFORE:

- ❏ Make sure all leaders and teachers have last-minute supplies.
- ❏ Conduct training workshop(s).
- ❏ Distribute theme buttons and/or T-shirts to all staff members to wear to church from now through the end of VBS.
- ❏ Mail postcard invitations to invite prospects to attend and/or deliver flyers/door hangers throughout neighborhood.
- ❏ Check and adjust time schedules and supplies.
- ❏ Plan for extra staff and special procedures needed for first-day registration. (See *Opening-Day Registration*, p. 123.)
- ❏ Update bulletin insert to provide final request for items still needed.
- ❏ Make and photocopy any flyers or announcements that will be going home with the children each day.
- ❏ Finalize date, time and arrangements for closing program.
- ❏ Make arrangements for sound system and custodial support during and after VBS.
- ❏ Order any extra materials needed based on preregistration indicators.
- ❏ Assign rooms and places for each class/center.

1 WEEK BEFORE:

- ❑ Hold dedication service for volunteers.
- ❑ Hold a preparation day for staff to decorate and arrange indoor rooms (if possible). (See *The Week Before: Have a "Prep" Rally*, p. 124.)
- ❑ Plan for first-aid needs and disciplinary problems.
- ❑ Assign preregistered children to classes or groups.
- ❑ Distribute class rosters/attendance sheets to teachers or counselors. (See *Roster/Attendance Form,* p. 196.)
- ❑ Assign volunteer(s) to make or purchase name tags for each class.
- ❑ Assist leaders or teachers in last-minute preparations.
- ❑ Plan morning staff devotions. (See *Conduct Morning Staff Devotions*, p. 130.)
- ❑ Hold an all-staff meeting to discuss any last-minute changes, announce room assignments and answer any questions.

DURING VBS:

- ❑ Continue all staff support functions. Pray with and for them. Communicate with them and work at maintaining their spirit of enthusiasm.
- ❑ Conduct morning staff devotions.
- ❑ Lead all or a portion of the opening and closing assemblies. Present VBS awards and certificates to staff and children on last day of VBS.
- ❑ Make sure teachers are present and on schedule. If using the activity center method, signal appropriate times to rotate to the next center.
- ❑ Arrange for substitutes when needed.
- ❑ Visit departments; make any necessary adjustments.
- ❑ Be an "evangelism booster." Encourage all the children to bring new friends throughout the week. Pray for and remind your staff to prepare for the evangelism emphasis of your VBS.
- ❑ Secure additional supplies as needed.
- ❑ Assist with discipline problems and emergency situations as needed.
- ❑ Make sure registration and attendance records are being properly kept.
- ❑ Have someone available to run errands.
- ❑ Distribute any announcements and flyers for children to take home on the appropriate days.
- ❑ Supervise preparations and build enthusiasm for the closing program.
- ❑ Send home special invitations to your closing program. (See sample p. 191.)
- ❑ Supervise the ongoing photography/video taping of the VBS activities.
- ❑ Make sure all VBS volunteers clean up their areas on the last day of VBS. (See *Preparing for Cleanup*, p. 136.)

AFTER VBS:

- ❑ Thank the Lord for His blessing. (Pray for the follow-up efforts. These are the fruits of your Bible ministry.)
- ❑ Make sure facility is cleaned up and returned to original condition.
- ❑ Express appreciation to all workers. (See *Appreciate Your Volunteers*, p. 143.)
- ❑ Have staff perform an evaluation of your VBS program. (See *Evaluating Your Program*, p. 142.)
- ❑ Prepare slide show or video presentation showing VBS highlights.
- ❑ Publish outcome of VBS successes in church bulletin or post on bulletin boards.
- ❑ Begin follow-up efforts.
- ❑ See that supplies are packed, labeled and stored for future use.
- ❑ Compile and file all records, receipts and publications.
- ❑ Create a "debriefing file" complete with your checklists, communication records, personnel lists, etc. Note how problems were solved and how to avoid similar ones in the future. Include notes of necessary adjustments in schedules, additional supplies needed, etc. Write down good ideas for next year.
- ❑ File names/addresses of workers to be contacted next year.

Director's Master Checklist by Categories

ADMINISTRATION/LEADERSHIP DUTIES

24 WEEKS BEFORE:

- ❑ Begin regular prayer for VBS. Ask church groups to pray for VBS from now until the program is over.
- ❑ Determine type of VBS (mornings, evenings, camp format, Backyard Bible School, etc.).

20 WEEKS BEFORE:

- ❑ Meet with church leaders to discuss your role as VBS director.
- ❑ Decide on possible dates for VBS.

18 WEEKS BEFORE:

- ❑ Appoint VBS committee (assistant director, department leaders, publicity coordinator, etc.).
- ❑ Set goals and determine unique needs of your VBS.
- ❑ Choose setting and location for your VBS. Reserve area if needed.
- ❑ Meet with church leaders and secure a VBS budget.
- ❑ Establish and announce VBS dates in church bulletin/newsletter.

16 WEEKS BEFORE:

- ❑ Meet with VBS committee (including all department leaders) to:
  1. Pray for VBS.
  2. Outline time schedules for both self-contained classrooms and activity centers.
  3. Set deadline dates for all activities.
  4. Estimate VBS enrollment and determine staff needs (departmental and general).
  5. Compile lists of prospective workers.
  6. Schedule training workshop(s).
  7. Make a list of supplies to be purchased.

8 WEEKS BEFORE:

- ❑ Plan dedication service for workers; secure minister's approval and help.
- ❑ Plan closing program.
- ❑ Plan follow-up efforts with Sunday School leaders.

6 WEEKS BEFORE:

- ❑ Plan all activities for opening and closing assemblies and for any special mid-week events.

4 WEEKS BEFORE:

- ❑ Check and adjust time schedules if necessary.
- ❑ Plan for extra staff and special procedures needed for first-day registration.
- ❑ Finalize date, time and arrangements for closing program.
- ❑ Make arrangements for sound system and custodial support during and after VBS.
- ❑ Assign rooms and places for each class/center.

1 WEEK BEFORE:

- ❑ Plan for first-aid needs and disciplinary problems.
- ❑ Plan morning staff devotions.
- ❑ Hold an all-staff meeting to discuss any last-minute changes, announce room assignments and answer any questions.

DURING VBS:

- ❑ Conduct morning staff devotions.
- ❑ Lead all or a portion of the opening and closing assemblies. Present VBS awards and certificates to staff and children on last day of VBS.
- ❑ Make sure teachers are present and on schedule. If using the activity center method, signal appropriate time to rotate to next center.
- ❑ Visit departments; make any necessary adjustments.
- ❑ Be an "evangelism booster." Encourage all the children to bring new friends throughout the week. Plan for and remind your staff to prepare for the evangelism emphasis of your VBS.
- ❑ Assist with discipline problems and emergency situations as needed.
- ❑ Have someone available to run errands.
- ❑ Distribute any announcements and flyers for children to take home on appropriate days.
- ❑ Supervise preparations and build enthusiasm for the closing program.
- ❑ Supervise the ongoing photography/video taping of the VBS activities.

AFTER VBS:

- ❑ Begin follow-up efforts.
- ❑ Compile and file all records, receipts and publications.
- ❑ Create a "debriefing file" complete with your checklists, communication records, personnel lists, etc. Note how problems were solved and how to avoid similar ones in the future. Include notes of necessary adjustments in schedules, additional supplies needed, etc. Write down good ideas for next year.

VOLUNTEER RECRUITMENT/ TRAINING

16 WEEKS BEFORE:

- ❏ Meet with VBS committee to estimate enrollment and determine staff needs (departmental and general), compile lists of prospective workers and schedule training workshop(s).
- ❏ Send letter and response postcards to veteran VBS volunteers you want to return.
- ❏ Begin personal contacts to recruit rest of staff.

12 WEEKS BEFORE:

- ❏ Publicize in the church bulletin the need for workers. Give names of department leaders as "persons to see."

10 WEEKS BEFORE:

- ❏ Meet with department leaders to work out training workshop procedures. Discuss the overall goals and aims for VBS and the individual lesson aims.
- ❏ Outline and prepare for training workshop(s).
- ❏ List all VBS staff in church bulletin, asking prayer for them and for any remaining vacancies.
- ❏ Contact all recruits, confirming preliminary assignments, notifying them of training workshop(s).

8 WEEKS BEFORE:

- ❏ Publicize training workshop(s) in church bulletin. Identify new staff additions and remaining vacancies.
- ❏ Enlist qualified crew of child-care workers for volunteers' children.

6 WEEKS BEFORE:

- ❏ Meet with the leaders (missions, publicity, finance, crafts, snacks, transportation, etc.) for prayer and to determine if they are accomplishing their assignments. Use the checklists from this section for evaluations.
- ❏ Plan for and enlist substitutes.

4 WEEKS BEFORE:

- ❏ Conduct training workshop(s).

1 WEEK BEFORE:

- ❏ Hold dedication service for volunteers.
- ❏ Distribute class rosters/attendance sheets to teachers or counselors.
- ❏ Assist leaders or teachers in last-minute preparations.

DURING VBS:

- ❏ Continue staff support functions. Pray with and for them. Communicate with them and work at maintaining their spirit of enthusiasm.
- ❏ Arrange for substitutes when needed.
- ❏ Visit departments; make any necessary adjustments.
- ❏ Present VBS awards and certificates to staff and children on the last day of VBS.

AFTER VBS:

- ❏ Express appreciation to all workers.
- ❏ Have staff perform an evaluation of your VBS program.
- ❏ File names/addresses of workers to be contacted next year.

PUBLICITY

16 WEEKS BEFORE:

- ❏ Plan publicity with publicity coordinator.
- ❏ Order publicity materials.

10 WEEKS BEFORE:

- ❏ Begin displaying banners and posters throughout church building and community.

8 WEEKS BEFORE:

- ❏ Make VBS flyers for church members to use for invitations.

4 WEEKS BEFORE:

- ❏ Distribute theme buttons and/or T-shirts to all staff members to wear to church from now through the end of VBS.
- ❏ Mail postcard invitations to invite prospects to attend and/or deliver flyers/door hangers throughout neighborhood.
- ❏ Make and photocopy any flyers or announcements that will be going home with the children each day.

DURING VBS:

- ❏ Distribute any announcements and flyers for children to take home on the appropriate days.
- ❏ Send home special invitations to your closing program.

AFTER VBS:

- ❏ Prepare slide show or video presentation showing VBS highlights.
- ❏ Publish outcome of VBS successes in church bulletin or post on bulletin boards.

PREREGISTRATION/ REGISTRATION

8 WEEKS BEFORE:

- ❑ Plan and prepare preregistration activities.

6 WEEKS BEFORE:

- ❑ Begin preregistration.

4 WEEKS BEFORE:

- ❑ Plan for extra staff and special procedures needed for first-day registration.

1 WEEK BEFORE:

- ❑ Assign preregistered children to classes or groups.
- ❑ Distribute class rosters/attendance sheets to teachers or counselors.
- ❑ Assign volunteer(s) to purchase or make name tags for each class.

DURING VBS:

- ❑ Make sure registration and attendance records are being properly kept.

AFTER VBS:

- ❑ Compile and file all records, receipts and publications.

CURRICULUM

20 WEEKS BEFORE:

- ❑ Compare and evaluate VBS curriculum choices.

18 WEEKS BEFORE:

- ❑ Decide on a VBS curriculum and return all unused kits to publisher.
- ❑ Order basic VBS curriculum (such as a Starter Kit).

16 WEEKS BEFORE:

- ❑ Order curriculum materials.

12 WEEKS BEFORE:

- ❑ Distribute curriculum materials to department leaders.

4 WEEKS BEFORE:

- ❑ Order any extra materials needed based on preregistration indicators.

SUPPLIES

16 WEEKS BEFORE:

- ❑ Publish bulletin insert listing craft supply needs, refreshment donations and other materials needed.

10 WEEKS BEFORE:

- ❑ Distribute second notice regarding supplies.
- ❑ Distribute supplies to department leaders.

8 WEEKS BEFORE:

- ❑ Purchase remaining craft supplies.

4 WEEKS BEFORE:

- ❑ Make sure all leaders and teachers have last-minute supplies.
- ❑ Check and adjust supplies as needed.
- ❑ Update bulletin insert to provide final request for items still needed.

DURING VBS:

- ❑ Secure additional supplies as needed.

AFTER VBS:

- ❑ See that supplies are packed, labeled and stored for future use.

FACILITIES

18 WEEKS BEFORE:

- ❑ Choose setting and location for your VBS.

6 WEEKS BEFORE:

- ❑ Plan theme-decorating ideas. This may include having backdrops painted.

4 WEEKS BEFORE:

- ❑ Make arrangements for sound system and custodial support during and after VBS.

1 WEEK BEFORE:

- ❑ Hold a preparation day for staff to decorate and arrange indoor rooms (if possible).

DURING VBS:

- ❑ Make sure all VBS volunteers clean up their areas on the last day of VBS.

AFTER VBS:

- ❑ Make sure facility is cleaned up and returned to original condition.

The Care and Feeding of Volunteers

Determining staff needs and recruiting are just the beginning of your involvement with volunteers. The deeper you get into planning for VBS, the more you realize how crucial your volunteers really are to the success of the program. It is to your advantage to make sure that your volunteers have the support and respect they deserve.

The Key to this is really very simple—communicate with them.

Delegation does not end your responsibility. You cannot hand someone a booklet and expect him or her to have everything prepared and ready to go by day one. Keeping in touch with your volunteers is a tangible means of supporting and ministering to them.

It is your job as VBS Director to keep the lines of communication open. Make proactive efforts to meet or talk periodically with each volunteer, and make sure he or she knows how to get in touch with you. Volunteers are bound to feel more confident and prepared when they are encouraged to come to you with any questions, problems, prayer requests or ideas. There are a variety of ways to maintain contact:

- **Meet personally with each of your volunteers.** This is especially important when you are not familiar with the person. You may want to meet with an entire department to build unity and generate ideas; or you may want to meet with some volunteers on a one-to-one basis.
- **Call them.** Try to telephone each volunteer at least once every four to six weeks before VBS starts. Check on their progress, ask if they have any questions, ask for feedback on how the process is going, ask how you can better assist them and then pray with them over the phone. If you find that a volunteer is going through a personal crisis or having a hard time coping with the extra stress, trust God to find a replacement. Be sensitive to the Holy Spirit's leading!
- **Write to them.** This may be done through encouraging personal notes or via a monthly newsletter that includes current lists of volunteers, a highlight on one of your volunteers, upcoming training meetings, prayer requests, list of requested items and an uplifting devotional. If your curriculum doesn't provide one, you may also want to put together a volunteer handbook that contains an encouraging letter from the director, a description of the VBS theme, the daily schedule, all scheduled meetings, closing program information, volunteer roster and job descriptions. Give the handbook to volunteers when they sign up.

You may want to keep a record of your communications with your volunteers (see sample form, p. 164). A simple note as to when you met/called/wrote, what was communicated and what response was made will keep you more consistent in your efforts. It may also keep problems from arising and will certainly serve as a good prayer reminder as you proceed through your VBS planning. Beyond that, regular personal communication from you will make all your volunteers feel valued and appreciated—as they ought to be!

Nursery and Child Care

Providing child care for your volunteers during meetings and at VBS is one of the most overlooked areas in planning a daytime VBS. However, if you have parents in your church with young children, this is an extremely important issue in recruiting. Very few parents will be willing to sacrifice the care of their own child in order to volunteer. Therefore, it is a good idea to make your plans for child care while you are still in the recruiting stages. For helpful information on the quality of your nursery facility, see *Health and Safety Precautions,* pages 85-86.

Choosing Caregivers

Depending on the ages your VBS program includes, you may need to provide child care for children anywhere from newborn to 5 years old. If you expect to have quite a few children in this range, consider asking your nursery coordinator or a similarly experienced volunteer to help coordinate this area. The child care coordinator will be responsible for creating a safe and interesting environment with age-appropriate activities and should assist in recruiting other caregivers to serve. You will need at least one caregiver for every three or four babies and toddlers (use the lower number for infants, the higher number for the oldest toddlers). Always plan for at least two caregivers to work together in the nursery, no matter how few children are present.

Churches have a variety of options when choosing caregivers for a daytime VBS: paid workers, volunteer workers, junior workers or a combination. Using paid caregivers has some advantages:

* It creates higher expectations of a quality program.
* It provides continuity of caregivers in the nursery each day.
* It fosters dependability on the part of caregivers to be there promptly each day.
* It provides more responsible oversight of volunteer caregivers.

Volunteer caregivers are more likely to view their job as a ministry and will not want to be paid. You may decide to have one paid caregiver and several junior volunteers; or if you have a dependable adult volunteer who wants the responsibility, you may be able to staff your nursery entirely with volunteers. The important thing is to make sure your main caregiver is totally qualified. He or she should be prepared to arrive at least 15 minutes (or more if you have morning staff devotions) before VBS starts each day. As the director, you want your VBS staff to be comfortable leaving their little ones in the nursery, knowing they are being well cared for and nurtured, so that they can freely give their energies to their tasks.

Planning a Schedule

Child care for nursery-aged children should be more than just baby-sitting. Considering that in the average VBS the children are in the nursery (or other classroom) for more than three hours each day, an interesting schedule of activities is an absolute must. Many publishers have become aware of the need to provide nursery activities and include curriculum for children as young as 12 months in their VBS materials. The goal of this curriculum is not to get a baby or toddler to spout theological concepts! Instead, it is to teach individually each baby and toddler through natural learning processes what he or she can begin to learn about God. Do not force a child to sit still or participate in any activity in which he or she is not interested. Here is a sample VBS nursery schedule for children newborn to 3 years. Follow it loosely and adapt it to fit your needs.

VBS NURSERY SCHEDULE (0–3 years)

8:30–9:00AM	Parents drop off children. Soft music or a soothing video. Independent play.
9:00–9:30AM	One or two caregivers bring 3-year-olds into Opening Assembly. Under 3 years, continue independent play.
9:30–9:45AM	Puppet Welcome Time. Story Time (use curriculum or own resources). Movement activities (stretching, finger play, copy cat).
9:45–10:00AM	Art activities (coloring page or simple craft from VBS craft book).
10:00–10:30AM	Free play or video.
10:30–10:45AM	Snack Time.
10:45–11:15AM	Outdoor walk and play.
11:15–11:30AM	Return to room. Circle Time. (Lay a large blanket on the floor and have children sit in a circle. Bring a special toy, book or other object for children to look at. Sing songs together.)
11:30–12:00PM	Free play and cleanup.
12:00–12:15PM	Parents pick up children.

Publicity Coordinator

Well-planned publicity is critical to the success of any event—especially Vacation Bible School. After identifying your target audience and determining how to appeal to them, you are ready to plan your attack. The goals are to build excitement and spread the information about your event. There are hundreds of ideas and tools to help you in your planning.

Promoting Within the Community

Vacation Bible School is one of the church's best opportunities for outreach to children and families in the community. With that in mind, you will need to give some attention to making contact with people in the community. The following list suggests a variety of exciting ways to reach this goal:

* **Purchase or make a large VBS theme banner.** (See *How to Make a VBS Banner,* p. 59.) Display the banner on a visible spot on your church property.
* **Place VBS theme posters in conspicuous places in your community** such as grocery store windows, businesses, recreation centers, libraries, shopping malls, restaurants, day-care centers and schools. Make sure you ask permission before posting them.
* **Present VBS skits in parks and neighborhoods.** Wherever children and families gather can provide a setting for a brief skit and announcement. A portable cassette player can be used to play the VBS songs to help draw a crowd.
* **Distribute promotional flyers or door-knob hangers throughout the community.** Be sure to print dates, time and place information on flyers. Consider handing out flyers in shopping centers (check with management first).
* **Submit promotional ads and/or short news releases about your VBS to your local newspaper(s).** Include a black-and-white glossy picture of some of your staff and children involved in a VBS activity. Use your VBS skit characters, mascot or puppet for an interesting photo! Ask for specific submission procedures from each publication before you begin. (See p. 59 for sample copy and hints.)
* **Publicize your VBS over local radio stations and/or television.** Some radio stations and public access television stations will announce your event for free.
* **Hold a special kickoff promotional event a few days before VBS begins.** Invite all 4- through 12-year-olds to come to your church parking lot for a morning of games, refreshments, crafts, skits and other fun activities. (See *Planning a Kickoff Promotional Event,* pp. 60-66.)
* **Duplicate and send a direct letter to all the homes in the community.** (See p. 190 for a sample letter.)
* **Print and distribute coupons or tickets to your promotional event or VBS.** Attach them to flyers or letters. Tickets are good on the first day of VBS or for whatever special activity you have planned.

Promoting Within the Church

It is not wise to neglect promoting VBS within your church body, as it is quite possible that many people in your own congregation may not know what VBS is about, let alone its times and dates. Getting your congregation excited about VBS will be a great boost to recruiting volunteers and spreading the word. Take advantage of every available means to promote VBS within your congregation.

* **Show slides of last year's VBS,** concluding with shots of this year's theme poster. Play your VBS theme song to go along with the presentation.
* **If available, show portions of the VBS publisher's preview video to build enthusiasm and recruit helpers.**

* **Make a coloring poster.** Photocopy and distribute coloring posters to Sunday School classes. Display completed posters in church foyer or well-seen window.
* **Have Sunday School teachers and VBS staff wear VBS theme buttons and/or VBS T-shirts to church for three to four weeks preceding VBS.**
* **Ask church leaders, Sunday School teachers and others to encourage the congregation to be involved in VBS.**
* **If you have a VBS mascot, clown or puppet, have the character make regular appearances in children's and adult Sunday School classes.**
* **Make a theme-decorated, giant registration booth out of cardboard or wood.** Place the booth in a visible area to capture attention. Use it to display T-shirts, tote bags, theme buttons and sample crafts. This booth could be moved to the kickoff event to serve as an information/registration booth.
* **Play music from your VBS music cassette in all Sunday School classes or during worship breaks for several weeks before VBS.** Have VBS staff sing one of the VBS songs during a morning or evening service.
* **Distribute recruitment flyers to everyone in the church.** (See pp. 162-163 for sample insert/flyers.)
* **Duplicate and send a direct letter to all the homes in your congregation.** (See p. 189 for a sample letter.)
* **Visit each Sunday School department and display VBS promotional items** such as T-shirts, tote bags, theme buttons and craft samples.
* **Promote the special kickoff promotional event** as an opportunity to get everyone involved.
* **Make creative, exciting VBS announcements in the church bulletin and/or newsletter.**
* **Make catchy bulletin board displays.**
* **Establish a telephone chain to invite all children within the church.** Keep details brief.
* **Invite previous VBS volunteers and/or students to give testimonials of the impact VBS had in their lives.** Ask permission to have testimonials presented during a worship or other adult service.

Publicity Materials

Most VBS publishers offer a variety of promotional items to help you in your publicity efforts. If they are not available, however, consider making your own. Here is a list of materials that have proven to be effective. Choose the ones which work best for your VBS.

* **VBS theme posters**—Advertise VBS in your community with a colorful poster. Include dates, time and location.
* **Outdoor banner**—Display a large colorful banner on the outside of your church building.
* **Ads**—Publicize your VBS through local newspapers and/or radio stations. (See *How to Use a News Release*, p. 59.)
* **Direct mail**—Use the suggested direct mail letters for church and community outreach.
* **Invitation postcards**—Mail postcards to prospective students.
* **Coloring posters**—Invite children to join the fun by holding a coloring contest.
* **Theme buttons**—Use buttons as attention-getters to promote VBS.
* **Promotional flyer/bulletin insert**—Use attractive inserts for your church bulletins preceding VBS. Also use flyers door-to-door in neighborhood outreach.
* **Clip art** (conventional or computerized)—Use clip art for your newsletters, bulletins and promotional materials. (See p. 58 for help on using clip art.)
* **Door-knob hangers**—Use hangers for advertising door-to-door in your community.
* **Promotional T-shirt**—and/or iron-on transfers. Have volunteers and preregistered children wear their shirts as walking billboards.
* **Preview video**—Use this video to give viewers a glimpse of the fun to be had at your VBS.
* **Theme music audiocassette or CD**—Play music to build interest for any promotional activity you plan.
* **Tote bags**—Give tote bags to volunteers to build team unity.

How to Use Clip Art

With clip art you can let your imagination do the walking to produce super flyers, bulletin inserts, postcards, posters, handbills, newsletters, overhead transparencies, T-shirt art and much more.

First, you should decide exactly what you are going to make. The following seven questions are good to work through for any printed piece you want to do, whether done in-house with computers and/or copiers or sent out to be done by a professional printer. Answer only the questions that are applicable. Place a check mark in each box as you make these important determinations.

1. What is the size of the publication (before folding)?
   - ❑ $4^1/_4$"x$5^1/_2$" (Postcard)
   - ❑ $5^1/_2$"x$8^1/_2$" (Bulletin Insert)
   - ❑ $8^1/_2$"x11" (Flyer)
   - ❑ $8^1/_2$"x14" (Small Poster)
   - ❑ 11"x17" (Large Poster)
   - ❑ Other ______

   (May require trimming from a printer or copy center at extra cost.)
2. On how many sides will it be printed?
   - ❑ One side
   - ❑ Both sides
   - ❑ Both sides of multiple sheets
3. How many copies will be printed? ______
4. What kind and color of paper will be used?

   ______

   (If your piece is being professionally printed, be sure to review sample stock at the printers.)
5. What color(s) of ink will be used (if professionally printed or done on a color printer)?
   - ❑ One. Color ______
   - ❑ More than one. Colors ______
6. Date publication must be printed ______
7. Date publication must be mailed ______

If you are using conventional clip art and doing your project in-house, you will need these materials:

- ❋ Clip art from publisher or other clip art resource book.
- ❋ Word processor or typewriter
- ❋ Photocopy machine
- ❋ Scissors
- ❋ Rubber cement, transparent tape or glue stick
- ❋ White paper

Follow these five easy steps to create your piece:

1. Choose the artwork you would like to use. Make a few sketches of the basic layout on scratch paper, including all text and position of all artwork. Don't leave any element out of this layout sketch. Plan to leave a one-half inch (or more) margin on your paper.
2. Use a word processor or typewriter to create the text you would like to include. Set margins to the width of the text area on your layout. (When using a word processor, take advantage of the variety of fonts and sizes available to create interest.) Print out and cut around shape of text.
3. Photocopy the clip art that you will be using. You may want to enlarge or reduce the artwork to fit your layout. Cut out around shape of artwork.
4. Position the art and text on a sheet of white paper following your layout. When you are satisfied with it, use tape, glue or rubber cement to attach the artwork and text to the paper. (Prevent the pick up of lines from the glued paper by taping all edges completely.)
5. Make as many copies as you need.

Another alternative to cutting and pasting is to use a computer publishing program. If your church does not have a publishing program of its own, find out if someone in your congregation has access to one. Many copy centers also have publishing programs available for your use. Chances are you will probably be able to find someone who can scan in your clip art and create the entire project on the computer.

How to Make a VBS Banner

A large outdoor banner will help to advertise VBS in your community. Use a 3x4-foot (.9x1.2-m) sheet of plastic, durable fabric or coated paper. Recruit a volunteer who is familiar with painting on the material you have chosen. Use clip art or other art to sketch out the banner design on paper. Photocopy the sketch onto a transparency sheet and use an overhead projector to project the image on the banner material. Outline the image with chalk or pencil. Then paint the banner with oil-based or acrylic paint.

How to Use a News Release

Adapt this sample news release to send to the local events editor of your local newspaper, or use it as a script for a short radio or television spot.

Sample News Release Copy

(Church's name) invites children to an exciting adventure. "We have a tremendous program planned for the children in our community," said (minister's name) of (church name). "This summer we will be transforming the church into a (theme name) where children will discover the truth from God's Word. We will be having great songs, skits, crafts, games, Bible studies and snacks—all of the things that make Vacation Bible School so popular with children and their parents. On top of that, we will be helping kids grow in their love for God and learn to share His love with others.

"Everything draws to a joyful conclusion at the closing program on (date and time of closing program)—a musical event that's fun for the whole family.

"We're looking forward to this very special opportunity for us to reach out to parents and children in our neighborhood and share with them the joy of developing a personal relationship with God."

The (theme name) Vacation Bible School begins (date) and continues through (closing date). It will be held at (church address) from (opening and closing times). For information, call (church phone number).

Remember these hints when preparing your ads:

- Newspapers operate on inflexible schedules, so be sure to deliver your press release on time. Call your local newspaper(s) to double-check deadlines.
- Type and double-space the press release and be sure to include your name and phone number.
- Don't be wordy. Include only pertinent information about your event—the newspaper editor will cut out the fluff anyway.
- Include a nonreturnable black-and-white glossy photo (with identifying names and information on the back) or ask the newspaper to send a photographer to your event.

Planning a KicKoff Promotional Event

Kick off your VBS with a special event combining your VBS theme with lots of fun activities for children and adults. Choose a weekend afternoon a week or two before your VBS program. Transform your church parking lot into a carnival, full of balloons and festive decorations. Set up booths for playing games, creating crafts, making discoveries, enjoying refreshments and, of course, registering for VBS (see the following suggestions). Perform parts of your VBS skits periodically throughout the day and have skit characters wander through the crowd answering questions and making people feel welcome.

Admission should be free. In this informal atmosphere unchurched parents will feel comfortable visiting your church with their children and will appreciate the good time you provided at no cost. Church members who help out will become excited. After all the fun, children won't want to miss a moment of the VBS program. And of much greater importance, your church will have made positive, friendly contact with a large number of families in your neighborhood, registered many children for VBS and opened the door for further ministry in the months ahead.

Information/Registration Is the Goal

The primary goal of this promotional event is to motivate parents and children to attend your upcoming VBS program. One of the things you can do to ensure that this is accomplished is to place your information/registration booth near the center of all the action. If possible, arrange it so that each person who arrives has to pass through this booth. Consider giving each child a "Party Pack" with tickets for all event activities and refreshments, Vacation Bible School registration forms and a small gift such as a button to wear. (See p. 66 for sample ticket/passport.)

When children do register for VBS, be sure to mention that VBS will not be just like the promotional event. Explain that while there will be many fun things to do at VBS, there will also be times of listening and learning about God's love and how to show His love to others. Consider giving each registrant a coupon redeemable for some feature on the first day of VBS.

Follow up each registration with a phone call or postcard from the VBS teacher of the child's age group. A simple, "I'm going to be your teacher and just wanted to say 'Hi,'" will encourage the child to come expecting good things.

In the midst of all the festivities, be aware of opportunities to talk informally with children and parents. Help them feel accepted by showing interest in them as individuals. A cold drink, a snack, a smile and conversation—all can be given in Jesus' name in a spirit of concern for children and their families.

Booth Ideas for Your Promotional Event

Information/Registration Booth
This should be the most prominent and gaily decorated booth of them all. Volunteers at this site should be friendly and well-informed about all facets of both the kick-off event and VBS itself. Keep this booth well-staffed at all times so volunteers will sense freedom to talk individually with those who arrive.

Refreshment Booth
Who can resist free drinks and snacks—especially on a fine summer day? Use ideas from your VBS snack guide or make up your own theme-oriented snacks.

Discovery Booth

Have children participate in a theme-related science discovery. Children may enjoy identifying places on maps or animal noises on tape; or have someone demonstrate a hands-on science project.

Photo Booth

Paint a cardboard backdrop with an VBS theme-related scene. Set props and potted plants in front of the backdrop. Provide costumes for children and then photograph each one in front of the backdrop. An instant-picture camera is suggested; however, you can use a regular camera and send photos to families or have the photos picked up when developed.

Go Fish

Make a fishing booth from plywood, cardboard or a sheet. Paint the front of the booth as an underwater scene. Children use a fishing pole with a clothespin hook to "cast into the sea." They catch a treat such as a plastic sandwich bag filled with fish-shaped crackers.

"Be Cool" Dunk Tank

Set up a dunking tank device in which a hit on the metal bull's-eye causes a person to drop into the tank of water. Encourage well-known people such as your Christian education director, pastor or Sunday School teachers to be targets.

Chalk Walk

With chalk, draw 10 to 20 small circles on the ground. Number each circle. While playing the VBS music tape, children hop from circle to circle. When the music stops, the leader draws a number out of a hat. Whoever is standing on the number drawn wins a prize.

Basket Toss

Paint the back wall of a booth with an appropriate theme design and attach baskets of various sizes to the wall. Children attempt to pitch objects into the baskets.

Search 'n Discover Booth

Fill a child's wading pool with water or sand. Add a few dozen colorful marbles or painted pebbles. Children can walk barefoot in the pool and attempt to pick up objects with their toes. Children see how many objects they can gather within a set time limit. Make a chart and place each child's name and number of objects gathered on the chart.

Fun on Wheels

Decorate tricycles, wagons or go-carts with crepe-paper streamers, ribbons and balloons. Let children race on a designated course.

Lights Out

Children stand behind a designated line and with a squirt gun attempt to extinguish a row of lighted candles several feet away. Take all necessary safety precautions for dealing with an open flame.

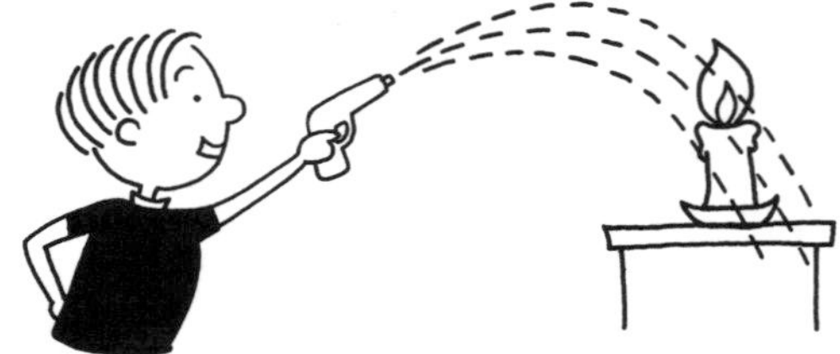

Pinwheel

Children cut and fold paper, and then tack to doweling to create pinwheels. You may want to have an electric fan on hand to provide a breeze.

Bangles and Beads

Provide dyed macaroni, beads and natural objects such as seed pods or flowers for children to string into necklaces and bracelets.

Beautiful Bouquets

Provide fresh and/or dried flowers and leaves to make bouquets. Children put their bouquets inside paper doilies that are cut in half and rolled into a cone shape. Children give their bouquets to a family member.

Bubble-Blowing Contest

Give each child a piece of bubble gum and several minutes to chew. Then have the children blow bubbles and measure them with a ruler. Record names and sizes of bubbles on a chart.

Apple Clowns
Decorate apple "faces" with raisins, marshmallows, carrot curls, coconut, grapes, etc., for eyes, nose, mouth and hair. Tooth-picks and peanut butter can be used to attach the facial features. Add a paper clown hat decorated with tiny stickers. You'll also need construc-tion paper, scissors, a stapler and stickers.

Water Jug Relays
Children hold water-filled plastic gallon milk jugs (with tops cut off) on their heads and race from the "well" to finish line.

Balloon Creatures
Cut shapes and eyes out of fun foam or colored card stock. Children can use felt markers to decorate eyes and fins and then tape them to a helium-filled balloon to create a colorful creature on a string.

Face-Painting Booth
Children choose from a variety of designs to have painted on their faces.

Potter's Place
Invite a potter to bring a potter's wheel and demonstrate his or her craft. Children take turns molding pots. If potter or wheel is unavailable, children can shape clay by hand into simple pots.

Bobbing for Apples
Float apples in a washtub filled with water. Children can take turns bobbing for apples.

City Zoo
In shaded area, have a variety of animals available for children to look at and pet.

Tie-Dyed Bandanna Booth
Children tie-dye 18-inch (45-cm) squares cut from white sheets. You'll need containers of fabric dye, rubber bands, rubber gloves, tongs or wooden spoons and a line and clothespins for drying.

Balloon Booth
Children can use permanent felt pens to decorate helium-filled balloons. A metal washer at the end of each balloon string will keep the balloon from floating away.

Snakes Alive
Set up a hands-on display with small animals and other safe caged reptiles. Children observe and may even touch the specimens. You may want to provide small leaves, flowers, bark, etc., and a magnifying glass with which to get a close-up look.

Human Statues
Have two or three people pose as statues or mannequins. Children take turns trying to make statues laugh without touching them.

Keepsake Collage
Children glue a variety of throw-away items to a cardboard base to make a collage. In addition to throw-away items, provide glue, paint, scissors, markers, etc.

Pony Rides
Children can take turns riding on a pony or horse.

Helpful Hints for Your Promotional Event

Staffing

Each activity needs at least one adult or responsible teenager to be in charge. Encourage all helpers to dress the part of the character or booth they are representing. You may want to ask individual families or Sunday School classes in your church to sponsor booths. Each family or class would be responsible for purchasing supplies, setting up and staffing the booth during the event. In addition to those running the booths, you may want to have several helpers who can be free to greet parents and encourage children to try an activity that is low on participation. These special personal touches will help make your big event a big success.

Setup

Each activity needs a designated area. In most situations, the booths should be set up outside, preferably on a lawn or in the parking lot. One simple way to designate each area is to mark the ground with colorful chalk and add an awning. Or mark the boundaries by placing stakes or cones in each corner of the area, tying brightly-colored crepe paper from stake to stake or cone to cone to make a booth. For a more durable enclosure, build or borrow actual booths. To build, use 8-foot-long 2x2s. Consider attaching small clusters of helium-filled balloons to the front corners of each booth and painting structures with theme-related scenes. Each booth needs a large sign identifying the activity. Restrooms need to be plentiful, open and clearly marked.

Live Characters

Have a VBS mascot, clown or skit characters make your event extra special. They can join helpers in greeting arrivals and in running booths. In addition, characters can perform mini-skits from your VBS curriculum or others you have created especially for the event.

Music

Live music will add a festive feeling and is something everyone will enjoy. If possible, use live musicians to play theme music. If you can't arrange for live music, play the VBS audiocassette or CD over a sound system.

Passports/Tickets

Make a passport for each child—a giant ticket that will allow him or her to participate in all games, crafts and refreshments. This ticket can be given out as children pass through the information/registration booth. It could also be given out in advance at Sunday School, parks, shopping centers or even door-to-door in various promotional activities.

The child can either carry or hang the passport around his or her neck. As children visit a booth, the volunteer rubber-stamps or punches a hole in the corresponding square on the ticket. Encourage children to visit every booth before repeating an activity.

Publicity Coordinator's Countdown Schedule

16 WEEKS BEFORE:

- ❑ Plan publicity with VBS Director.
- ❑ Order publicity materials.

10 WEEKS BEFORE:

- ❑ Begin displaying banners and posters throughout church building and community.
- ❑ Photocopy and distribute coloring posters.

4 WEEKS BEFORE:

- ❑ Distribute theme buttons and/or T-shirts to all staff members to wear to church from now through the end of VBS.
- ❑ Mail postcard invitations to invite prospects to attend and/or deliver promotional flyer/bulletin inserts throughout neighborhood.
- ❑ Update bulletin inserts to provide final details to congregation.
- ❑ Display completed coloring posters.
- ❑ Submit promotional ad for a newspaper article.
- ❑ Send direct mail letters to church and community members.
- ❑ Arrange to air a VBS promotional spot on local radio station.

Sample Ticket for Promotional Event

(VBS Theme Name)

Your ticket to the
(name of promotional day).

(name of booth)	Date:	(name of booth)
(name of booth)		(name of booth)
(name of booth)		(name of booth)
(name of booth)	Time:	(name of booth)
(name of booth)		(name of booth)
(name of booth)	Place:	(name of booth)
(name of booth)		(name of booth)
(name of booth)		(name of booth)
(name of booth)		(name of booth)

Missions Coordinator

The purpose of Vacation Bible School is to reach children with the message of Christ and to teach them what it means to live for Him. A VBS missions project is an excellent way for children to experience sharing God's love with the world around them. When projects are well-chosen and creatively presented, children respond naturally and enthusiastically. You may be sparking an interest in missions that will literally change the world.

A successful missions project will include two key elements: missions teaching and missions involvement. This section contains many ideas for both teaching and involving children in missions. Use those ideas that best fit your situation.

Choosing the Right Missions Project for Your Kids

In choosing a missions project, you may want to consider these factors before making your final decision:

* **The tangible, reachable nature of your goal.** Children respond better to meeting a specific need than giving to the general fund of an organization or missionary. It's even better if the need is one they can directly relate to as children, such as a car for a missionary family, food or clothing for an orphanage, books for a school, etc.
* **The appeal of the project to parents of unchurched children.** A project that assists people with physical needs (feeding the hungry, clothing the homeless, providing medical aid, etc.) is most easily presented to families who may not be involved in your church.
* **The availability of visual information about the missionary and/or project** (photos, posters, artifacts, maps, letters, etc.). These visual resources are absolutely necessary to increase children's understanding and maintain their interest. A missionary may be very worthy and a project very commendable, but your children will not "get it" without lots of visual help.
* **Your ability to visualize creatively the progress of your project to create suspense throughout the week.** For example, if you are helping to buy a vehicle, collect offering in hubcaps. One VBS gathered money to buy powdered milk for an overseas orphanage, illustrating each day's giving by pouring an appropriate amount of powdered milk into a transparent container so students could see the result of their offerings. A large treasure chest could be filled with "coins" to represent each day's offering. Be sure to display your visual at the closing program.

When you think you know what you want to do, be sure to consult your pastor and the missions committee of your church (or denominational headquarters). Then write to the missionary, asking ways VBS students may give assistance; also ask for specific prayer requests. Suggest the missionary send a videocassette of his or her work, prayer letters and personal stories if at all possible.

Teaching Children about Missions

With so many activities competing for a child's time and attention at VBS, you will want your missions teaching times to be brief but interest-catching. A short presentation made with enthusiasm will be very effective. Your aim should be to teach children a few simple facts about missions and about your particular project during each day of VBS. The following ideas may be used in a five-minute "Moment for Missions" during your opening assembly times, a longer session in individual classrooms, a missions activity center visited by individual classes each day, or any combination.

Sample Schedule for Five-Minute "Moment for Missions"

(during opening assembly)

DAY 1:
Display a large poster with the name and picture(s) of the missions organization or missionary you have chosen to support. Briefly tell how the organization or missionary shows God's love to children in need. Introduce your missions project for the week.

DAY 2:
Tell a specific story of how your missions organization or missionary shared God's love with children and what resulted. Explain how your missions project will help the organization or missionary to continue showing God's love. Display the visual device that will record the progress of your missions project during VBS.

DAY 3:
Show several slides of the work done by your missions organization or missionary. Report on the progress of your missions project. Update visual accordingly.

Day 4:
Play a brief tape-recorded message to the children from a person within the missions organization or your missionary. Ask a volunteer to update your missions project visual.

DAY 5:
Conclude missions project by displaying visual and giving a final report. Encourage children by explaining what their efforts will mean to the organization or missionary. End by leading in prayer that the children's gifts will be useful in helping children discover God's love.

Sample Schedule for Missions Session

(during individual classes or at a Missions Activity Center, 15–25 minutes)

DAY 1:
Children unscramble lettered cards to spell "missionary." Discuss what it means to be a missionary. Children use Bibles to locate and read 1 Timothy 2:3,4. Ask, "What does God want all people to know?" (The truth.) Explain that many missionaries share the truth about God and His Son, Jesus, with people who have never heard it before. Tell a true missionary story. Display a large poster with the name and picture(s) from the missions organization or missionary you have chosen to support. Introduce your missions project for the week.

DAY 2:
Lead children in a prayer time for the missions organization or missionary and the children to whom they minister. Tell a missionary story. Children begin their missions projects.

DAY 3:
Show slides of the work done by the organization or missionary. Ask, "What are some ways our organization (or missionary) shares the good news with children?" Tell a missionary story. Children continue working on their project.

DAY 4:
Display a map marking locations where the completed missions projects might go or the location of your missionary. Tell a missionary story. Children continue work on missions projects.

DAY 5:
Children complete missions projects. Encourage children by explaining what their efforts will mean to the recipients. Lead children in prayer that their projects will provide encouragement to the people in the community that will receive them. Pray for the missions organization or missionary family that has been highlighted throughout the week, that God would continue to protect them and strengthen their faith.

Involving Children in Missions

Children will become aware of the needs of missionaries and the people they minister to through your teaching times. However, the key to developing a lasting interest in missions is hands-on involvement. Your children will respond well to the following ideas:

* Write a letter to parents about ways to involve their children in your missions project. Send the letter home with children on the first day of VBS.
* Children do jobs for their parents to earn money for the missions project. Send home a list of suggested jobs.
* Children collect aluminum cans or other recyclable materials to raise money for missions.
* Children present a musical program at a retirement center, hospital or other local ministry.
* Older children prepare food and serve it at a local rescue mission, soup kitchen or recovery center.
* Volunteers participate in a prayer time for your missionary.
* Children communicate directly with missionaries through letters, videos or tape recordings. They might enjoy singing songs, reading Scripture and introducing themselves. A class photo could be enclosed in a letter.
* Children prepare materials for crafts to be made by children in mission Bible schools.
* Children decorate and prepare boxes packed with useful and fun items to be distributed in your local community or across the world! Boxes may be filled with small toys, toiletries, individually wrapped non-perishable food items, stationery and other small gifts. You may give your boxes to local shelters or to a missionary whom your church supports.

Other Ideas

* Display a colorful poster lettered with the word "missionary." Point out that a missionary is someone who is sent on a special mission or job and the most special job anyone can be sent to do is to tell people about Jesus. Explain that all believers can be missionaries wherever they live. Tell how your church sends missionaries to many places where people need to hear about God and His love.
* Tell a true missionary story (see resource list at end of article).
* Set up a room or corner of a room as your missions activity center. Decorate according to the country or project on which you will be focusing. Prepare a missions listening post. Record a missionary story on cassette tape for children to listen to with earphones.
* Set up a missions book corner in your classroom. Purchase or borrow children's books about the lives of famous missionaries.
* Display a map or globe and place a colorful marker to indicate where your missionary lives or where your missions organization supplies help. On photocopied maps, children can mark the location of your town (or church) and the location of the organization or missionary you are supporting.
* Invite a visiting missionary to come to your VBS to tell a true mission story. Your guest may be a missionary or one who has visited a mission field. Use high school or college students who have been on short-term mission assignments. Before the guest arrives, have the children write or dictate questions to ask. Have the missionary briefly tell about his or her work and then answer the questions. Communicate with your guest beforehand about the age level of the children he or she will be speaking to and the type of information they would be interested in hearing. Don't assume that the missionary is skilled at dealing with children.
* Present a brief slide show or video of the work done by a missionary or a missions organization.
* Visit a local mission agency and take a tour of the facilities.
* Have a church member who enjoys writing and illustrating create a simple booklet to tell about a missionary your church supports. Make a copy for each child. Read through the booklet with children and allow them to color the pictures.

Gospel Light's Children's Missions Resources for Grades K-6

Missionary Adventure Stories on Audiocassette

Six dramatic missionary adventure stories are told by Ethel Barrett, one of America's favorite storytellers. Sound effects and animated dialogue add to the suspense and drama of these true-to-life adventure stories. Some are short stories (five to eight minutes). Others are longer stories with several five- to seven-minute segments that can be used either in serial form or all in one sitting.
Code #75116.00042

The Great KidMission

This resource book is full of stories, games and crafts designed to acquaint children with different parts of the world and to build their enthusiasm for sharing the gospel.
Code #08307.17617

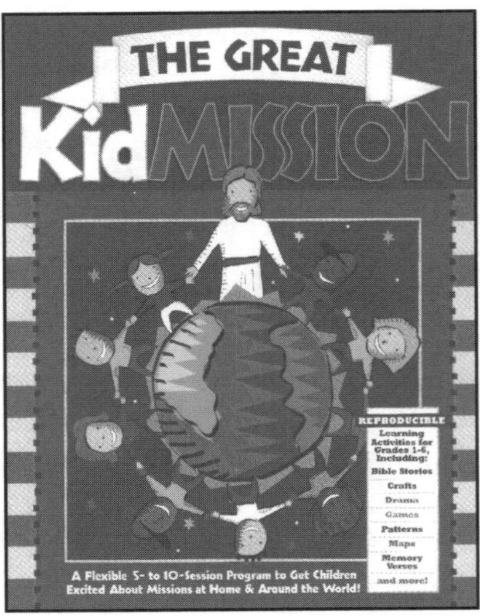

Christian Mission Agencies

Contact these missions agencies for information about their ministries and the people groups or countries they serve.

Africa Inland Mission International, Inc.
P.O. Box 178
Pearl River, NY 10965

Arab World Ministries
P.O. Box 96
Upper Darby, PA 19082

Bible Christian Union, Inc.
P.O. Box 410
Hatfield, PA 19440-0410

Euromission
Postbus 32
3950 AC Maarn
The Netherlands

Frontiers
Jill Harris
Coordinator of Children's Missions Education
325 North Stapley Dr.
Mesa, AZ 85203

GLINT
Gospel Literature International
(909) 481-5222

Indonesian Missionary Fellowship
P.O. Box 4, Batu 65301
E. Java, Indonesia

Interserve
239 Fairfield Ave.
P.O. Box 418
Upper Darby, PA 19082

IVS
Mr. Irving Sylvia
18134 Woodbarn Lane
Fountain Valley, CA 92708

Korean American Society for World Mission
1605 Elizabeth St.
Pasadena, CA 91104

Leprosy Mission International
Goldhay Way,
Orton Goldhay,
Peterborough,
PE2 OGZ, England

Mission Aviation Fellowship
P.O. Box 3202
Redlands, CA 92373

Navajo Gospel Mission
P.O. Box 3717
Flagstaff, AZ 86003

Overseas Missionary Fellowship
404 S. Church St.
Robesonia, PA 19551

OMS International
P.O. Box A
Greenwood, IN 46142

Partners International
P.O. Box 15025
San Jose, CA 95115-0025

Red Sea Mission Team
P.O. Box 16227
Minneapolis, MN 55416

Society for International Ministries
P.O. Box 7900
Charlotte, NC 28241

The Evangelical Alliance Mission
P.O. Box 969
Wheaton, IL 60189-0969

Wycliffe Bible Translators International
7500 West Camp Wisdom Road
Dallas, TX 75326

WEC International
P.O. Box 1707
Fort Washington, PA 19034-8707

World Gospel Mission
P.O. Box WGM
Marion, IN 46952

Youth With a Mission
P.O. Box 55309
Seattle, WA 98155

Craft Coordinator

Crafts are one of the most popular VBS activities. Children welcome the creativity and teachers appreciate the opportunity to reinforce a lesson objective. Most publishers do a thorough job of creating a variety of interesting, meaningful craft ideas. However, it is your responsibility to make sure that the suggested crafts work specifically for your unique VBS as far as time, materials and age capabilities are concerned. The following pages will give you guidelines to choose and plan the best crafts for your students!

Four Keys to Success

As craft coordinator, you play a key role in determining the quality of your craft program. Here are four crucial parts in achieving success at your task:

1. **Plan ahead.** Choose projects far enough in advance to allow time to gather all needed supplies in one coordinated effort. Familiarize yourself with each day's craft project, make a sample of each one and plan any necessary changes.

2. **Be well organized.** Follow your count-down schedule (see p. 76).

3. **Secure your supplies in advance.** Make an inventory list to help you keep track of the items needed for each group.

4. **Communicate with everyone involved.** If there is a possibility someone may not know what to do, be assured there will be someone who does not know what to do.

Choosing the Right Crafts for Your Kids

What can you do to make sure craft time is successful and fun for your students? First, encourage creativity in each child! Keep in mind that the process of creating is just as important as the final product. Here are some other helpful hints:

* **Choose a range of crafts that use a variety of materials with which children may work.** Allow children to make as many choices as possible on their own.
* **Choose projects that are appropriate for the skill level of your students.** Children become easily discouraged when a project is too difficult or too simple for them. Finding the right projects for your students will increase the likelihood that the children will be successful and satisfied with their finished products.
* **Choose activities that reinforce the biblical aim of each VBS session.**
* **Choose projects that work.** Make a sample of each craft to be sure the directions are easily followed and potential questions can be addressed. Adapt projects and vary the materials as needed. Use your own creativity to enhance the given crafts.

Helpful Guidelines for Choosing Crafts

Young Children (Pre-K and Kindergarten)

Craft projects for young children are a blend of "I wanna do it myself!" and "I need help!" Each project, because it is intended to come out looking like a recognizable something, usually requires a certain amount of adult assistance—in preparing a pattern, in doing some cutting, in preselecting magazine pictures, in tying a knot, etc. The younger the child, the more the adult will need to do; but care must always be taken not to rob the child of the satisfaction of his or her own unique efforts. Neither must the adult's desire to have a nice finished project override the child's pleasure at experimenting with color and texture. Avoid the temptation to do the project for the child or to improve on the child's efforts.

If you find a child frustrated with a structured craft, it may be a signal the child needs an opportunity to work with more basic materials—blank paper and paints, play dough or abstract collages (gluing miscellaneous shapes or objects onto surfaces such as paper or cardboard). Remember the cardinal rule in any task a young child undertakes: The process the child goes through is more important than the finished product.

Younger Elementary (Grades 1–3)

Children in the first few years of school delight in completing craft projects. They have a handle on most of the basic skills needed, they are eager to participate and their taste in art has usually not yet surpassed their ability to produce. In other words, they generally like the things they make.

Since reading ability is not a factor in most craft projects, crafts can be a great leveler among a group. Some children excel here who may or may not be top achievers in other areas.

Older Elementary (Grades 4–6)

Trying to plan craft projects for older children has driven many teachers prematurely gray. The challenge is that while these children have well-developed skills to complete projects, they also have well-developed preferences about what they want to do. Thus a project that stretches their abilities may be scorned because it is somehow not appealing to these young sophisticates; or a project will seem too juvenile to the adult leader, but it will click with the kids!

A sense of humor will surely help. Try filtering craft ideas through a panel of experts—two or three fifth graders. If they like a craft, chances are the rest of the group will. Also, the better you get to know your particular students, the better your batting average will be.

Gathering Supplies

Once you have chosen the crafts you will do, make a list of the supplies you will need for the number of children you expect. In making your supplies list, distinguish between items that each individual child will need and those that will be shared among a group. If you are using the activity center method, many materials may be shared among more than one age level. However, self-contained classrooms will need their own supply of basic materials such as glue, scissors, pencils, etc. (See *Supply Checklist* on p. 185.) Teachers should not be frustrated by supply glitches.

Distribute the supply list to everyone in your church family about 16 weeks before VBS begins (see sample copy below). Repeat the distribution at least once or twice, removing from the list the items already provided.

Many items can also be acquired as donations from people or businesses if you plan ahead and make your needs known. In addition, some items can be brought by the children themselves.

Expect that some items will not be donated. But before you rush out to buy them, give a little creative thought to people or places where items can still be obtained at little or no cost: wood is often available from cabinet shops or carpenters; a variety of paper products can usually be rounded up from printers, etc. Some people who would not take the initiative to secure materials from home or work will feel included if you make a point to ask them personally for help in getting a specific item.

After exploring these avenues, if some items are still not available, be sure you have some money budgeted for purchases. If you discover there are some things you simply cannot afford, consider choosing an alternate project or substituting less costly materials.

Sample Bulletin Insert Copy

CRAFT SUPPLIES

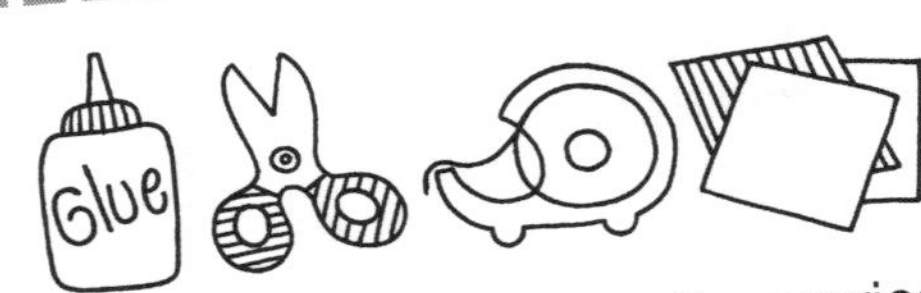

We are getting very excited about our VBS and the great discoveries our children will make. One important part of VBS is crafts—opportunities for children to learn by using their senses, working on projects that creatively reinforce the important lessons studied that day.

Your help is needed to make this our greatest VBS ever! All you have to do is look through this list of craft supplies and discover the items you have around your home. Perhaps you see something here that could be donated from your place of employment. We welcome financial contributions as well, which will enable us to purchase materials we do not receive as donations.

(Include a checklist of items needed.)

Please bring your donations to the church office.

Setting Up a Craft Center

Crafts can be done as part of the lesson in self-contained classrooms or in a designated crafts center where the different age groups of children rotate through according to a set schedule. Begin your work by assembling your team. Recruit adults and/or youth to assist you in gathering supplies, preparing materials and running your center. Then, designate one room in your church or school as the craft center. Choose a creative, theme-oriented name for your center and decorate it with samples of the crafts the children will be making. As classes visit the craft center, lead them in making projects, tailoring your instructions and conversation to the age level of children with whom you are working. Make sure you select craft projects that will appeal to several age levels. Sometimes you'll find one project that all children will enjoy making. Other times you'll need to select one project for the younger children and one project for the older children.

To set up a workable center:

- Place newspaper or butcher paper on floor to protect carpeting.
- Cover work area with newspaper or butcher paper.
- Have a sink with soap and water and towels or provide wet wipes for cleanup.
- Provide large trash cans for trash and paper towels after cleanup.
- Post word charts on wall explaining craft instructions.
- Hang craft sample (from ceiling, etc.) next to word chart so children can read instructions and refer to the completed craft as needed.
- Set up extra tables for craft projects to "dry."

Helpful Hints for Leading Crafts

If you are planning to lead a group of children in doing craft projects, keep the following hints in mind.

Preparation:

- In the weeks before VBS begins, make as many preparations for crafts as possible to allow craft time to run smoothly and to avoid last-minute hassles.
- Purchase card stock, etc., at paper discount stores and reduce photocopying costs by using a church photocopier.
- Have plenty of masking tape on hand.
- With groups of children, provide enough small containers to hold supplies for 2 to 3 children to share—glue, beads, etc.
- Have available in your classroom two or three pairs of left-handed scissors. These can be obtained from a school supply center.
- Have classroom and supplies set up before children arrive.

Leading:

- Ensure sufficient helpers for hands-on participation.
- Ensure that teachers or counselors coming through craft center assist their children while they are working on their crafts.
- Use positive reinforcement at every opportunity. Don't expect every child's project to turn out the same. Show an interest in the unique way each child approaches the craft. Affirm the choices he or she has made. Treat each child's final product as a "masterpiece"!
- Look for ways in which children are exemplifying biblical characteristics. Encourage positive behaviors.
- Make sure each student's name is on his or her project.
- If acrylic paints are required for some of your VBS craft projects, the following suggestions will help:
  1. Provide smocks or old shirts for your children to wear, as acrylics may stain clothes.
  2. Squeeze a small amount of paint into a shallow container and add a small amount of water to make paint go further; or use acrylic house paints.
  3. Fill shallow containers with soapy water. Clean paintbrushes before switching colors and immediately after finishing project.
- Clean up as you go as much as possible.

Craft Coordinator's Countdown Schedule

16 WEEKS BEFORE:

- ❑ List all staff needs. (Will crafts be led by regular teachers or by special craft leaders?) Meet with VBS Director to compile list of prospective staff.
- ❑ Begin personal contacts to recruit needed staff.
- ❑ Review VBS craft book.
- ❑ Select projects to do and make a sample.
- ❑ After finalizing selected projects, make a list of needed supplies.
- ❑ Determine what needed items are already on hand and which need to be secured.
- ❑ Distribute first bulletin notice regarding needed supplies.
- ❑ Begin organizing supplies as they are acquired. (Separate inventories for each age group are often helpful, especially in large programs.)

10 WEEKS BEFORE:

- ❑ Review staffing needs with VBS Director and plan involvement in training session.
- ❑ Distribute second notice regarding supplies.

8 WEEKS BEFORE:

- ❑ Make any needed personal contacts to gather added supplies.
- ❑ Purchase remaining craft supplies.

6 WEEKS BEFORE:

- ❑ Assign staff to make a sample of each craft project. (In most cases this should be done by the person who will actually guide children in completing the project.)

4 WEEKS BEFORE:

- ❑ Participate in training workshops, showing samples of at least the first day's craft projects.
- ❑ Distribute third notice regarding supplies.

2 WEEKS BEFORE:

- ❑ Purchase any last-minute supplies.
- ❑ Check and adjust time schedules and supplies as needed.

DURING VBS:

- ❑ Make sure needed supplies are available for staff.
- ❑ Secure additional supplies as needed.
- ❑ Clean up craft area and supplies each day.

AFTER VBS:

- ❑ See that leftover supplies are packed, labeled and stored for future use.
- ❑ Clean up and restore room to original condition.

Music Director

Music is one of the richest and most natural forms of expression for both young and old. Scripture is filled with references to God's people responding in melody and rhythm. Unfortunately, music is often used with children as merely "something to do until all latecomers arrive" or as a change of pace from the "real learning" going on in the session. Such a limited view misses the powerful impact music can have on children. Music can help a child learn Bible truths, memorize Scripture, remember to display Christian conduct, feel an atmosphere of quietness and worship, move smoothly from one activity to another and enjoy relaxation and activity. While music is always an important ingredient in the larger context of a learning session, it is a valuable learning experience on its own.

Chances are, if you have volunteered for this position, you probably have some experience with or at least a keen interest in music. Either of these can be helpful, but they are not necessary and do not guarantee success in a VBS setting. While it is good to have a pleasant, strong singing voice for leading, the essential quality is the ability to teach children songs with affection and enthusiasm—often without a professional accompanist to "hide" your mistakes. A joyful heart and uninhibited spirit will do much to ensure your success. The following paragraphs will offer some practical help.

Choosing the Right Music for Your Kids

Ask the following six questions about any song you intend to use:

1. Is the meaning obvious to children?
2. Is it easy to sing?
3. Does the song relate to the current unit of Bible lessons?
4. Are the words scripturally and doctrinally correct?
5. Does the song build positive attitudes?
6. Will children enjoy it?

Learning a New Song

Many teachers tend to use a few songs again and again. "Those are the ones children like," is the common explanation. This comment, when interpreted, usually means, "Those are the ones the children—and the teachers—know best." These suggestions will be helpful to you as you learn new songs:

* Listen to the song recorded on the music cassette provided with your curriculum. Then sing along as you play the song again. Sing the song several times to become familiar with the words and the melody. If you do not have a cassette tape of the song you wish to use, find a friend who plays an instrument to play the melody for you or ask a friend who likes to sing to teach you the song. Use a cassette tape recorder to preserve your friend's music.
* Practice the song until you can sing it easily and confidently. Learn the song well enough so that as you sing, you can maintain eye contact with the children rather than look constantly at the songbook.
* When you can sing the song well, learn the motions. Practice until they feel natural and you can do them without thinking.

Teaching a New Song

When you are familiar with a new song, use the following steps to teach it to the children:

* Letter the words on a large chart or overhead transparency, possibly decorating it with appropriate pictures. Hang the chart or project the words where children can easily see.
* Capture the children's interest before you introduce the song. You may connect the song to a learning activity in which children have participated that morning. For example, you might say, "We've been talking about names the Bible uses for God's Son, Jesus. Listen to this song to find another name for Jesus."
* Present the song. Play the cassette as you and other teachers join in and sing along as a group. If you use an accompanist instead of the tape, be sure the accompaniment is simple, emphasizing the melody line.

* Discuss children's answers to your previous questions or listening assignment. Focus first on the points of the song which children do understand. Then discuss any parts of the song that might be unfamiliar or difficult to understand. Ask questions such as, "What did the writer of this song want us to think about while we sing? Does the music sound happy? Serious?"
* Ask children to join in singing the song. Sing only one stanza and/or chorus the first time. Plan to repeat the song in each session of the unit.
* Teach motions when children are familiar with the words and melody. Use masking-tape guidelines on the floor, especially when children are forming circles or lines. Then demonstrate steps or motions and have children repeat several times with you. Finally, children do movements with the music. They will gradually grow comfortable with singing and moving at the same time.

Adding Variety to Your Music

You may use the following suggestions to add variety and to encourage even more participation.

* Create new words to songs by leaving blank spaces for children to fill in, or create a phrase in a song by letting children sing their own answers to a question in the song.
* Provide other instruments such as chimes, melody bells or a keyboard for children to use.
* Lead children in choral speaking. Children respond well to the rhythmic speaking of songs. Any song can be used in this way. You may divide the class into two or more groups and assign each group parts of the song to speak.
* Invite a member of your church choir or a parent who is musically skilled to lead a music activity during one or more lessons.
* Use the song as a discussion prompt. Let children share what they have learned about the Bible through the song or compare it with Bible verses to help them understand and recall the words of Scripture. They can identify times during the coming week when it would be helpful to remember a song they have learned in VBS.
* Ask a child in your class to accompany a song.
* Combine art and music.
  1. Make a rebus chart of the words of a song. Letter the words on a chart, leaving blank spaces where children can glue appropriate magazine pictures to represent words.
  2. Make an illustrated songbook or frieze (a series of pictures on a strip of paper). The words of each phrase are written beneath a picture which illustrates them. Children may draw pictures or cut them out of magazines.
  3. Make a mural about a song. Choose a song with beautiful imagery. Songs describing God's creation would be especially good. Use butcher paper and colored chalk or tempera paints. Display in your music center or use as a decoration for your closing program.

Setting Up a Music Center

A music center should be one of your interest areas if you are using the activity center method, with groups of children rotating through on a set schedule. A music center is recommended for primary, middler and junior age levels. Younger children need the security of a consistent classroom setting. The center is staffed by a music director and several helpers. Counselors accompany their children to the center, participating in activities and maintaining discipline.

To set up a workable center:

* Choose a room big enough to accommodate your largest size age group with lots of space to move around while doing motions. It should be well-ventilated and comfortable, with all the electrical outlets you need for your musical equipment.
* Decorate the center according to your VBS theme.
* Place your accompanist (whether it is a person or a cassette player) where you can easily direct him or her. If speakers are necessary, place them where they can't be disturbed by active children.
* Have other instruments you will need available for easy retrieval but not out where they can become sources of distraction.
* Be sure charts and/or overheads can easily be seen by all the children.
* If you are combining art and music, have tables and all necessary art supplies at hand.

Helpful Hints for Leading Music

Preparation:

* Be totally familiar with each session's theme so you can maximize tie-ins to the lessons.
* Be totally familiar with all the songs and motions yourself. Know exactly what instruments, props and room arrangements are needed every day.
* Prepare charts and/or overheads for each song. Make them as attractive and legible as possible.
* Train your helpers in use of the overhead. Keep transparencies labeled, filed and readily available for each day.

Leading:

* Have a clearly established signal for "Quiet" or "Restore to Order." This doesn't have to be heavy-handed, but it will be helpful in the "active fun" of your center.
* Sing the songs every day.
* Take advantage of every opportunity to discuss the meaning of the songs and reinforce the day's Bible focus.
* Have fun!

Presenting Your Closing Program

Music is easily everyone's favorite VBS activity. Children love learning and singing the songs during each day's opening assembly and at music time in their classes or activity centers. But the highlight of all their hard work is the opportunity to perform the songs in grand finale style. This kind of celebration event provides a wonderful climax to your VBS.

Many curriculum publishers include a closing program that brings together all the skit and music elements from the entire week. As music director, you may be put in charge of the whole program. If so, be sure to work with the skit director and any event coordinators appointed by your VBS Director. Step 9 will give you more information and ideas for planning the closing program activities.

Whether you are responsible for the entire program or only the music elements, the following tips will help you keep everything running smoothly.

1. Make sure all of the VBS students will be included in at least a portion of the program. Parents are coming to see their children.
2. Give actors any scripts you are using several days before the event and be available to work with them if necessary until they know their lines.(This may be handled by the skit director.)
3. If you are having solos, duets, trios or class groups, let each department or class know the part(s) they will perform well in advance.
4. Be sure to have an adequate sound system and experienced technicians lined up well in advance. This may require coordination with your church staff.
5. If you don't have a stage, set up bleachers or risers on which kids can sit and stand. Place the VBS backdrop behind them.
6. Reserve an area of seats for VBS students to sit in while waiting for their performance time. Have teachers/counselors sit with their classes to help with control and cueing.
7. Rehearse the entire closing program with all children before the actual performance.
8. Be sure children sing facing the audience, even if they have faced another direction on other days.
9. Practice having groups of children move on and off stage. For younger children, use masking tape to mark where they will be standing.
10. Allow preschoolers to perform first and then sit up front with their teachers or with their parents for the duration of the program.
11. During the program, have children who are not singing sit down in reserved seats or on the risers, allowing parents easily to see those who are actually performing.
12. Use slides or videotape from the week's VBS activities and a music background both before and after the program. Be sure to run through this beforehand and have everything cued and ready to go. Be sure all equipment is securely plugged in and working.

Skit Director

As the skit director, you have the opportunity of being involved with VBS and making an impact on children without having to actually work directly with children. Most published curriculums already contain a skit that introduces and develops an important theme or idea throughout the entire week. How these skits are presented directly affects their impact. Here are some ways that you can make your VBS skits top-notch!

Rehearsals

Rehearsals are essential to the success of your skits. Actors must be totally familiar with characterizations, spoken lines and positions on stage; otherwise they may stumble over lines, causing uncomfortable pauses, and the skits will lose some of their impact. Rehearsals also allow actors the opportunity to be creative and flexible. They can add their own expressions, gestures or movements to customize skits.

Have someone watch each rehearsal and make comments. This person should observe if actors can be seen by the audience at all times and if they are speaking clearly and expressively.

Casting

Make every effort to cast all the parts. You may even want to choose a substitute for emergencies. If you have a limited number of volunteers, you may need to adapt the skits to accommodate the gender of your actors or the need for dual roles. Choose people who have a sense of humor and some dramatic ability. They need to be willing to rehearse in order to be fully prepared for each skit.

Making Your Characters Come Alive

The key to making your skit characters come alive is to have each one develop a clearly defined personality. The students will "get to know" the characters and enjoy anticipating how each one might react in different situations. Development of a character includes:

* **Movements**—Each actor should develop a pattern of unique, stylized movements—such as a way of walking, a stance, a gesture of the hands—that reflects his or her character's personality. These movements should include a strong, emphatic way of entering and leaving the stage.
* **Speech**—Each actor should have a distinctive way of talking that will accentuate his or her character's personality. Also, each actor should take note of repeated phrases that are typical of his or her character and practice saying them in a way that will be memorable to the children.
* **Costumes**—Enhance each character with an individualized costume. Thrift stores are good resources for inexpensive costumes.

Props

For a more realistic effect, use various props and costumes for each character. Gather props and garments well ahead of time by asking your church congregation for assistance. If some items can't be located, modify the skit to use something else. Make a complete list of props for each day's skit.

Skit Backdrop

A large painted backdrop will add color and excitement and provide an excellent setting for the opening assembly. Determine the material that you want to use for the backdrop and talk with someone in your church or community who is familiar with painting on that material. Paper, fabric, muslin and wood react differently to various kinds of paints. Backdrops should be at least 8x10 feet (2.4x3 m).

When you are ready to paint, use an overhead opaque projector or transparency projector to project your design onto the backdrop. Trace outlines with pen or pencil. Then paint background colors. Add details after background has dried.

Additional Ways to Utilize Skits

Skits are excellent devices for building excitement in your church and community in the weeks before VBS. To make the most of your hard work and practice, try using the following ideas:

- **Present skits to congregation before VBS.** Get the attention of your entire congregation by presenting one or more of the skits during a worship service or other congregational event. The excitement of the skits helps to build interest among children and motivates adults to volunteer their services.
- **Present skits to Sunday School classes before VBS.** Instead of, or in addition to, presenting skits in a worship service, have the actors visit children's and adult Sunday School classes in advance of VBS. Don't worry that children will lose interest if they have already seen a skit. Actually, most children enjoy the skits at VBS even more if they have already seen one or two before they come. Excitement will build more quickly if children have already met the main skit characters.
- **Present skits in parks and neighborhoods.** Skits are also an excellent means of capturing the attention of unchurched families. Wherever children and families gather can provide a setting for a brief skit and announcement. A cassette tape player can be used to play the VBS songs to help draw a crowd. Then you may distribute information about the upcoming VBS.
- **Present skits at your closing program or on the Sunday after VBS.** Many unchurched people feel uncomfortable coming to church after VBS is over. The skit characters are proven bridge builders at this crucial time. Announce that favorite skit characters will be at the closing program—or at church next Sunday—and that they will be looking for all their friends to be there too. When added to your other invitations to children and parents, these characters will help your visitors feel more comfortable about attending.

Skit Director's Countdown Schedule

12 WEEKS BEFORE:

- ❏ Coordinate appearances of skit characters with your publicity coordinator for pre-VBS activities. You may want to have portions of the actual skits prepared for these appearances.

10–12 WEEKS BEFORE:

- ❏ Familiarize yourself with the skits from beginning to end. If you are using a published curriculum, make sure you have everything you need from the publisher.
- ❏ Choose a rehearsal site and times and book them on your church calendar if necessary. The last few rehearsals should be held on the stage or platform where the actual production will occur. Be sure this is booked on the church calendar as well.

10 WEEKS BEFORE:

- ❏ Coordinate with your music director if your closing program involves both a skit and music.

8–10 WEEKS BEFORE:

- ❏ Make a master list of characters and begin "advertising" for the roles.
- ❏ Be willing to adjust the script if necessary to accommodate the number/gender of your actors. Try to have all roles filled and begin rehearsing at least four weeks before VBS begins.

6–8 WEEKS BEFORE:

- ❏ Make a master list of props, scenery and costumes needed for each day. Prioritize the list and present it to your congregation. Make the backdrop first—it can be used in promotional activities before VBS.

4–6 WEEKS BEFORE:

- ❏ Verify permission to present a skit before the congregation.
- ❏ Begin rehearsals.

Snack Coordinator

For many years, snacks at VBS simply meant providing children with a supply of punch and cookies. As with crafts, however, the process of creating a snack can be a valuable learning experience of its own. Many publishers provide a variety of great snack ideas from which to choose, or you may decide to choose your own snacks using resources such as cookbooks and magazines. The process of making creative snacks together can be almost as much fun as eating them! Use the following suggestions to help you plan your snack attack.

Four Keys to Success

As snack coordinator, you play a key role in determining the quality of your snack program. Here are four crucial elements in achieving success at your task:

1. **Plan ahead.** Make your selection of all snack recipes far enough in advance to experiment with the recipe.
2. **Be well organized.**
3. **Secure your ingredients and supplies far enough in advance to purchase ingredients in bulk** (see p. 186). Make an inventory list to help you keep track of the items needed for each group.
4. **Communicate with everyone involved.** If there is a possibility someone may not know what to do, be assured there will be someone who does not know what to do.

Choosing the Right Snacks for Your Kids

What can you do to make sure snack time is successful and fun for your students?

* Choose a variety of snacks using items from each of the four food groups. Allow children to create, decorate or personalize their snacks.
* Choose snacks that will appeal to the majority of students. Choosing all-healthy, unfamiliar snacks may backfire if most of the children are opposed to eating them.
* Choose snacks that are fairly simple and appropriate for the skill level of your students.
* Know the learning aim for each VBS session. Look for snack activities that might allow a child to demonstrate a biblical virtue or attitude such as patience, perseverance or kindness.
* Choose snacks that work. Make a sample of each to be sure the estimated time and instructions are correct. You may want to adapt some snack ideas to simplify procedures or vary the ingredients required.
* Use your own creativity to enhance the given snacks. Adapt snack ideas, ingredients and instructions to suit your children's needs. Substitute ingredients that may work just as well or better. Just make sure they work.

Food Safety

* Always wash hands before handling food.
* Things that are hot don't always look hot. If someone gets burned, immediately hold the burned area under cold running water.
* When chopping, cutting or peeling food, use a cutting board.
* Keep pot handles on the stove turned away from you.
* Turn the burner or oven off before removing pans.
* Stand mixing bowls in the sink as you stir to avoid splashes.
* Use hand beaters, a large spoon or a wire whisk instead of electric beaters. This way, children have a chance to get the feel of the batter.
* Demonstrate and let children practice using utensils.

* Store sharp utensils out of children's reach.
* Keep hands dry while working in the kitchen. Wet, slippery hands can cause spills and accidents.
* Keep pot holders dry. If damp, they will absorb heat and lead to burns.
* When cutting with a knife, always cut away from yourself and keep fingers away from the blade.
* To help prevent steam burns, tip the lid away from you whenever you raise the cover of a hot pan.
* Electrical appliances should be used by ADULTS ONLY.
* Young children should not use the stove at all.
* Make sure hot foods are thoroughly cooked and any leftovers are quickly refrigerated.
* Instruct children in advance how to deal with a sneeze or a cough.
* When outdoors, keep all refrigerated items in a cooler.
* Don't allow children to touch uncooked poultry or raw eggs.

Setting Up a Snack Center

The snack center is usually set up in a kitchen or dining area where children can gather at tables to prepare and eat their snacks. However, if your church kitchen is too small or you don't have one, consider setting up your snack center outside. Place picnic benches under an awning and use a rolling cart to bring items back and forth from the kitchen. Having your snack center outside also makes cleanup much easier.

The snack coordinator should have one helper for every six to eight children who are in the snack center at one time. Groups of children will rotate through the snack center.

To set up a workable center:

* Choose an area where children can gather around child-sized tables easily.
* Electrical appliances to be used should be readily available but not out where children can reach them.
* Choose a catchy, theme-oriented name and decorate the center. Use paper, cardboard or dough samples of the treats you will be making. Post a menu board that features the "daily special."
* If indoors, place newspaper or butcher paper on floor to protect carpeting.
* Cover work area with butcher paper.
* Have a sink with soap and water and towels or provide wet wipes for cleanup.
* Provide large trash cans for trash and paper towels after cleanup.
* Provide a large container with drinking water or lemonade. Don't forget paper cups.

Helpful Hints for Leading Snacks

Preparation:

* Be totally familiar with each day's snack. Know exactly what needs to be done and in what order.
* In the weeks before VBS make as many preparations for snacks as possible. Premeasure, prebake and store appropriately.
* Have all ingredients/supplies arranged on tables or ready to pass out to each group.
* If your snack involves baking, be ready with a game for children to play while they wait.

Leading:

* Review safety rules.
* Go over snack instructions together.
* If children are going to be measuring ingredients, show them the correct way and let them practice a few times.
* Ensure sufficient helpers for hands-on participation.
* Ensure that teachers or counselors coming through snack center assist their children while they are working on their snacks.
* Use positive reinforcement at every opportunity. Don't expect every child's snack to turn out the same. Show an interest in the unique way each child approaches the project. Affirm the choices he or she has made. Treat each child's final product as a "masterpiece"!
* Look for ways in which children are exemplifying biblical characteristics. Encourage positive behaviors.
* Clean up as you go along.

Recreation Coordinator

Play and learn! Often children are not aware of the direct learning value of a game, but they participate enthusiastically because they enjoy it. Recreation time can help children learn social skills, sportsmanship, fair play and sensitivity to others' feelings. See page 187 for a helpful schedule worksheet.

Tips for Leading Games

Explain rules clearly and simply. It's helpful to write and post the rules to the game. Make sure you explain rules step by step.

Offer a "practice round." When playing a game for the first time with your class, play it a few times "just for practice." Children will learn the rules best by actually playing the game.

Vary the process by which teams are formed. Allow students to group themselves into teams of three or four members each. Play the game one time. Then announce that the person on each team who is wearing the most (red) should rotate to another team. Then play the game again. As you repeat this rotation process, vary the method of rotation so that students play with several different children each time.

Choose games appropriate to the skill level of the class. If you know that some children in a class are not able to read or write as well as others, avoid playing games which depend solely on that skill for success. Avoid highly competitive games with children younger than age seven.

Health and Safety Precautions

Part of preparing for VBS includes dealing with potential health and safety concerns ahead of time. Some of the information in this section requires consideration by you, the director. The other part requires information and training to be passed on to your volunteers.

Ensuring Safety on Campus

Making sure your facilities are safe inside and out is part of being well-prepared. Check every area that will be in use. Things to check for are:

* **Objects that cause a child to trip.** Make sure all cords are taped down securely. Remove any protruding tree roots or rocks that may be tripped on. Mark anything that cannot be removed with brightly colored flags.
* **Items that could cause head or eye injuries.** Look for broken items that have sharp edges. Do a walk-through of each area considering all protruding items that may be directly at children's eye-level.
* **Harmful chemicals or electrical hazards** that may be easily accessed. Inform your church custodian about the areas that will be in use during VBS. Verify that these areas will be safe from such hazards.
* **Rotted wood, peeling paint or rust that could cause splinters.**
* **Outdoor areas that may be infested by harmful insects.** Make sure that grass areas will be mowed and trees trimmed prior to your VBS to protect children from unseen insects.

Special Safety Concerns for Preschoolers

Inspect all areas that preschoolers will be using. In addition to the aforementioned concerns, check the following:

* **All exposed outlets should have plug covers.**
* **Small items or toys with pieces on which a child could choke should be removed.** Also verify that snack, craft and game items are safe from choking hazards.
* **Plants that are poisonous if ingested must be removed.** Check with your local green nursery if you have any questions.
* **Safe playgrounds should have a ground cover of at least 2 inches of sand, mulch or pea gravel or have rubber tiles.** All ramps, platforms and bridges should have guardrails with slats no more than 3½ inches apart.

Dealing with Sick or Injured Children

Prepare a first-aid station or at least have a kit in a central location, such as your church office, along with children's registration forms. Check to see that the station or kit is well-stocked with the following items: adhesive bandages in a variety of sizes, antibacterial ointment, sterile gauze pads, first-aid tape, ipecac syrup, thermometer, disposable gloves, tweezers and a first-aid manual. Post the phone numbers for the nearest poison control center, fire station and police station where they can be easily seen. Keep an ice pack in a nearby freezer or purchase ice packs that need no refrigeration. You may also want to provide a comfortable place for a child to lie down, if needed.

Have a volunteer who is trained in first-aid be the "on-call nurse" in case he or she is needed. By law, the only care he or she can give is providing ice, soap-and-water cleanup and bandaids. Ask the volunteer to review all of the registration forms and to mark clearly the cards of children who have a potential health problem. Make sure there is a working phone near your first-aid area so he or she can call parents or caregivers in case of an emergency.

Administering Medications

All medications and prescription drugs should only be administered when there is written request from the child's parent or guardian. The request will need to be signed and dated and should include written directions on how and when to administer the medications. Make sure all prescription drugs are labeled with the child's name and pharmacy instructions. When a child does receive medication, the person administering the drug will need to record the time and dosage.

Preventing Child Abduction

Preventing child abduction should be a concern in every VBS program, regardless of size or location. Plan your drop-off and pick-up procedures ahead of time so that they are clear to all parents from the start. Make sure your teachers and counselors also know what is expected from them during those times.

Resist the temptation to allow the children to disperse on their own. Have each teacher or counselor be responsible for ensuring that each of their students is picked up by the person who brought him or her. Also ensure that two adults stay with any child who is not picked up on time.

Special Prevention Concerns for Preschoolers

Preschoolers require additional safety procedures. Do not excuse the children to find parents on their own. Use a claim ticket or token system to ensure that a preschooler is released only to the person who is responsible for him or her. Check to see what kind of security system is used in your church's regular weekly programs for preschoolers. Preschoolers should be dropped off or picked up in a contained classroom to ensure safety. Use one of these two options:

- As children arrive, have a designated person (either preschool teacher or assistant) hand a claim ticket to the adult who is dropping off the preschooler. Prepare the tickets ahead of time with your VBS logo or class name and each day's date already stamped or preprinted on them. Before distributing the ticket, write the preschooler's name on it. At the end of the VBS session, the preschooler may only be released to the person presenting the ticket.
- Prepare a sign-in/sign-out roster for each day of VBS. As children arrive, have the parent or caregiver sign his or her name next to the child's name and note the time dropped off. At the end of the VBS session, ensure that the same person signs the child out.

Preventing Child Abuse

Preventing child abuse by screening questionable volunteers is only half of the responsibility the church has to protect children. It is also the director's job to make sure that all volunteers who will be working with children are adequately informed about avoiding inappropriate behaviors. Much of this information is given to protect your volunteers from false allegations. Check to see if your church already has an established policy. If not, here are some tips to help you:

- **Establish a "Buddy/Witness Policy."** Always have at least two adults present at all times in every activity involving children. This means there will always be a witness built into the situation.
- **Develop an "Appropriate Touching Policy."** Think about, talk about and agree upon what is "appropriate touching" at your church. Kids need love, but it is wise to guard against false accusations over displays of physical affection. Perhaps you can decide to give children the affection they need only where groups of four or more adults are present.
- **Write down your policies.** Once you've carefully thought through and established appropriate guidelines, make them a matter of record. Have your policies available for all parents, caregivers and volunteers to review.

Preparing Your VBS Volunteers

It goes without saying: prepared volunteers are successful volunteers. Effective volunteer training is crucial in the total preparation of VBS and so requires careful planning. The amount of training to offer depends largely on the experience level of your staff. New, inexperienced staff deserve assistance in developing the skills necessary to succeed. However, even experienced teachers need opportunities to be refreshed and reminded of essential goals and procedures. Teacher training will also help build team unity, provide encouragement and communicate the VBS vision.

Training volunteers is a responsibility that both you and your department leaders can share. Once you have equipped and trained your leaders, they can then train their teams in specific areas. The first section of this chapter provides general information on how to conduct training meetings. The second and third sections provide a variety of helpful articles on specific issues that can be used in departmental or age-group training meetings. We recommend you photocopy them for your department leaders to use in their training.

How to Conduct a Training Meeting

There are basically two types of training sessions that should be conducted: general (for all staff) and specific (departmental or leadership staff).

A general meeting for all volunteers is absolutely necessary for dispersing basic VBS information. One or two meetings are all that you will probably need to have. These meetings should include:

- ✻ introduction to the curriculum (theme, lesson focus, theme verse, etc.);
- ✻ pertinent general information (dates, time schedule, locations, supplies, future meetings, etc.);
- ✻ opportunity to fellowship.

Specific training sessions should then be conducted by the director or by department leaders. The nature of these meetings depends on the needs of the staff. Topics that may be covered in these sessions include:

- ✻ planning and preparing lessons
- ✻ decorating and preparing your classroom
- ✻ use of the curriculum
- ✻ age-level characteristics
- ✻ how to lead a child to Christ
- ✻ dealing with discipline
- ✻ building relationships
- ✻ storytelling techniques
- ✻ following up after VBS

Preparing for Your Meeting

- ✻ **Schedule the meeting for a time you think most volunteers will be able to attend.** Many churches schedule their meetings on Saturday morning or Sunday, after church. Keep child-care issues in mind if you schedule a meeting during the week. Reserve your chosen date on the church calendar.
- ✻ **As you begin recruiting, make sure you let all volunteers know the date(s) of your meeting(s)—either in person, by phone or by mail.** Publicize the meeting in your church bulletin. Then mail reminder notices at least five days in advance. Make your notices look attractive and exciting, and be sure to include the date, time and place. (See sample p. 176.)
- ✻ **Plan your meeting agenda.** Write down all the information and topics you wish to cover. Have specific goals and specific steps to meet them. If other individuals will lead parts of the meeting, make sure you give them plenty of advance notice. Begin brainstorming ideas on how to add excitement and variety to your presentation. Consider using visuals, skits, games, videos, etc.
- ✻ **Make a list of all the supplies you will need for the meeting.** Secure important curriculum items such as the preview video, musical tape or CD, posters, teacher manuals and any other helpful promotional items. Also make sure you have tables, chairs, cassette or CD player, a television, VCR and overhead projector, if needed. (See p. 177.)
- ✻ **Plan to serve refreshments.** Refreshments show your volunteers you appreciate their attendance. The food can be as simple as coffee, iced tea and cookies or be expanded to include theme-oriented munchies.
- ✻ **Personalize the meeting.** Purchase or make name tags for all your volunteers—don't assume everyone knows each other. Provide a sign-in sheet to give your volunteers a sense of accountability. Purchase little treats for each participant such as candy, VBS pencils or pins, note pads, tote bags, etc.

A Sample General Training Meeting

The following is an example of a general staff training meeting. Adapt it to fit your particular needs.

Before the Meeting

* Display any promotional posters, banners or other promotional items from the curriculum.
* Place chairs in semicircles around tables so they face one wall.
* Arrange to have a cassette or CD player, a television and a VCR.
* Liven up the room with theme-oriented decorations.
* Place a sign-in sheet, name tags and pencils on a table.
* Set up a refreshment table.
* Place handbooks, handouts and a simple treat on each seat.

During the Meeting

* While waiting for volunteers to arrive, play the VBS music in the background.
* Greet each person by the door and invite each one to sign in, make a name tag and enjoy the refreshments.
* After volunteers are seated, enthusiastically welcome the group and open with prayer. Express appreciation for their attendance and assure them that this meeting will be worth their efforts.
* Play a brief, organized icebreaker game to allow volunteers to get to know each other (optional).
* Introduce the theme, content and key verse of your VBS.

* If available, show the VBS preview video.
* Introduce the VBS committee and each of the coordinators/directors. Ask each one to share in a few words their duties, with whom they will be working and any goals they might have.
* Review the daily time schedule (including devotions) and room assignments.
* Have your publicity coordinator share ideas and events for promoting your VBS. Explain how all the volunteers can participate in promotion.
* Have your music director teach and demonstrate the motions to your VBS theme song. Also have him or her share the date and events planned for the closing program.
* Have department leaders distribute any curriculum items or other important materials to their teams.
* Explain your procedure for securing and/or purchasing supplies. Distribute pertinent forms (see pp. 183-187).
* Allow teams about 15 minutes to meet with each other to review their job descriptions and deadlines and to schedule additional meetings.
* Bring groups together. Give individuals a chance to bring up any general questions.
* Close in prayer and dismiss.

After the Meeting

* List all items that require follow-up, with dates to be done and person responsible for the task. Check each item off as it is accomplished.
* Write a short summary of the meeting, noting topics discussed, decisions taken, etc. Include your evaluation of the meeting's success and thoughts on how to improve for the next one. Refer to this in planning for your next meeting.

A Sample Departmental Training Meeting

Before the Meeting

* Assign volunteers to prepare different elements of the lesson for Day One—visuals, crafts, snacks, students' papers, etc.—and be ready to explain how each one helps meet the lesson aim.
* Ask a volunteer(s) to read an article(s) from this book and be prepared to "teach" the content to the others.
* Arrange the room for the comfort and ease of volunteers. Make sure they can see and reach everything they need.
* Have all necessary equipment in place—overhead projector and screen, TV/VCR, cassette player/CD, pens, paper, etc.
* Have sufficient copies of all handouts ready to pass out.
* Have available all curriculum materials not already in the hands of teachers.

During the Meeting

* Begin on time. Pray together asking God to help you express His love to children in ways they can understand.
* Write learning aims for the course on an overhead transparency or on a chalkboard. Discuss aims to ensure that all staff members understand and share the same objectives for the course.
* Walk through the daily schedule for your department. This is especially important if you are using an activity center approach. Each class must know where it should be at all times.
* Walk through Day One together from the teacher's manual, emphasizing how to prepare the lesson from the manual instructions and using all the sample elements made by your volunteers.
* Have your volunteers "teach" the articles they read.
* Make any special assignments for the week. Discuss your department's role in opening/closing assemblies and closing program.
* Make plans for departmental follow-up of children.
* Answer any questions. Dismiss in prayer.

After the Meeting

* List all items that require follow-up, with dates to be done and person responsible for the task. Check each item off as it is accomplished.
* Write a short summary of the meeting, noting topics discussed, decisions taken, etc. Include your evaluation of the meeting's success and thoughts on how to improve for the next one. Refer to this in planning for your next meeting.

Hints for a Successful Meeting

* Arrive ahead of time. Having everything planned and set up in advance provides a positive example to your volunteers. You can't expect more from your volunteers than you're willing to do.
* Use your VBS theme to build excitement. Reinforce the theme through the use of decorations, attire, refreshments, prizes, etc.
* Provide some time for fellowship. Start your meeting with an icebreaker game or other fun event. This will help your volunteers become familiar with one another, build friendships and foster team unity.
* Make the meeting worth their while. Though "fun" can be on the agenda, volunteers should not feel that they have wasted their time. Make sure all information is clearly presented.
* Start and end the meeting on time. This shows your volunteers that you respect their schedules. Allow about five minutes for volunteers to arrive before beginning the meeting.

Training Information for Elementary Workers

Age-Level Characteristics

Effectively instructing children of varying ages requires that a teacher recognize and accept wide individual differences in skills, abilities and interests. God has entrusted us with a wonderful opportunity to help children learn vital scriptural truths. An effective teacher is aware of children's needs and how children grow and develop. An effective teacher is also aware of how these processes influence children's attitudes and actions—particularly as related to ways children learn best. Regardless of the level at which a child works, a teacher can use that child's interest in an activity to guide his or her thinking toward understanding a Bible truth.

Before you lead children through the daily activities of VBS, consider the following age-level characteristics of the children in your department.

Grades 1 and 2 (Primary)

PHYSICAL

Children need opportunities for movement each day. Small muscle coordination is still developing and improving. Girls are ahead of boys at this stage of development.

Teaching Tips: Encourage activities that involve cutting and simple writing skills; give alternatives for children who do not write well (e.g., drawing); give children opportunities to vary their activities.

EMOTIONAL

Children are experiencing new and frequently intense feelings as they grow in independence. Sometimes the child finds it hard to control his or her behavior. There is still a deep need for approval from adults and a growing need for approval by peers.

Teaching Tips: Seek opportunities to help each child in your class know and feel you love him or her. Show genuine interest in each child and his or her activities and accomplishments. Learn children's names and use them frequently in positive ways.

SOCIAL

Children are concerned with pleasing their teachers. Each child is struggling to become socially acceptable to the peer group. The Golden Rule is a tough concept at this age. Being first and winning are very important. Taking turns is hard. This skill improves by the end of the second grade. A child's social process moves gradually from *I* to *you* to *we*.

Teaching Tips: Provide opportunities for children to practice taking turns. Help each child accept the opinions and wishes of others and consider the welfare of the group as well as his or her own. Call attention to times when the group cooperates successfully.

INTELLECTUAL

There is an intense eagerness to learn and children of this age ask lots of questions. They like to repeat stories and activities. The concept of time is limited. Thinking is here and now rather than past or future. Listening and speaking skills are developing rapidly; girls are ahead of boys. Each child thinks everyone shares his or her view. Children see parts rather than how the parts make up the whole and they think very literally.

Teaching Tips: Consider the skill and ability levels of the children in accomplishing activities. For example, some can handle listening and writing activities and others may do better with music or art. Use pictures to help them understand Bible times and people. Avoid symbolism!

SPIRITUAL

Children can sense the greatness, wonder and love of God when helped with visual and specific examples. The non-physical nature of God is baffling, but God's presence in every area of life is generally accepted when parents and teachers communicate this belief by their attitudes and actions. Children can think of Jesus as a Friend, but they need specific examples of how Jesus expresses love and care. This understanding leads many children to belief and acceptance of Jesus as personal Savior. Children can comprehend talking to God anywhere, anytime, in their own words and need regular opportunities to pray. They can also comprehend that the Old Testament tells what happened before Jesus was born and the New Testament tells of His birth, work on earth, return to heaven and the works that occurred afterwards on earth.

Teaching Tips: The gospel becomes real as children feel love from adults. Teachers who demonstrate their faith in a consistent, loving way are models through which the loving nature of God is made known to children.

Grades 3 and 4 (Middler)

PHYSICAL

Children at this level have good large and small muscle coordination. The girls are still ahead of the boys. Children can work diligently for longer periods but can become impatient with delays or their own imperfect abilities.

Teaching Tips: Give clear, specific instructions and allow children as much independence as possible in preparing materials. Assign children the responsibility for cleanup.

EMOTIONAL

This is the age of teasing, nicknames, criticism and increased verbal skills to vent anger. At eight years children have developed a sense of fair play and a value system of right and wrong. At nine years children are searching for identity beyond membership in the family unit.

Teaching Tips: Here is a marvelous opportunity for the teacher to present a Christian model at the time children are eagerly searching for models! Provide experiences that encourage children's creativity and self-concept. Let all the children know both verbally and by your actions that "love is spoken here"—that you will not let others hurt them or let them hurt others. Make your class a safe place to be.

SOCIAL

Children's desire for status within the peer group becomes more intense. Most children remain shy with strangers and exhibit strong preferences for being with a few close friends. Some children still lack essential social skills needed to make and retain friendships.

Teaching Tips: This age is a good time to use activities in which pairs or small groups of children can work together. Create opportunities for each child to assume increased responsibilities.

INTELLECTUAL

Children are beginning to realize there may be valid opinions besides their own. They are becoming able to evaluate alternatives and are less likely than before to fasten onto one viewpoint as the only one possible. Children are also beginning to think in terms of "the whole." Children think more conceptually and have a high level of creativity. By this stage, however, many children have become self-conscious about their creative efforts as their understanding has grown to exceed their abilities in some areas.

Teaching Tips: Encourage children to look up information and discover their own answers to problems. Activities such as art, music and drama help children learn Bible information and concepts. Encourage children to use their Bibles by finding and reading portions of Scripture. Bible learning games are good for this age; these are also good years for Bible memory work. Help children understand the meaning of the verses they memorize.

SPIRITUAL

Children are open to sensing the need for God's continuous help and guidance. They can recognize the need for a personal Savior. There may be a desire to become a member of God's family. Children who indicate an awareness of sin and concern about accepting Jesus as Savior need careful guidance without pressure.

Teaching Tips: Give children opportunities to communicate with God through prayer. Help them understand the forgiving nature of God. Talk personally with a child whom you sense the Holy Spirit is leading to trust the Lord Jesus. Ask simple questions to determine the child's level of understanding.

Grades 5 and 6 (Junior)

PHYSICAL

Children have mastered most basic physical skills, are active and curious and seek a variety of new experiences. Rapid growth can cause some 11-year-olds to tire easily.

Teaching Tips: Ten-year-old boys will still participate in activities with girls, but by 11 years they tend to work and play better with their own sex. This is a good age for exploration and research activities. Use active, creative ways to memorize Bible verses.

EMOTIONAL

Children are usually cooperative, easygoing, content, friendly and agreeable. Most adults enjoy working with this age group. Even though both girls and boys begin to think about their future as adults, their interests tend to differ significantly. Be aware of behavioral changes that result from the 11-year-old's emotional growth. Children are experiencing unsteady emotions and often shift from one mood to another.

Teaching Tips: Changes of feelings require patient understanding from adults. Give many opportunities to make choices with only a few necessary limits. Take time to listen as children share their experiences and problems with you.

SOCIAL

Friendships and activities with their peers flourish. Children draw together and away from adults in the desire for independence. The child wants to be a part of a same-sex group and usually does not want to stand alone in competition.

Teaching Tips: Children no longer think aloud, so keeping communication open is of prime importance. Listen, ask questions and avoid being judgmental.

INTELLECTUAL

Children of this age are verbal! Making ethical decisions becomes a challenging task. They are able to express ideas and feelings in a creative way. By 11 years children have begun to reason abstractly. They begin to think of themselves as adults and at the same time question adult concepts. Hero worship is strong.

Teaching Tips: Include lots of opportunities for talking, questioning and discussing in a safe, accepting environment. These are good years for poetry, songs, drama, stories, drawing and painting. Give guidance in a way that does not damage children's efforts in becoming thinking, self-directed people.

SPIRITUAL

Children can have deep feelings of love for God, can share the good news of Jesus with a friend and are capable of involvement in evangelism and service projects. The child may seek guidance from God to make everyday and long-range decisions.

Teaching Tips: Provide opportunities for children to make choices and decisions based on Bible concepts. Plan prayer, Bible reading and worship experiences. Involve children in work and service projects.

Differences in Religious Backgrounds

Your VBS children can be divided into four general categories of religious backgrounds:

* **Children who attend your church regularly.** These children know all the ins-and-outs of your church and are probably well-known by most of your staff. These are the children who will be bringing the bulk of visitors. To these children, Vacation Bible School is like a super-fun, extended Sunday School. They've probably heard the Bible stories before, know the Bible memory verses and can give the "correct" answer to most questions (which can be quite helpful at times). Do the following to keep them from getting bored: (1) capture their attention during story time by relating new, interesting facts; (2) explain why you believe the story is worth hearing again; (3) remind them of the importance of their testimony; (4) encourage them to bring unchurched friends and to pray for those who don't know Christ; and (5) help them to make others feel welcome.
* **Children who have never attended church.** These are the children who make your VBS a wonderful and exciting outreach experience.

Usually they are hungry, or at least curious, to hear the Word of God for the first time. For many the whole package of playing games and making crafts and snacks is a brand new experience. Fortunately, most curriculums design their stories and activities with these children in mind. However, these children often require special attention to feel loved and welcomed. You will have only a few days to build relationships with them. Make the most of this opportunity, as you can have a tremendous, life-long impact on them and their families.

* **Children who attend your church infrequently.** These children are often grouped with "church kids" because their faces are familiar. However, these children may know little about what it means to have a personal relationship with Jesus Christ. The Bible stories and verses will probably still be interesting to them. VBS may be just the thing they and their families need to feel comfortable in your church. Make an effort to get to know these children better, talk to their parents and answer their questions. Encourage churched children to form friendships with them.
* **Children who attend other churches.** While many of the new faces you see might be considered unchurched children, several of your VBS students may come from local churches. Some families send their children to all the VBS programs in your areas as an inexpensive day-care program. Some have even been to the same VBS program at another church and already know all the songs. In addition, these children may come from many different religious persuasions with varied interpretations of who God is and what the Bible says. Respect these differences and be available to answer any conflicting questions. Make their experience at your church a positive one.

Helping the Hurting Child

Due to the variety of family backgrounds and home-life situations of your VBS students, you may encounter some disturbing things. The National Foundation to Prevent Child Sexual Abuse reports that one in three girls and one in six boys will be subjected to some form of sexual abuse by the age of 18. These statistics are shocking and, unfortunately, real.

What do you do when a child shows signs of problems or trauma at home? How can you be sure? What is your responsibility? How involved should you get? These are the questions that you need to be able to answer *before* your VBS begins!

What to Look For

The problem situations your VBS children face may range anywhere from divorce or death in the family to physical or mental abuse. Some of these tragedies are a part of life and require only sensitive understanding and support. However, other circumstances require immediate intervention for the protection of the child. How do you know what to look for?

Signs of Children Coping with Divorce or Death

* The child may be moody, withdrawn and depressed.
* The child may be irritable and/or striking out at other children—hitting, biting, kicking and/or name-calling.
* The child may refuse to enter into sharing times with others.
* The child may have a hard time separating from the parent and may become frightened, crying until the parent returns.
* The child may feel rejected and unloved. He or she would tend to withdraw from anything that could lead to a disappointment.

Signs of Abused Children

* The child's emotional and physical makeup appears different from other children.
* The child may seem fearful of his or her parents. (The fear may be expressed through hesitancy to go to the parent.)
* The child shows extremes in behavior such as crying too easily or being overly sensitive, or they may block emotions and appear not to care.
* The neglected child will show evidence of poor overall care.
* The child may be cautious or wary of physical contact. The opposite extreme of appearing

starved for adult affection is also symptomatic, but the methods of getting affection are inappropriate.
* The child uses sexual terms uncommon to most children.

What to Do/Where to Go

If a volunteer has a strong suspicion of child abuse, don't try to intervene personally. It is your responsibility to report suspicions to the child protective services in your area. In fact, the failure to report such knowledge could make a volunteer criminally liable. For more information on what to do, contact your state's child protective service.

Helpful Resources

Recognizing and Helping Hurting Children by Norm Wright.

How to Protect Your Children's Ministry from Liability by J. David Epstein, J.D.

The Good Shepherd Program by William Stout and James Becker (a program designed to help churches develop strategies to reduce the risk of abuse or injury to kids). Call (888) 639-8788.

Building Relationships in the Classroom

All good VBS teachers conduct classes. They tell the Bible stories, lead activities and keep order. Some teachers, however, change lives. The children who are in their classes are never the same afterwards. We've all known teachers like this who attract children like the proverbial Pied Piper. They seem to be gifted with a natural talent which others can only envy. But are they so gifted? What really makes the difference?

Fortunately, it often boils down to a few basic, easily learned skills—nonverbal and verbal in nature. Teachers who practice these skills find their teaching is dramatically changed. It becomes more enjoyable and the children begin to respond more openly because they sense the teacher cares.

NONVERBAL SKILLS:

* **Expression**—Greet each child with a big smile and a warm greeting—and don't let it be the last smile of the day!
* **Posture**—Sit at the student's eye level. Avoid hovering over children or moving mysteriously behind them. Join in the lesson activities whenever you can.
* **Touch**—Touching says, "I like you, you are worthwhile." Look for appropriate ways to build contact with each child through touch. (See *Preventing Child Abuse*, p. 86.)
* **Gestures**—Nod your head in response as a child talks with you. Lean forward to show interest. Make movements with an open hand. Include each child in the group with a broad sweep of the arms or indicate specific children with a wave or nod.

VERBAL SKILLS:

* **Accepting feelings**—This means listening deeply, sensing and "feeling" the child's real emotions, and then responding with honest empathy, even if not always with agreement. Say, "Kelly says she sometimes hits her brother when he takes her toys. Kelly, I know you must feel angry when your brother bothers your things." Then discuss the situation by asking, "What is something helpful to do when your brother or sister makes you angry? What advice does today's Bible memory verse give for a situation like that?"
* **Accepting ideas**—Accepting children's ideas helps them dare to think out loud. It provides freedom to ask questions or express thoughts, enabling children to expand their concepts.
* **Praise and encouragement**—All children (as well as adults) need to feel good about themselves and what they are accomplishing. The most precious gift we can give a child (short of leading him or her to Christ) is a positive and realistic sense of worth and value.
* **Open questions**—Most teachers ask questions. However, questions that require one correct answer can be threatening to children. Open questions remove pressure by asking for opinions, feelings or ideas, not just facts.
* **Enabling directions**—Instead of always telling a child exactly what to do, pose a question that allows the child to decide on a course of action. Instead of saying, "Put the glue on the shelf," you can ask, "Where does the glue need to be put?" Enabling questions help a child develop responsibility for his or her own behavior, building feelings of success and value.

These verbal and nonverbal skills are helpful for every adult who works with children. They can help you more effectively communicate Bible truths and enjoy shared experiences with your students. Initially, some of these techniques may seem awkward. However, with practice they will become natural and effective ways of building positive relationships with children—relationships that will carry over beyond the classroom.

Tips for Effective Teaching

* **Learn all you can about the age group you will be teaching.** Begin to pray for God to prepare the hearts of those who will be your students.
* **Read the entire teacher's manual.** Note all the learning aims, activities and schedules. Know exactly what you're doing in each day's session and how each element of your teaching fits in with that day's focus.
* **Become totally familiar with each Bible story and memory verse for the week.** Know the lesson aim for each day and keep everything you do focused on that one thing.
* **Learn and practice good storytelling techniques.** Be confident, focused and interesting as you communicate the Bible part of your lesson. (See pp. 109-110 for practical helps in this area.)
* **Pay particular attention to guided conversation opportunities in your lesson.** Plan to listen as much as you talk and look for ways to involve your students in the lesson both verbally and actively.
* **Be prepared before each day begins.** Have all materials at hand, ready for use, so you can focus on the children and the learning that is taking place.
* **Know and use each child's name in positive, loving, affirming ways throughout the lesson.** Greet and dismiss each one with a personal word and appropriate touch, if possible.

Guiding Conversation

Conversation is an important part of a child's learning process. "Guided conversation" refers to informal discussion during class activities that directs the child's thoughts, feelings and words toward the lesson focus. Think carefully about your conversation during the activities, because those moments are filled with the potential for meaningful learning. Be alert to ways of relating the present experience to what God's Word says, thus helping that child understand Bible truth.

Conversation with individuals and small groups also helps a teacher build a good relationship with each child. Children need to feel that you love each of them and are interested in the things that interest them. As you guide the conversation, look for opportunities to express praise and encouragement. Each child needs to know that you recognize his or her honest efforts and the things he or she does well.

Here are some helps for using guided conversation effectively:

* **Be prepared.** Read the information in your teacher's manual. Become familiar with the lesson focus. Review any conversation suggestions provided. Think of ways you might tailor or build upon any conversation ideas in your curriculum to meet more specifically the needs of your own kids. Write down any other ideas or questions you might ask. Keep these with you during the session.
* **Stay with your children as they work.** They need to know that you are there, ready to listen and ready to talk.
* **Know the characteristics of the children you teach.** Be aware of individual differences in maturity. Be sensitive to each child's home situation and plan your conversation to include the variety of family situations represented in your class. Your conversations will help you discover what information a child knows (or doesn't know) about a particular topic.
* **Recognize and accept the ways children respond to guided conversation.** Some children are quite verbal. Others may respond

with nods or other motions. Engage children in a dialogue rather than a monologue. The conversation should stimulate rather than interfere with the child's learning experiences.

* **Spend more time listening than you do talking.** Look directly at the child who is talking. Demonstrate your interest in what was said by responding to the specific ideas the child expressed.

The opportunities for guided conversation with children are endless. Prepare thoughtfully and prayerfully before each session. The Holy Spirit will use your words to reveal God's love and truth to your students.

Reinforcing the Bible Memory Verse

Discovering truths from God's Word can be an exciting and rewarding experience for all the children in your class. Some children may memorize easily as they enjoy these activities. Other children may have difficulty recalling all the words but can still clearly understand the meaning of the passage. Be sensitive to the learning level and learning style of each child. Each is an individual and has a different capacity to memorize and recall. Here are some ideas for helping children understand and memorize God's Word:

* **Use the Bible memory verse as often as possible.** Your natural conversation and discussion during each activity should reinforce the words and meaning of the verse.
* **Ask questions to check a child's understanding of a specific Bible passage**. For example, "How would you say this Bible verse in your own words? What are ways these verses can help you at school? In the neighborhood? With your family? What do you think is the most important word in this Bible verse? Why?"
* **Occasionally share situations in which knowing God's Word has helped you**. Repeat a specific Bible verse that has special significance for you.
* **Use the variety of ways Bible verses are presented and discussed in your curriculum**. Games, worksheets, Bible learning activities and songs encourage children's understanding and practical application of each Bible memory verse. As you lead children in activities, encourage them to memorize God's Word and give honest praise for each child's efforts.
* **Challenge your students to work together to achieve a class goal.** Individual contests often discourage children for whom memorization is difficult. For example, explain that when 10 verses have been memorized by the class, a special treat will be provided. Make the goal achievable for the size and skill of your group. The next day, make the goal a little harder.

Above all, remember that your own attitude toward God's Word and your memorization of Bible verses will have the greatest effect on children as you encourage them to hide God's Word in their hearts (see Psalm 119:11).

Leading a Child to Christ

One of the greatest privileges of serving in VBS is the opportunity to lead children to Christ. Most VBS curriculums introduce and build on what it means to be part of God's family and then conclude the last day with a clear explanation of the gospel (Christ's death and resurrection). This is a very special day that really is the high point of your entire program. Inform your VBS staff, church leadership and congregation of when this day will be and ask prayer for the teachers and the students.

Also, make sure you have trained your volunteers on what to do if a child does want to accept Christ into his or her life. Oftentimes, we get so caught up in all the other areas of VBS that we neglect to be prepared for someone actually making a decision! Don't let this happen to you! Be prepared.

The following steps (next page) will help you lead a child to Christ. Know them well and communicate them to your staff (especially your Bible story teachers and counselors). You may even want to train additional volunteers to help out on this special day.

How to Lead a Child to Christ

1. **Pray.** Starting at the initial planning of VBS, ask God to prepare the hearts of your children to receive the good news about Jesus. Ask that He prepare the staff to communicate effectively with the students. Pray that the Holy Spirit will give you and your volunteers wisdom and keep you sensitive to every child's spiritual needs. Always remember that salvation is a supernatural work of the Holy Spirit.

2. **Prepare the foundation.** The children at VBS will be evaluating everything they see your staff say and do. They will recognize people who show a living, growing relationship with God, people whose lives show that knowing God makes a noticeable difference, people who love them and listen to them the same way God loves them and listens to them.

   Learn to listen with your full attention. Learn to share honestly both the joys and the struggles you encounter as a Christian. Be honest about your own questions and about your personal concern for students. Learn to accept your students as they are. Christ died for each one while he or she was yet a sinner. (See Romans 5:8.) You are also called to love each one as is.

3. **Be aware of opportunities.** A child may show an interest in salvation by a direct question or a seemingly indirect one. If you sense a child is searching, try to find some time to talk to him or her one-on-one so that you can share what it means to be a Christian and to answer any questions.

4. **Create a relaxed atmosphere.** Here are some tips to keep in mind when you talk with a child:
   a. *Put the child at ease.* Be perceptive of his or her feelings. Be relaxed, natural and casual in your conversation and avoid criticism.
   b. *As the child talks, listen carefully to what is said.* Children sometimes make superficial or shocking statements just to get your reaction. Don't begin lecturing or problem-solving. Instead, encourage the child to keep talking and express him- or herself.
   c. *Be gently direct.* Do not overpower the child with demands from the gospel. But make no apologies either. God does not need to be defended and neither does the truth. If a child does not bring up the topic of salvation, a simple question such as, "If a friend wanted to know how to become a Christian, what would you say?" can unlock a life-changing conversation.

5. **Clearly and simply explain how to be a Christian.** Discuss these points slowly enough to allow time for thinking and comprehending.
   a. God wants you to become His child (John 1:12). Do you know why God wants you in His family? (1 John 4:8)
   b. You and all the people in the world have done wrong things (Romans 3:23). The Bible word for doing wrong is "sin." What do you think should happen to us when we sin? (Romans 6:23)
   c. God loves you so much He sent His Son to die on the cross for your sin. Because Jesus never sinned, He is the only one who can take the punishment for your sin (1 Corinthians 15:3; 1 John 4:14).
   d. Are you sorry for your sin? Tell God that you are. Do you believe Jesus died to be your Savior? Tell God. If you do believe and you are sorry for your sin—God forgives all your sin (1 John 1:9).
   e. The Bible says that when you believe in Jesus, God's Son, you receive God's gift of eternal life. This gift makes you a child of God. This means God is with you now and forever (John 3:16). He wants you to spend time with Him by praying and reading the Bible.

(NOTE: The Bible uses many terms and images to express the concept of salvation. Children often do not understand or may create misconceptions about these terms, especially those that are highly symbolic. [Remember the trouble Nicodemus, a respected teacher, had in trying to understand the meaning of being "born again"?] Many people talk with children about "asking Jesus into your heart." The literal-minded child is likely to develop strange ideas from the imagery of the words. The idea of being a child of God [see John 1:12] is perhaps the simplest portrayal the New Testament provides.)

How to Follow Up

Following up on the boys and girls who have made a decision is especially important at VBS. In some cases, you may never see that child again. Follow-up helps the child really understand the decision he or she just made and gives him or her guidance on how to grow in Christ.

After a child has made a decision, quietly have two counselors or other person(s) familiar to the child talk with him or her. It is best to get together with the child away from the group to prevent distractions. Follow these steps:

* **Silently pray that the Lord would speak through you and give you the right words.**
* **Congratulate the child**. Let him or her see how happy you are and hear from you the importance of his or her decision. Be careful not to embarrass the child. Present the child a certificate with the date and his or her name on it (see sample pp. 225-226). This helps to commemorate the event and also gives the child a reminder of when he or she made the decision.
* **Briefly review the decision he or she made**. This helps give the child a better understanding of what he or she did.
* **Explain that Jesus is a friend to us and that, like a friend, He want us to spend time with Him**. Be careful not to talk in abstract or "church" terms. If you do use words such as "grow" or "born again", explain what they mean.
* **Give practical ways that a child can "grow" in Christ.**
  1. Spend time with God by reading His letter to us, the Bible.
  2. Obey what God tells us to do in the Bible.
  3. Spend time with God by praying to Him.
  4. Pray and ask God's forgiveness when we do wrong things.
  5. Learn more about God at church, Sunday School or Bible club.
  6. Tell others about God.
* **Encourage the student to tell his or her family about the decision**. Offer to go with the child to answer any questions. However, use good judgment in doing this. Some parents will be excited to hear the news, but others may not be too happy.
* **Stay in touch with the child and parents through phone calls, visits or postcards**. Invite the child to attend Sunday School. Continue to pray for him or her.

Gospel Light Resources

* *God Loves You* is an effective evangelism booklet to use with a child.
* *God Wants You to Grow as His Child* is a booklet to help children know what to do after their initial decision.

Discipline in the Classroom

"Why do they act like that?" comments a frustrated teacher.

"Why can't they just sit still?" sighs another.

"What these kids need is discipline!" states another.

Why is a child's behavior sometimes so puzzling? Why do children "act like that?"

No two children are alike. We cannot begin to number the different experiences each child has had in the early years of life. Nor can we fathom the varying family backgrounds of each of these children. Still, even knowing these things, we continue to be surprised when children do not act the way they are "supposed" to act.

So what's a leader to do? Where can the weary teacher find help? Is discipline the answer? And just what *is* discipline?

Many people use the words "discipline" and "punishment" to mean the same thing. In so doing they confuse their meanings. "Punishment" is retaliation for wrong doing. "Discipline" is the process of providing guidance. Discipline helps a child acquire self-control—an inner commitment to do what is right.

For a child to grow into a thoughtful and loving adult, he or she needs to begin developing self-control—direction from within. To accomplish this lifelong task, the child needs loving adult guidance until he or she is mature enough to handle the task alone.

Learning to get along with others and to use materials and equipment creatively help a child enjoy the classroom. VBS can be an important, positive contribution to a child's educational experience.

Preparing to handle the inevitable discipline issues that will occur during VBS is part of the planning. Be sure to have a clear plan of action designating who is responsible for discipline and what they are to do. If you have enough volunteers, it is a good idea to assign one or two people to handle major disruptive problems. This will give a level of comfort to your teachers, counselors or other volunteers who often aren't prepared to handle such problems and will help you to establish a positive learning atmosphere in your classroom.

Preventing Unacceptable Behavior

"An ounce of prevention is worth a pound of cure." How much better for children when things go well and episodes of misbehavior and punishment are avoided! Consider the following ideas to make your VBS a "good place to be."

* **Develop an atmosphere of love and acceptance.** Each child who enters your VBS program needs to feel loved and wanted. Children long to feel that someone cares about them, that they matter. Sitting down and listening attentively to what a child has to say or kindly but firmly redirecting a child's out-of-bounds activity demonstrates your love and care in ways a child can understand.
* **Set realistic standards that can be enforced.** A child feels secure with limits. He or she needs to know what you expect. Establish a few basic rules from the start. Phrase the rules in a positive way whenever you can. Help children remember and observe the rules during their work and play. Give each child consistent and positive guidance. Find a middle ground between rigid authority and total permissiveness. Most VBS programs intersperse physical activities throughout the schedule so that children can release pent-up energies. Children need the freedom to move around and make choices within limits. But children also need the security of a consistently maintained standard of behavior.
* **Recognize accomplishments and good behavior.** Look for ways to encourage all children. Problem children will always be recognized, but those who have already achieved a high degree of self-control will also need to be noticed. Affirm them by such comments as, "I really appreciated how you..." or "You're really good at..." When children know they will receive attention for positive behavior, their display of disruptive behavior often diminishes.

Correcting Unacceptable Behavior

There are occasions when corrective measures are necessary. In dealing with a behavior challenge, we can do one of two things—ignore it or respond to it. There are times when ignoring the problem will be the best solution. Many children would prefer negative attention to no attention. Often we are guilty of creating a power struggle over issues that would be better left alone.

Sometimes, though, we cannot ignore misbehavior. Here are some helpful steps to follow in correcting the situation.

* **Deal with the problem individually.** Avoid embarrassing the child in front of friends. When possible, talk with him or her alone.
* **Have the child tell what he or she did.** Don't ask why the child behaved in that way. A "why" question merely invites the child to attempt to justify the offense. Perhaps you will want to tell what you saw and then ask, "Is that what happened?" Deal only with the current situation. Do not bring up past offenses.
* **Be sure the child understands why the behavior is not acceptable.** Either ask the child to tell why the action is a problem or offer a clear explanation of the reason you intervened. Phrase your explanation so the child can recognize that the problem is his or her own and that it results in a loss to both the individual and the group.
* **Redirect the child toward positive behavior.** Focus on good behavior. For example, ask, "Max, can you think of a better thing you could have done?" or "What can you do about it now?" Then help the child implement positive changes. As the child makes these changes, give honest and sincere encouragement to reward acceptable behavior.

* **Let the child experience the consequences of negative behavior.** Attempt to tie a child's actions to natural consequences. When materials are being misused, remove the materials from the child or remove the child from the materials. Let the child choose to correct the behavior voluntarily or to experience the appropriate result.

Dealing with Distracting Behavior

Activity does not prevent a child from listening or learning. When a child's "active-ness" is not interfering with another child's attention, let that child do what his or her energy is requiring at that time. The following general guidelines can help limit distractions during large group times.

* **Signal a helper to sit beside or behind the active child**. He or she can gently guide arms and legs back into the child's own space or provide a productive alternate activity the child can do.
* **Simply state what the child is to do with his or her hands**. It is often appropriate to tell the child what will happen if he or she continues to disturb (e.g., be moved to another place).
* **If the disturbing actions continue, follow through and do *exactly* what you said you would do**. Your effectiveness depends on your ability to follow through on your promise.
* **If more than one child is showing signs of restlessness, realize that it's time to do something else** (e.g., sing an active song, stand and stretch, etc.).
* **If a child consistently misbehaves during activities, remove the child from the scene of the difficulty**. Try to redirect the child's interest in something else. Keep conversation cheerful.
* **Watch to determine what makes the child want to continue negative behavior**. Sometimes misbehavior is simply a bid for attention. Quite often a child would rather be punished (which is one kind of adult attention) than receive no attention at all.
* **Avoid repeated threats**. There is a difference between a threat ("Wesley, if you do that again, I will...") and explaining consequences ("I cannot let you do that because...."). A threat is a kind of dare that increases tension, while an explanation of consequences (in terms a child can understand) defines limits.

A Final Reminder

A positive, loving approach to the needs of your students is one of the most important factors in making VBS a safe place to be. In all your actions and words, reflect the unconditional love you yourself have experienced from God. Pray for understanding, wisdom and patience. Be a loving, caring person both inside and outside the classroom, no matter what the behavior challenge may be.

Helping Children with Special Needs

The Hyperactive Child

A clinically hyperactive child is different from a child who simply can't sit still for very long. The hyperactive child reacts to life the way you would respond to being closed in a room with the television, radio, stereo system and two vacuum cleaners all turned up full blast. Sound like too much for you? A classroom often seems like "too much" for the hyperactive child.

Hyperactive children are unable to sort out and concentrate on one thing at a time. They are in constant motion mentally and often physically as well. Since such a child is unable to sit and listen or even to work on one project for any length of time, he or she leaps from one distraction to another, often distracting others in the process.

Try to steer hyperactive children primarily toward quiet activities which can help them keep their energies channeled. Hyperactive children function best with a minimum of distraction and an activity which captures their attention.

As you show love to hyperactive children, be aware of the needs of the other children in your class at the same time. If your guidance is to have maximum effectiveness, you cannot allow one or a few children to distract others unnecessarily or reduce your classroom to chaos.

A hyperactive child may need individual attention from another adult or VBS leader. In some cases, it may be beneficial to enlist a caring adult assistant specifically to focus on meeting the needs of the hyperactive child.

It may be helpful to talk privately and in a loving and understanding manner with parents. Get firsthand information on the most effective ways to care for their child. You will find most parents highly appreciative of your concern for the child's well-being. Since they know their child better than anyone else, they will likely be able to suggest approaches which have proven helpful.

The Shy Child

A shy child may often feel insecure and afraid. He or she may be a natural introvert. It is difficult for these children to feel safe and loved. Encourage the children in your group to help everyone feel welcomed and important by modeling those behaviors for them.

Never label a child "shy." (The child may try to live up to it!) Do not push a shy child to talk in a large group and never shame him or her for not responding. A rather quiet child will usually feel more free to talk in a small group in which every child is freely participating. Such a child may eventually feel free to speak up in a large group after some successful experiences in smaller groups. Look for appropriate situations to make that happen. Encourage the child to talk about things with which he or she is familiar and secure. The child may only be willing to give short replies, but each successful expression will build acceptance and security.

Be sure that quiet children receive your personal attention and encouragement. It's easy to overlook them. Consistently help shy children feel welcome and important without being made the focus of group attention.

The Aggressive Child

The child who most needs love and acceptance is often the one whose behavior makes others feel anything but loving! Unfortunately, the natural tendency to withhold love from such a child is likely to produce even more aggressive, unacceptable behavior as the child desperately seeks to be noticed.

As with any other child, the rule is to accept the aggressive child as he or she is, not requiring that the child change in order to earn your affection. But every time there is positive behavior, be sure the child knows you appreciate his or her efforts. Your good example of showing love to aggressive children by encouraging and affirming them will also help teach all children ways to relate to each other.

At the same time, you need to be concerned with the welfare of all children. If a child is being aggressive enough to upset or harm another child, firmly remove the aggressive child from the situation and clearly explain the behavior necessary in order to return. Give the child the choice between obeying or "cooling off" for a longer period.

The Child Who Says, "I Can't"

The "I can't" attitude is built on fear of failure. Children need the freedom to fail without loss of acceptance or status. Teachers can help children understand that "failure" is part of learning. Often it is necessary to discover what does *not* work in order to find out what *does*.

"I can't" is often the student's way of saying, "Give me the attention I need to feel I can do this. Help me try a new experience."

Some examples of beneficial phrases:

"It's hard to try something when you're not sure you can do it."

"Make a start and see how it goes. Your work doesn't have to be perfect."

"This is a good place to practice something like this. No one will give you a grade or criticize what you do."

Avoid platitudes like "Do the best you can!" or "It's easy." Acknowledge the child's feelings and be sure the child knows you're on his or her side.

Welcoming the Disabled Child to Your VBS

A Special Word from Joni Eareckson Tada

I remember the panic as if it were yesterday. My first day of class in a wheelchair—the desks were too short, the narrow aisles blocked my way and every student was staring. I stopped and stared back. Would I fit under the desk? Who would place my books in front of me? Would someone be willing to turn the pages? I needed help to take notes. And would I even be accepted? I was scared to death!

I was ready to turn and head the other way when the teacher confidently walked toward me with a happy smile and warm handshake. She welcomed me into the class and into a whole new adventure of learning. That teacher, with her friendly and accepting attitude, instantly set the tone not only for the rest of the students, but for me as well. Everyone, including myself, was part of the class.

Jesus approached disabled people in a very open, accepting way. And in Luke 14:12—14 He makes a special point of telling leaders to broaden their ministry to the blind, the deaf and the physically disabled. Sure, it takes a little creativity, lots of courage and an extra measure of effort, but as the Lord says, "You will be blessed. Although they cannot repay you, you will be repaid at the resurrection of the righteous" (Luke 14:14, *NIV*).

It's no different for you and your ministry with the young people in your Vacation Bible School. At first you may feel awkward and unsure of yourself when a disabled kid wheels through your classroom door. You may shrink at the idea of stretching your teaching skills to include a child who is physically or mentally impaired. *After all,* you may think, *I have enough to worry about with a bunch of energetic kids and a whole new series of lessons. Add a child with a disability and I know I'll blow a fuse!*

Take heart—God knows exactly how you feel. He knows all about your limited personal resources. But He also delights in using people who think they "just can't do it!" In fact if you feel unskilled, you are God's best candidate to get the job done. Why? Well, He enjoys displaying His power through the weak and untrained.

And as the story goes in Luke 14, it's not enough to merely wait passively until a disabled child shows up in your classroom. Jesus reminds us to "Go out to the roads and country lanes and make them come in, so that my house will be full" (Luke 14:23, *NIV*). God will give you the courage to actively seek out those young people who have special needs and invite them to Vacation Bible School.

Remember: The church is the most logical place for barriers to be broken. Right now, the world is doing a better job of it than we. It's up to us to make the difference!

In the Classroom

And once these children are in your classroom? Remember, kids who are disabled adapt easily to most new situations—they've been dealing with questions, stares, embarrassment and obstacles longer than you realize. Also, you may be surprised at how readily the rest of the class befriends the child who is disabled, once their questions and fears have been allayed.

Teaching Tips

As with any boy or girl, pinpoint the disabled child's strengths and weaknesses. Learn to work through his or her strengths rather than weaknesses, thus building a positive self-image essential for learning. A child with a disability can be God's best audiovisual aid of how His power shows up best through weakness.

- Praise the child for those things he or she does well.
- Seek advice from the child's parents. Ask about any special materials or helps to make learning enjoyable.
- Make your classroom as accessible as possible.
- Do not measure the child's achievements by those things that other children the same age do.
- Teach the child it is more important to compete with him or herself than with others. Reward the child for any improvement.

* Discover ways of adapting materials and activities so that *all* can participate. Does the material used or the action involved need to be: larger, smaller, higher, lower, easier, slower, more tangible, sung, clapped, tapped, reinforced more strongly, implemented in shorter time spans or in smaller group sizes?
* Don't forget your best resource—your students. They will often be quicker and more inventive than teachers in this kind of problem solving.

Different Disabilities

You will want to make God's Word and your lessons as accessible as possible to disabled children. But accessibility means different things to different people.

* The child in your class may be *physically* impaired. He or she may use crutches, braces, a wordboard (if he or she cannot speak) or a wheelchair. Ask questions about the adaptive equipment and then learn to look at the obstacles in your room through the child's eyes. Is a ramp needed? Wider aisles? Someone to help turn pages and take notes? Hold materials? Reading for or with? Choose an able-bodied child in your class to be a special helper, occasionally rotating the responsibility to others—that way you will raise the awareness of everyone.
* Is the child *deaf or hearing impaired*? Work with his or her parents to secure a qualified sign-language interpreter. Seat the child near the front of the room where he or she may watch your lips and facial expressions to gain more complete meaning. Speak slowly and expressively. Use lots of audiovisuals to stimulate the child's interest. Encourage the child to use any hearing aids or other specialized equipment he or she may have. Involve the child in as many activities as possible, designing games in which he or she can participate. Teach your class some of their songs in sign language!
* The child in your class may be *blind.* Again, work with parents and professionals to determine how you might best meet his or her needs. Do not be afraid to use "visual" language such as, "My, Jennifer, you look pretty today in your pink sweatshirt. Did you see your friend, Michael, outside on the playground?" If the child would like to have a special helper in class, teach his or her friend how to best help—never tugging the blind child, but always offering an elbow for guidance. A touch is so important. Remember to include the child in as many games, songs and activities as possible. Don't forget to translate the medium of message from sight to sound, or sound to sight.
* If your student is mildly *mentally handicapped,* please remember that he or she is neither mentally ill or emotionally disturbed. Mental handicaps such as Down's Syndrome or some kinds of cerebral palsy are organic (and not psychological) disabilities resulting in a lower functioning level. Although the child may show some difficulty in following group rules or maintaining a normal attention span he or she can still be integrated into class activities.
* Watch for a child who may be *learning disabled.* Symptoms include an inability to follow directions, a fear (or reckless fearlessness) of swings and slides, constant interrupting (or unusual quietness), poor handwriting, an inability to color inside lines, trouble in reading, difficulty in expressing ideas, and little understanding of the difference between up and down or left and right. All children exhibit some of these traits and it is important to separate the occasional from persistent behavior. Sensitively alert the child's parents if you spot these problems. Time and patience will help you modify your curriculum to best suit the child's needs. And Vacation Bible School may be just the place where a learning disabled child can perform successfully and gain new social skills.

In Closing

Although I am severely disabled, my classroom experience was a positive push in the right direction. I thank the Lord Jesus for linking me with a teacher who was able to envision success for me when I was too shortsighted to see it for myself. God's power not only showed up best through my teacher's weakness, but mine as well. With His grace, you and the disabled child can enjoy the same success. So, happy teaching! If you'd like more help, contact me at:

Ms. Joni Eareckson Tada
Joni and Friends
28720 Canwood St.
P. O. Box 3333
Agoura Hills, CA 91301
Phone: (818) 707-5664

Training Information for Early Childhood Workers

Knowing Your Kids

Age-Level Characteristics

Effectively instructing young children requires that a teacher recognize and accept wide individual differences in skills, abilities and interests. For example, a two-year-old will thoroughly enjoy stacking blocks in a random fashion while a kindergartner plans windows and doors for his or her building. Both children work successfully with blocks but at different levels of ability and interest. Regardless of the level at which a child works, a teacher can use that child's interest in an activity to guide his or her thinking toward understanding a Bible truth.

Before you lead children through the daily activities of VBS, consider the following age-level characteristics of the children in your department.

Two- to Three-Year-Olds

PHYSICAL

From two to three years the child is in constant movement. The child tumbles often. Large muscles are developing but small hand/finger muscles are not. Twos walk, climb, scribble on paper, build a tower with blocks, turn pages of a book and feed themselves snacks. Threes may build structures with blocks, draw pictures which they will name as objects/people, begin to count and may begin to use scissors on heavy, straight lines.

Teaching Tips: Plan for freedom of movement. Use simple finger fun and activity songs for stretching, stepping, jumping and clapping. Use simple puzzles, large blocks, jumbo crayons and large sheets of paper. Provide some quiet-time activities.

MENTAL/EMOTIONAL

Twos have short attention spans. They may say many single words and some sentences. The child is beginning to recognize his or her name in print. Two- and three-year-olds are explorers; they learn through their senses. They can learn rhymes, songs and finger fun.

Teaching Tips: Provide materials with interesting textures, smells, tastes, etc., for the child to explore. Tell stories in a literal, simple way—avoid symbolism. Be brief and use pictures or flannelgraph figures often. When telling them what to do, give one brief direction at a time. Wait patiently until they have responded before you continue with the next direction.

SOCIAL

Twos have little regard for the rights of others. Threes can interact in play with others. However, it's still a "ME, MY, MINE" world. Sharing and taking turns is hard to do. When a conflict arises, children respond better to distraction rather than reasoning.

Teaching Tips: Teachers need to be kind and patient. Offer opportunities for play with other children. Know each child as an individual and use his or her name often. Help each child to succeed by providing activities appropriate for the child's abilities.

SPIRITUAL

The two- and three-year-old can learn that God made all things and that God cares for him or her; that Jesus is God's special Son and that He did kind, loving things when He lived on earth; that the Bible is a special book about God and Jesus and that Bible stories are true.

Teaching Tips: The child's learning about God is dependent on not only what people say but also what people show about God. Your loving actions help the child understand God's love. Help the child experience God's presence in our world through a variety of seeing, touching, smelling, tasting and hearing activities. Talk and sing about God.

Four- to Five-Year-Olds

PHYSICAL

At this age children are in a period of rapid physical growth. Coordination is greatly improved. These children are still constantly on the move! Girls often mature more rapidly than boys. Fours and fives may be able to cut with scissors on a curved line and draw recognizable pictures of people and objects.

Teaching Tips: Freehand, creative art activities are best. Don't expect perfection. Children this age still need to be recognized for their work on the process of art, not the product. Large pieces of paper, jumbo crayons and heavy lines for cutting are needed. More sophisticated toys are appropriate: puzzles with 10 to 20 pieces; varieties of construction toys (various shapes and sizes); realistic home living accessories (dress-up clothes for boys and girls, kitchen utensils, food packages), etc.

MENTAL/EMOTIONAL

Fours and fives are curious and questioning. They may concentrate for longer periods, but their attention span is still short. Children will interpret your words literally. Fours and fives may recall short Bible verses, talk accurately about recent events and pronounce most common words correctly.

Teaching Tips: Use large teaching pictures to reinforce basic concepts. Set realistic limits and emphasize the behavior you desire. ("Raymond, running is a good thing to do outside where there is lots of room. Inside we have to walk so no one will get hurt." "Jasmine, you may only draw on your own paper. Are there any more places on your page that you want to make purple?") Supply a variety of materials for children to touch, see, smell and taste. Help children discover things for themselves by having the freedom to experiment (play) with a variety of safe materials.

SOCIAL

The four- or five-year-old child can participate with other children in group activities. The child actively seeks adult approval, responds to friendliness and wants to be loved, especially by his or her teacher. Some children may use negative ways of gaining attention from others.

Teaching Tips: Encourage opportunities for group singing, prayer and conversation. Give each child individual attention before negative behavior occurs. Make eye contact often, listen carefully to the child and smile and show that the child is special to you.

SPIRITUAL

The four- and five-year-old child can learn basic information about God—He made the world; He cares for all people; He forgives him or her when the child is sorry for doing wrong. A child this age can also learn that Jesus died to take the punishment for the wrong things we have done and that He rose from the dead and is alive. Fours and fives can be taught that the Bible tells us ways to obey God and that he or she can talk to God in prayer.

Teaching Tips: Because the child still thinks literally and physically, avoid the use of symbolic words such as "born again," "open your heart," or "fishers of men." When about to use a symbolic expression, think of the simplest, most literal explanation of what the expression means. Then use that simple explanation *instead* of the symbolic one which may confuse the child. Some children may respond to individual conversations by praying to become a member of God's family. Provide opportunities for children to hold the Bible.

Communicating Bible Truths to Young Children

Guiding children in their early years is an awesome task. Helping children learn basic scriptural truth is extremely important. Fortunately, God has not left us to accomplish this task in our own strength. He offers us the instruction of the Holy Spirit and the promise of His guidance: "If any of you lacks wisdom, he should ask God, who gives generously to all" (James 1:5, *NIV*).

With this assurance of guidance, how does one go about teaching little ones of God's love? How do we communicate Bible truth in terms a child can understand?

Learning by Doing

The Christianity we share with children must be more than mere words or knowledge. It is not enough for the young child to hear God's Word or even to memorize it. The child must *do* it. Hands-on activity is the young child's most effective way to learn. He or she is not yet able to play with ideas; the child must play with *materials*. The child must use all of his or her senses—seeing, touching, tasting, smelling and hearing—in order to learn effectively. Therefore, we must help the child learn Bible truths through active play experiences. As the child draws or builds with blocks or tucks a doll into bed, a teacher can link those activities to Bible words and events, creating an effective learning experience out of what may seem to be "just play."

For instance, a simple beanbag game can reinforce Bible learning with questions and comments like these: "Ashley, you tossed the beanbag into the basket! I remember when you were too little to do that. Now you've grown taller and stronger, just as God planned. You are even big enough to learn ways to be kind to others. You are big enough to take turns tossing the beanbag. Taking turns is a way to be kind. Our Bible says, 'Be kind to one another.'"

Attitude and Commitment

The best teaching methods, however, are only effective when the love and Christian commitment of the teacher shine through. Search your heart. Do you fully realize how much Jesus loves these little ones? Do you really want to share God's love with children to help them make a good beginning? The answers to those questions have nothing to do with the VBS program, class size or facilities. They are questions about attitude and commitment. Help for changing attitudes and creating commitment can come only through earnest prayer. Your vision of what God is doing through you can recharge your enthusiasm and change your attitude! Ask God to give you that vision.

Talking with Young Children

Those of us who work with young children often feel that they are like blotters, absorbing every word we say. Sometimes we talk from the moment the first child arrives until we tell the last child good-bye. But often a child simply tunes us out! Then, of course, the child misses hearing the very things we want him or her to learn. So it is important for us to choose our words wisely; we must learn to talk *with* a child rather than always *to* him or her.

* **Begin by listening.** Listen to a child as if he or she were the only one in the room. Give your focused attention even though you might not understand every word. Your sincere interest in what the child says gives him or her a model to imitate. This will help that child become a better listener when it's your turn to talk.
* **Let the child take the lead.** Every child has his or her own level of interest in what you say. Whenever you exceed that level, the child mentally flips the switch and tunes you out. When the child comes to you, he or she is showing you what his or her interests are. "Allison, I'm glad you showed me your picture. Tell me about it."
* **Get the child's attention before speaking.** Adults waste lots of breath talking when no one is listening. For instance, shouting across a room to a child results in confusion rather than communication. Go to the child. Bend down so your face is at his or her eye level. Speak the child's name. "Sammy, you need to look at me for a moment. That's right. Sammy, it's time for you to put your dishes in this cupboard." Phrase comments in positive terms. "Patrick, blocks are for building, not for throwing."
* **Say the most important words first.** After you've spoken the child's name, *briefly* state what action you want the child to do. Then you may add a reason. "Kylie, you may play with the blocks now. It's time for free-play."

* **Use simple words and a natural tone of voice.** Speak slowly and distinctly in a soft, yet audible tone. Let your voice express your enthusiasm and interest. Add a smile to your words. Avoid "baby talk" or "gushing."
* **Use specific words.** General terms leave a child confused, not knowing exactly what you mean. Rather than, "Put the toys away," say, "Alex, your red truck needs to go here on this shelf."
* **Tie words to experience.** Understanding comes when a child hears words at the same time he or she sees the words demonstrated. Show a child the appropriate action as you describe it. For example, "Eric, this is the way to rub the picture so your sticker will stick." Eric understands immediately.
* **Relate the child's activity to the lesson focus.** Keep in mind the lesson focus and Bible verse for each session. Then your natural conversation can tie children's activities and thoughts to the lesson's Bible truths. Briefly telling parts of the Bible story can also help make the connection. For example, while children are building with blocks during a session aimed at increasing awareness of God's love and care, say, "James, I like the way you are building. You're using your strong arms to lift those big blocks. God made your strong arms, James." Open your Bible and say, "Our Bible says, *God cares about you!*"
* **Make a clear distinction between times when a child may and may not have a choice.** Ask a question or offer a choice only when you are willing to let the child have an alternative. When his or her obedience is necessary, make a direct statement to that effect, assuming cooperation. Questions such as, "Colin, will you put away your truck?" leave the door wide open for an honest "No," which then needs to be respected. A positive statement, such as "Colin, you need to put away your truck," lets Colin know you mean business and he has no choice. A middle ground approach is possible through questions that focus the child's attention on the situation but leave him free to determine the action. "Colin, it is time for our snack. What do you need to do with your truck?" Or, "Colin, would you like to roll your truck or carry it to the shelf?"
* **Avoid shaming a child.** Sarcasm and ridicule have no place with young, sensitive children. Remember that children take your words literally. Their idea of humor is not the same as an adult's. Often adult attempts at humor result in hurt feelings. When a child makes a mistake, he or she most needs your words of encouragement. First, describe what you see. "Ashley, you seem unhappy because the juice spilled." Then offer a solution or let the child choose how to help. "We could use paper towels or the sponge to clean it up."
* **Show children the same courtesies you would adults.** A child is a real person with real feelings! These feelings are important to him or her. When we rudely interrupt a child's activity or conversation, we are showing our lack of consideration for that child. We are also modeling the kind of behavior we do not want imitated! Ask yourself before you speak or act, *Would I say that to a grown-up friend? How would I interrupt another adult?* Then go to the child. "Adam, you are working very hard on your picture. You may draw one more thing on it and then it will be time to clean up."

Use the conversation ideas in your curriculum as conversation "starters"—words and suggestions to spark your own imagination as you guide children's thoughts and activity. Adapt this suggested conversation to fit the particular interests and needs of individual children. Be alert and sensitive to each child. "How good is a timely word!" (Proverbs 15:23, *NIV*).

How to Get a Child's Attention

* "Danny, it's my turn to talk and your turn to listen."
* "I'll give stickers to the children who are sitting quietly at the table."
* "I see Nicholas waiting quietly for his turn to talk."
* "If you see someone helping in this picture, put your hand on your knee."
* "You've had a turn to talk, Megan. Now it's Brandon's turn."
* (Whispering) "I'm going to whisper a question. Whisper your answer to me."

Principles of Effective Storytelling

Storytelling scares more new teachers than perhaps any other facet of teaching. The prospect of having to capture the interest of squirming children and then sustain it for the duration of a story seems like a greater challenge than many people are ready to face.

Fortunately, effective storytelling is a skill that anyone can develop by practicing a few simple principles.

Preparing to Tell the Bible Story

* **Read the story from a current Bible translation**. Although you may have read the story many times, read it again from God's Word!
* **Then read the story as it is written in the lesson**. Usually this version has been prepared in words a child can understand. Reread and know your story well enough to talk *with* your students rather than read *to* them. When your eyes are not tied to the words of the story, you are free to focus on the faces of the children in your class. By *telling* rather than *reading* the story, you will be better able to express enthusiasm through your face and voice. Knowing the story well also frees your hands to move any Bible story figures on the flannel board.
* **Have confidence in the story**. Ask yourself, "Why is this story worth hearing?" People will listen to a story that offers them a benefit. A few moments spent reflecting on the value and appeal of your story will make you less concerned about your storytelling ability.
* **Focus the story**. No matter how skillfully you tell a Bible story, it will have little impact unless the point of the story is clear to you and your class. Unfortunately, some teachers get so involved in filling their stories with interesting tidbits and descriptions that when they come to the conclusion no one is too sure what the story is all about. To make sure the point does not get lost, tell the story so that the point is the focus of all that happens. As a general rule, the longer the story becomes, the harder it is to keep it focused. Therefore, keep your story brief.
* **Prepare the visual resources for the Bible story**. These visuals have been planned to reinforce and give meaning to your words. You may choose to use additional visuals such as puppets, clothespin people or a simple Bible-times costume.
* **Practice telling the story using the visual resources**. Tell it to someone in your family, to a tape recorder or to yourself in the mirror. If you feel it is necessary to use notes, write them on a small card and place it in your Bible. Know the story well enough so you can look directly at the children most of the time with only an occasional glance at your notes.
* **Be sure children are seated comfortably and can see the visuals you are using**. Remove distractions such as toys or papers. Then say, "When you first came this morning, it was my turn to listen and your turn to talk. Now it's my turn to talk and your turn to listen." Briefly remind children of activities they have done today that helped prepare them for this story. Then begin immediately with the opening sentence in your story.

Telling the Bible Story

* **Teach from the Bible**. Have your open Bible in front of you throughout the story and clearly state that the story is true. Children need to see you as a teacher of God's Word—not merely a reader of a curriculum product.
* **Capture interest at the start**. A good beginning is essential because it is much easier to capture an audience than it is to recapture them after their attention has wandered. The best way to begin most stories with children is through some type of experience interesting to everyone in the group. This experience needs to connect to some aspect of the story. The younger your children, the more crucial it is to start a story with a reference to something in their own experience.
* **Create interest in the story with your voice**.
  1. Try talking a little slower—or faster—to make parts of the story more dramatic.

2. When the suspense builds, talk softer. A whisper is the most dramatic sound the human voice can make.
3. On rare occasions, talk louder—but be considerate of other classes when you do.
4. Above all, avoid talking down to the children. Talk to them as you would to your best friend. Be careful to use words your listeners understand.

* **Create interest in the story with facial expressions**.
  1. Make a conscious effort to smile as you talk, especially if you have a tendency to be very intense.
  2. Occasionally, try matching your expression to the emotion of a character in the story.
  3. Work at maintaining eye contact with your children throughout the story. Know your story well enough that you can glance at your Bible and your notes and then look up.

* **Create interest in the story with gestures**.
  1. Avoid nervous habits such as scratching your head, rubbing your nose, fiddling with a tie or necklace, etc.
  2. Fold your hands in your lap or on your Bible until you need them to emphasize something.
  3. When you really want attention, gesture with your hands to invite the class to lean in closer to hear what you are saying.
  4. Occasionally touch a child's shoulder or hand to convey your interest and concern.
  5. Move closer to a child whose attention is wandering.

* **Create interest in the story with visuals**.
  1. Hold teaching pictures face down in front of you so that you can show them when you want to and then put them down when you want attention returned to you.
  2. Invite children who already know the story to place flannelgraph figures on the board as you talk.
  3. Mount flannelgraph figures on craft sticks and use them as puppets.
  4. Ask children to tell what they think happened just before or just after the scene in a teaching picture.

* **Be sure to end the story**. Use your closing sentence and then stop! Conclude the story before the children lose interest.

After the Bible Story

* **Ask questions**. Use any suggested conversation ideas from the curriculum to help review and reinforce the Bible story concepts.

* **Evaluate your storytelling experience**. Ask yourself these questions:
  1. Did the story hold the children's attention?
  2. Did I know the story well enough to have eye contact with the children?
  3. Did I stop when the story ended?
  4. Was I well enough prepared in the use of my visual resources so they did not distract from the story?

* **Keep the results of your evaluation in mind as you prepare your next Bible story**.

Music and the Young Child

In planning music for young children, the key word is "use." Music is a teaching tool to be *used* for accomplishing a specific Bible learning aim. Instead of asking children what they want to sing, select each song with a definite purpose in view. As you use the songs in your curriculum, keep in mind the following:

- **Songs can teach a Bible truth.** As the leader and children sing about God's loving care, the fact of God's love and care for each child becomes imprinted on young hearts and minds. When a child sings God's Word each day, those words become a part of his or her understanding. Words that are sung make a deeper impression than words that are spoken!
- **Songs can relate God's Word to a child's everyday experience.** Children are here-and-now people. They need to see clearly that God's Word speaks to their current situation. A song about family members, for example, gives children opportunities to tell then sing about the people God made to love and care for them.
- **Songs can help establish friendly feelings at VBS.** As children gather for group activities, the leader sings,

> "Eric's here; Sara's here.
> We're glad we are together.
> Marta's here; Jason's here.
> We're here in (sunny) weather."

Hearing his or her own name helps each child feel he or she is an important part of the group. The song also helps children learn each other's names.

- **Songs can provide meaningful activity.** After children have become familiar with a song, the leader asks, "Can you think of something to do with your feet that we can all do with you?" When a volunteer responds, the leader and children act on the child's suggestion. What a boost to a child's self-esteem when an adult uses his or her idea in the song!
- **Songs can guide activity.** For example, when it's time to put away toys, the leader (or a teacher) may sing a cleanup song several times. The words to this type of song direct children in putting away materials and equipment. The song is open-ended so the leader can sing about specific cleanup activities (e.g., "Let's put the blocks away...").

Don't worry if you don't read music or feel you can't sing well. You are *not* performing or providing entertainment—you are *using* a song to guide children in growing awareness of God's love and care within the everyday world of family, home and friends. Your musical perfection is unimportant. However, your enthusiasm and interest are vital! Be willing to make mistakes. If you forget the tune, keep going with the words. Children will be delighted that you, too, are learning. Relax and enjoy the children's response to the songs. When you truly sing from a heart of love for the Lord, children are quick to catch your feeling of joy.

The Fun of Finger Fun

- Before you use the finger fun suggested for a lesson, know it well yourself. Practice it at home.
- Encourage children first to join you in only the action, then in the words also. However, a young child may also "participate" by only observing you.
- Use action words the sketches suggest. You may want to make up additional actions or use the actions suggested by a child.
- Speak the words rhythmically, yet distinctly. Begin slowly and increase tempo as children become familiar with the movements.
- Be enthusiastic! Use an expressive voice, face and manner while leading a finger fun activity.
- Repeat the finger fun several times during the session. Plan to include it in future lessons. Children need and enjoy repetition.

Special Help for Young Children

For younger children to complete successfully some of the activities in your VBS curriculum, a few basic skills may be required. These skills—folding, taping, cutting and gluing—must be learned. And as you know, not all children learn at the same rate. There are a variety of ways to help children learn to succeed at these four tasks. Some of these ways are listed below.

Folding

1. Before giving paper to child, prefold paper as needed, then open it back up. Paper will then fold easily along the lines when child "folds" it.
2. Score the line to be folded by placing a ruler on it. Then draw an empty ballpoint pen along the ruler's edge. The line will fold easily into place.
3. Hold the corners of the paper in the folded position. Tell the child to "press and rub" where he or she wants to fold it.

Taping

1. Use double-sided tape whenever possible. Lay the tape down on the paper where it is needed. Child attaches the item that needs to be taped.
2. If double-sided tape is not available or is not appropriate, place a piece of tape lightly on the craft where indicated. Child rubs on tape to attach it securely to paper.

Cutting

1. Cutting with scissors is one of the most difficult tasks for any young child to master. Consider purchasing several pairs of "training scissors" (available at educational supply stores) to assist in teaching children how to cut.
2. Have available in your classroom two or three pairs of left-handed scissors (also available at educational supply stores). All scissors should be approximately 4 inches (10 cm) long and should have blunt ends.
3. Hold paper tightly at ends or sides while child cuts.
4. Begin to cut paper for child to follow. Child follows cut you have begun.
5. Draw simple lines outside actual cut lines for the child to follow. This will help a child cut close to the desired shape—though it will not be exact.
6. Provide scrap paper for child to practice cutting.

Gluing

1. Have child use a glue bottle to apply a spot of glue to a large sheet of paper before pressing a smaller piece of paper onto glued area.
2. Provide a glue stick for the child to use (available at variety stores). Take off cap and roll up glue for child. Child "colors" with glue stick over desired area.
3. Since preschoolers have difficulty applying glue on large areas, you may want to try the following procedure. Purchase glue in large containers (up to one gallon size). Pour small amounts of glue into several shallow containers (such as margarine tubs or the bottoms of soda bottles). Thin glue slightly by adding a small amount of water into each container. Children use paintbrushes to spread glue on their projects. 
4. To glue a smaller surface, pour a small amount of glue into a shallow container. Give each child a cotton swab. Child dips the swab into the glue and rubs on project. Excess glue can be poured back into the large container at the end of each session. 
5. When using glue bottles, buy the smallest bottles for children to use and refill them as needed. Adjust top to limit amount of glue that comes out. Instruct child to put "tiny dots of glue" on paper. Clean off and tightly close top of bottle when finished.

Remember not to expect perfection. Accept all attempts at accomplishing the task. Specific and honest praise will encourage the child to attempt the task again!

Art and the Young Child

Art experiences are among the most familiar—and most misunderstood—in a classroom for young children. Most young children are introduced to crayons at a very young age, but few adults take the time to observe the child at work, to see the real value of what is being done. The key word in a young child's art experience is *process*—not *product.* The work the child puts into the experience is of more value than the finished product. The skills, attitudes and understandings a child gains far overshadow the price of paper that adults often make the object of much attention.

Art activities offer the young child an opportunity to give expression to thoughts and feelings. A happy, secure child may express joy through the bright colors used in a painting. A shy or inhibited child may make just a few timid strokes with one finger on a finger painting. An angry child may release emotions by pounding, squeezing or twisting clay.

As a child works at art activities, he or she can learn basic concepts of sharing, taking turns, being kind and helping others. The child has opportunities to learn respect for the ideas and work of those about him or her. As a child and teacher use art materials together in a relaxed, creative way, opportunities for natural conversation with the child are likely to come. These "teachable moments" often are the best opportunities to help a child learn basic and vital scriptural truths.

Encourage the child's efforts at whatever stage of development he or she is at. Do not insist on perfection or correctness from an adult perspective. Avoid "improving" or "finishing" a child's work.

Always write the child's first name on artwork so it can be easily identified. Allow the child to write his or her name whenever possible, even if all the child can do is write the first letter. Give each child an enjoyable and lesson-related art experience.

Prayer and the Young Child

Prayer can be a meaningful form of worship for a young child. Unfortunately, it sometimes is presented as a boring, uninteresting activity. What are some ways we can help young children grow in their desire and ability to express themselves to God?

First, it's important to examine what young children can understand about prayer. They can know:

* God wants us to talk to Him, and He hears us;
* we can pray anytime, anywhere—not only at VBS or church but also in our homes, at school, in the car and at the store, etc.;
* we can pray silently, aloud or by singing;
* closing our eyes helps us think of what we are talking about instead of thinking about other things.

The following guidelines can help you teach these facts to young children:

* **Model meaningful prayer**. The way *you* talk to God shows that prayer is important in your own life. Your example shows what prayer is. If you pray long, adult-level prayers, you are teaching children that prayer is for grown-ups and is very complicated. However, if you pray short, simple, specific prayers that are within the child's capacity to offer, you are teaching that prayer is simple and deals with things of interest to the child.
* **Provide prayer opportunities throughout the session**. During many activities, you'll discover many natural opportunities to guide a child in brief prayer.
* **Encourage children to repeat short prayers after you**. This experience is the first step toward the child's using his or her own words in prayer. Keep the prayer short and use simple words that are clear to the child. For a prayer to be meaningful, a child should understand what he or she is saying or what is being said.
* **Sing your prayers**. Prayers need not always be spoken. Many songs are prayers in themselves. Ask children to listen carefully as you

read aloud the words of the song. Point out that the prayer song is addressed to God. Encourage children to close their eyes while they sing.

Remember: The most meaningful and trustworthy method of teaching children to pray is your example. Talking to God about things within the child's experience will increase his or her understanding about prayer.

Salvation and the Young Child

Examining the Issues

Christians have consistently maintained that the focal issue of one's spiritual life is a personal relationship with Jesus Christ. A definite individual commitment to follow Christ as Savior and Lord, based on acceptance of His sacrificial death, is proclaimed as humanity's only means of finding eternal life. Many Christians have thus advocated leading children into that commitment as early in their lives as possible.

How early in life is it possible for a child properly to make this commitment? Some people suggest children as young as age two are ready; others maintain any decision made before adolescence is suspect. Much of the disagreement seems to be focused on determining the age at which the child can actually be held accountable for actions and decisions.

There are some very real problems involved in applying the principle of accountability to children under age six. In order for a child to be considered guilty of sin, and thus in need of cleansing and forgiveness, the child must be able to understand the significance of his or her actions. More is involved than merely recognizing that certain actions are acceptable and others are not. The decision demands that the child be capable of accepting responsibility for acts and their consequences.

This is a critical point, for there are very few areas of life in which a child under the age of six is capable of personal responsibility. Is he allowed to settle the question of whether or not he will attend kindergarten? Is she considered mature enough to decide whether or not to brush her teeth? Is a visit to the doctor within his realm of choice? She may be allowed to choose the color of shirt she will wear, the flavor of ice cream she wants to eat or the games she will play with her friends. Can it be expected that these experiences give a child enough background in making choices to recognize personal responsibility before God?

The fact that a young child is easily manipulated further complicates the issue. Most young children keenly desire to please the adults in their lives. The teacher who asks the child, "Would you like to ask Jesus to forgive your sins?" is likely to have the child respond out of a simple desire to cooperate.

Repentance is another issue of importance, for it is frequently mentioned in the Bible as a necessary ingredient of salvation. While a child may express sorrow for a specific misdeed, it is often questionable that this sorrow is more than distress resulting from unpleasant behavior rather than a true desire to turn from sin.

This analysis, of course, is limited to a human perspective. The process of regeneration is in many ways beyond the realm of human understanding. Testimonials of parents, teachers and ultimately of the individuals themselves give support to profound spiritual encounters by children under the age of six. But the unique nature of the young child places a grave responsibility on teachers to be wary of manipulating the trusting responses of these little ones.

Explaining Salvation to Young Children

Most young children can understand that Jesus is always their Friend and Helper. The plan of salvation in Jesus Christ is simple and clear enough that some of these children can understand it and respond to it at their level of childlike faith (particularly those who receive Christian nurture at home).

As a VBS teacher of young children, you have been given an opportunity and responsibility to nurture a child's understanding of salvation. You may be the first person in a child's life to explain these spiritual truths to him or her. Keep in mind, however, that spiritual birth, like physical birth, is part of a process. A baby must develop in the womb before birth. Jesus compared the preparation of the heart to the planting of seed which later bears fruit. Ideas and attitudes that take root in the child early in life will produce a rich harvest in years that follow.

Most conversions among children are recorded between the ages of 10 and 12. However, children who attend Sunday School regularly during the early years—particularly if from a supportive Christian home—often are capable of an earlier meaningful response to Jesus' love. All children, no matter what their backgrounds, need Christian nurture to develop a personal faith.

Parents and teachers alike must be sensitive to the guidance of the Holy Spirit in leading a young child to Christ, for unless God Himself is speaking through His Spirit to the child, there can be no genuine heart experience. Parents and teachers also have the responsibility to ask questions that will reveal the degree of understanding the child has about salvation, plus the level of commitment he or she has to that belief. (Avoid asking leading questions or questions that can be answered "Yes" or "No".)

Your prayers for the Holy Spirit's guidance, along with your wise use of the following principles, will have far-reaching results in the lives of the children you teach, including those you are preparing for an encounter with Jesus at a later stage of development.

Explaining Salvation to Young Children

* **Be clear about what a child needs to know**. It must be simple yet complete:
  1. God loves you.
  2. You have done wrong things (sinned).
  3. God says that sin must be punished.
  4. God sent Jesus to take the punishment for your sin.
  5. Tell God you have sinned and want to stop doing wrong things.
  6. Ask Jesus to be your Savior.
  7. Then you are a member of God's family.
* **Be familiar with key Scripture passages.** God's Word is powerful. Use the Bible in sharing salvation's message with children. Mark these key verses: John 3:16; Romans 3:23; Romans 5:6; 1 Corinthians 15:3; 1 John 4:14. Use the simplest, clearest version you have available.
* **Avoid symbolism.** Use words whose meanings are clear to a child. Phrases such as "born again" or "asking Jesus into your heart" are meaningful to adults but create misconceptions in children's minds.
* **Explain key terms to lay the foundation**. For example, briefly explain these terms: "*sin*"—doing wrong things or disobeying God's rules; "*saved*"—to become a part of God's family; "*forgive*"—to take away the punishment for doing wrong; "*everlasting life*"—to live now and forever with Jesus.
* **Talk individually to a child who expresses interest in becoming a member of God's family.** Something as important as a child's personal relationship with Jesus Christ can be handled more effectively alone than in a group.
* **Allow for free choice.** A child needs to respond individually to the call of God's love. This needs to be a genuine response to God—not because the child wants to please peers, parents or you, the teacher. Be willing to allow the Holy Spirit to work within the child. A child may come to you for information, not necessarily to make a decision. Allow the Holy Spirit to lead; don't feel that a child must "do something." Be a faithful planter of the seeds of God's truth.
* **Focus on God's love and forgiveness.** Let the child know there will still be times when he or she does wrong things. Remind him or her that God doesn't stop loving us when we sin. If we are sorry for the wrong things we do, God will forgive us.

Discipline and the Young Child

Good discipline is what you do *with* and *for* a child, not what you do *to* him or her. Discipline, then, is the guidance an adult gives so a child knows what he or she *may* do as well as what he or she *may not* do.

Preventing Unacceptable Behavior

* **Love and care for each child.** This love is not the gushy kind, but a love that gives a child what he or she needs to grow and develop. Children long to feel that someone cares about them, that they are people of worth and value. Demonstrate your love and care in ways a child can understand. Sit down at the child's eye level and listen attentively to what a child has to tell. Kindly but firmly redirect a child's out-of-bounds activity. When you redirect a child's disruptive or unacceptable activity, do not scold or shame the child. Scolding or shaming makes the child feel excluded from your love. Focus on the child's *behavior*, not on the person. Let the child know you love him or her but that you cannot allow the misbehavior. In all your actions and words, reflect the unconditional love you yourself have experienced from God.
* **Help children feel a sense of security and order**. Tell them by your actions and your words that they are safe in your care and that you will allow no harm to come to them. Children also find security in knowing you are nearby to assist when they need help. When they are assured you will be there to help, they will be more willing to try a new activity or experience.
* **Establish and maintain a comfortable routine**. Children like to be fairly sure of what will happen next. Follow the same schedule of activities each week. Of course, there will be times when you will need to be flexible by shortening or lengthening parts of the schedule, depending on the interest and attention spans of the children.
* **Set reasonable limits**. A child feels secure with limits. He or she needs to know what you expect. Establish a few basic rules, such as, "Dough stays on the table." Phrase the rules in a positive way whenever you can. Help children remember and observe the rules during their work and play. Give each child consistent and positive guidance. Find a middle ground between rigid authority and total permissiveness. Children need limits; but they also need freedom to move around and make choices within those limits.
* **Create an ordered environment**. Children respond in a positive way to a neatly arranged room with fresh and interesting things to do. An unorganized room filled with clutter and "off-limits" items is almost certain to invite misbehavior.

When a child receives an adult's thoughtful and consistent guidance, he or she is on the way to understanding what it means to be responsible for one's own behavior. From this responsibility grows self-control—discipline from within.

Correcting Unacceptable Behavior

Sometimes a teacher's most thoughtful preparation and guidance does not keep a child from misbehaving. With most preschoolers, you have only about 10 seconds to do the correcting. Avoid long explanations. There are no surefire guarantees for these special situations, but these brief suggestions may help you:

* **When a child hits (kicks, scratches)**—Say, "That hurts. I cannot let you hit Brian. And I cannot let Brian hit you. You may not hurt other people here. Use words to tell Brian what you want." Then, separate the two children. Redirect the offender's activity to another area of the room. Stay with the child until he or she is constructively involved.
* **When a child bites**—Say, "Biting hurts. We use our teeth only to chew food." Never encourage a child to bite back to "show how it feels."
* **When a child spits**—Say, "Your spit belongs in your mouth. If you need to spit, you may spit in the toilet."

* **When a child uses offensive names**—Say "Do not call Jami stupid. She is not stupid. Jami is doing a good job of drawing. And you are doing a good job of drawing."
* **When a child has a tantrum**—This is no time for words. The child is too upset to listen. Hold the child firmly until he or she calms down. When you hold the child, you are offering protection as well as control. If other children are frightened by the tantrum, take the child to another area with an adult to supervise. Explain to children, "Kevin is having trouble now. He will be all right in a little while."

A Final Reminder

A positive, loving approach to the needs of your students is one of the most important factors in making VBS a safe place to be. In all your actions and words, reflect the unconditional love you yourself have experienced from God. Pray for understanding, wisdom and patience. Be a loving, caring person both inside and outside the classroom, no matter what the behavior challenge may be.

The Early Childhood Classroom

Setting Up Your Classroom

Young children have unique needs for security, open space and a wide variety of materials. Before setting up your classroom, it's a good idea to remove any unnecessary furniture (e.g., piano, large tables, extra chairs, etc.). Classrooms often become storage areas for unwanted items. Put items not in use out of children's reach. Reserve low shelves for materials children will use in the current session. Room furniture should be appropriate for the size of your little ones: chairs—10–12 inches (25–30 cm); tables—20–22 inches (50–55 cm); and table tops—30x48-inches (75x120-cm) to 36x60-inches (90x150-cm).

Organizing Your Classroom

The most important feature of a room for young children is the clearly defined learning activity areas. These are places in the room where a teacher and children can actively explore and experiment. A well-designed room for young children is equipped to provide all of these experiences. In most cases, all of these activities would not be available in any one session, but each could be offered at different times.

*** Blocks, Games and Skill Toys**

These activities help a child learn to reason and solve problems as well as develop coordination. They also bring pleasure and, with guided conversation from a sensitive teacher, will stimulate curiosity about the Bible, family, the world, God and Jesus.

Blocks may be purchased from school equipment suppliers or toy stores; or they can be made from half-gallon (1.9-l) milk cartons. To do this, open tops and rinse thoroughly. Cut off flaps at top. Insert open end of one carton into open end of other until one carton is inside the other. Provide enough blocks so several children can build at the same time.

*** Accessory Toys**

Accessory toys are cars, trucks, and stand-up figures of people, animals, trees, etc. Children under three tend to use each toy—a block or a truck—independent of other toys. However, older children will enjoy using accessory toys in the same area with the blocks. Dramatic play is enhanced by a variety of accessory toys. Sturdy transportation toys should be a part of every block area. (Wooden cars and trucks are preferable to most metal ones for safety and durability.) Fours and fives enjoy using signs ("Airport," "Gas Station," "Stop" and "Go") in dramatic play.

✻ Discovery Center

These activities help children understand the world God made. As the teacher guides the conversation, the children also learn of the care provided by their parents, teachers and God.

✻ Home Living

Dramatic play in the home living area can help children relate their everyday lives to the Bible truths they learn at VBS. These experiences help children express their feelings and ideas.

✻ Large Group Area

In addition to these activity areas, the room should also allow all teachers and children in the department to meet together for a time of music, sharing and group activities. The Bible story can also be told in this large group time. From the large group, teachers and children can then move into small groups to complete a variety of activities. These groups can either sit around tables or on the floor. Dividers between groups are usually not necessary.

If Your Space Is Limited

Here are some specific suggestions for adapting activity centers to limited facilities.

✻ Art

Painting—Spread newspapers over a section of the floor (away from the flow of traffic in your room). Paintings may be done on paper placed on newspapers. If weather permits, children may paint outside. Allow pictures to dry outside. Or string clothesline in the hall or high in the classroom. Attach pictures to line with clothespins. For cleanup, provide paper towels and two plastic tubs half full of water. Children wash paintbrushes in one tub and their hands in the other. You may wish to substitute crayons, felt pens, or chalk for paint in the art activities.

Murals—Attach paper to the wall with masking tape or thumbtacks. Place pictures, glue and scissors on small trays. Children complete activity without taking up valuable table space. Children may also work on the floor to complete a mural or collage.

✻ Blocks

If you have limited space for storing blocks or for building with blocks, purchase small wooden or plastic "alphabet blocks" that easily fit in small hands. Less storage space will be needed and children will still be able to build any of the structures suggested in the block activities.

✻ Books

Display only those books which highlight the lesson focus. These may be placed along a section of the wall or in a small bookrack. Teacher and children may sit on the floor or on carpet squares (available from carpet stores) to read.

✻ Discovery Center

If table space is not available for a science/discovery activity, use a shallow box or tray in which to place items. Children relax on the floor or sit on carpet squares as they look at items. For planting activities, use trays placed in a less traveled area of the room.

✻ Home Living

Doll and cooking play may be done on table tops instead of in a special home living area. For cooking play provide pans, spoons and other utensils. Use masking tape to section off a portion of the table for a stove. Use a plastic dish pan as a sink. Push two chairs together for a baby bed. Place dress-up clothes in a box or small suitcase. Store box until clothes are needed. Drape blankets over tables to make tents. Stores can be set up on table or floor by stacking empty boxes for shelves.

✻ Skill Toys

If table activities take up too much space, remove the table. Activities can be done easily by children sitting on the floor.

Remember—children have great imaginations. Even when the materials are not elaborate, children will still have meaningful learning experiences.

Last-Minute Preparations for VBS

The excitement is building! Your VBS program is just around the corner. All the tough stuff has been dealt with and you're ready to roll, right? Well, not exactly. There are still a few last-minute preparations that need to be made. But take heart and read on—you're almost there!

Preregistration

To simplify first-day procedures and to aid in your last-minute planning, begin to preregister students at least four weeks ahead of time—the earlier, the better! Preregistration is not just making a list of names—it involves obtaining all pertinent information necessary to help you conduct your VBS.

Registration Forms

Before you begin to preregister children you need to give some thought to the forms you want to use. A good registration form will include all the information you will need to have before, during and after VBS. (See sample registration form on p. 193.) The following is a list of information you may need or want and why such information is helpful.

* **First and last name**
  Too obvious to mention!

* **Grade level in school**
  To categorize into grade-appropriate classes or groups. (Most VBS curriculum publishers gear their lessons to the average students who have just completed a specific grade, i.e., first and second grade lessons are geared for students who would have the knowledge of a child who has just completed first and second grade.)

* **Street address, city, state, and zip code**
  To send a greeting letter or other information to the child prior to VBS and future promotional notices after VBS.

* **Parents' names and home and work phone numbers**
  To reach during VBS in case of illness or emergency and for personal contact after VBS.

* **Birthdate**
  To help categorize children into appropriate age groups and to contact children on their birthday.

* **Church affiliation**
  To inform teachers of the religious background of child and family; to keep track of VBS outreach effectiveness; to put unchurched families on future mailing list.

* **Emergency contact name and phone number**
  To contact if parents cannot be reached in the event of an emergency.

* **Doctor's name and phone number**
  To contact student's doctor in case of illness or emergency.

* **Allergies or other special conditions**
  To prevent allergic reactions and be aware of any special concerns about the physical condition of a child.

* **School child attends**
  To form school support groups based on information.

Procedures

Once you have your registration forms ready, you need to consider the actual process of preregistration. Obviously, you will need volunteers to assist in the effort. Choose well-organized individuals with a good working knowledge of how your VBS will run. An experienced VBS volunteer will be able to answer lots of unanticipated questions.

You will also need to plan ways to publicize preregistration. Work with the publicity coordinator in your planning. In addition to a kickoff promotional activity (see pp. 60-66), here are a few other suggestions:

* Set up a brightly-decorated registration booth in Sunday School departments, in the church foyer or parking lot, at a nearby shopping center or some other convenient location.
* Include an attractive display of VBS promotional items, student books and craft samples on or near the booth or registration table. Play VBS theme music.
* Offer simple, complimentary refreshments at your preregistration booth.
* Create a life-size cardboard mascot or other character that relates to your VBS theme.
* Have volunteers wear VBS T-shirts and buttons to promote preregistration.
* Offer a prize (stickers, buttons, T-shirts) or incentive (reduced registration fee) to all who sign up in advance and attend the first session.
* Show a clip from the VBS preview video in your church worship service to kick off preregistration.
* Have an all-church dress up day when people can dress in clothing appropriate to your VBS theme.

Preregistration should also be accessible through your church office on weekdays and by mail. Those in your church visitation/outreach ministry should also know how to handle preregistration requests. Continue preregistering children until the day before your VBS begins.

Assembling Class or Group Rosters

Preregistration allows you to assemble roster lists in advance. Class or group rosters should be prepared a day or two before your VBS begins. You may want to create a preliminary roster earlier for your teachers. However, everyone should know that the roster will probably change and be added to each day. See sample on page 196.

To assign children to their appropriate classes, collect all the current preregistration forms and follow these steps:

1. Categorize registration forms by age or group classifications.
2. Make several photocopies of a blank roster form—one for each group (don't forget nursery and preschool classes).
3. Label the top of each form with age/grade level, teacher/counselor's name, class/group name, class/group color and class location (if applicable).
4. Write each student's name on the form, last name first, in alphabetical order. Include parent's name and phone number under each name. Record any special health or physical concerns next to the child's name.
5. Leave sufficient lines to add newcomers.
6. Record the total number of pre-enrolled students at the end of each form.
7. After you have completed each of the roster forms needed, make two photocopies of each list. Give one copy to the appropriate teacher or counselor. (If possible provide a clipboard and attached pen.) Keep one copy for yourself. The original copy will go to volunteers at the registration table.

(NOTE: Compare the total number of students in each group with your desired teacher-student ratio [p. 31]. Allow for students to be added during the week. If class sizes appear too large and unmanageable, you will need to recruit additional volunteers.)

Preparing Name Tags

Name tags are a necessary part of any Vacation Bible School. They are a first step in helping to build the relationships that are at the heart of VBS.

In choosing name tags, consider that a good name tag should be: (1) durable enough to wear each day; (2) large enough to be readable from a feasible distance; (3) able to attach securely to a child's clothing or hang around the neck; (4) safe for wearing; and (5) able to be permanently written on.

Many publishers and party or office stores have name tag packs that you can purchase, or use your own creativity to make unique name tags that fit your VBS theme. You can also match the colors and shapes of your name tags to identify team colors and names. If you are making your own, here are a few ideas to get you thinking:

- Trace a theme-related pattern onto poster board. Laminate or cover poster board with clear Con-Tact® paper and cut out shapes. Punch two holes at the top of each cutout and use safety pins to attach to children's clothing.
- Look through business promotional catalogs for some unique name tag products.
- Make photo-ID tags. Have one or two volunteers with instant cameras take pictures of each registered student. Trim each picture and put next to child's name and team or class. Use a plastic laminate or clear Con-Tact® paper over the cards. Poke a hole near the top and thread yarn or string through the hole to hang around the child's neck.
- Use a button-maker to make personalized badges for each child. You can vary the color of buttons according to team colors or have your VBS theme printed near the outer edge.

Name tags can be prepared one or two days before VBS begins. Keep in mind that some preregistered children may not actually attend VBS (especially if no fees were paid). Use a dark-colored, wide-tip, permanent marker for writing names. If you need help writing the names on the name tags, let teachers or counselors do their own students' tags. Otherwise, pass out completed name tags to teachers/counselors on the first day. All volunteers should also wear name tags.

Remind staff to collect name tags at the end of each day. Store them in teachers' classrooms or in counselors' bins, or place them alphabetically by last name on a table or bulletin board. Put the tags near the entrance so each child can retrieve his or her tag upon arrival.

Opening-Day Registration

First-day registration can be a real disaster if it is not well-planned. No matter how successful your preregistration activities are, you are bound to get a steady influx of unenrolled students. Keep in mind that first impressions are important, so begin planning now how to register everyone efficiently and in a warm, friendly manner.

Procedures

Before each session set up an adequately sized table in a central area where each newcomer can register. Decorate the table with balloons and streamers, at least on the first day. Give each volunteer at the registration table the original class rosters so they can add newcomers' names to the appropriate lists. Have parents completely fill out registration forms and submit any registration fees.

Children who are preregistered should be able to go directly to their assigned groups. Letter the words "Preregistered Students" on a large poster board. Display the class rosters and meeting locations so that parents can easily drop off their preregistered children in the appropriate places. If needed, post a volunteer near the display to help direct parents and answer any questions.

To simplify walk-in registration details:

* Prepare an ample supply of registration forms in advance so they can be filled out easily. Don't forget to provide lots of pens.
* Arrange for additional volunteers to assist in first-day registration.
* Form more than one line, categorized alphabetically by last name or by grades.
* Post a large sign with registration procedures and other information to help parents fill out cards.
* Provide an information sheet with details on picking up and dropping off children, the time VBS ends, etc.
* Have additional blank name tags for newcomers.
* Hand out a VBS button to each child who registers.
* Set up an additional table with registration forms and pens so parents can fill forms out before standing in line.
* Make your campus as user-friendly as possible with building signage, maps and facility directories clearly posted.
* Have volunteers available to guide children into their assigned groups.
* If classes have group colors, have teachers or counselors wear corresponding colors so they are easy to identify.
* Give classes group names or numbers and make signs for teachers to hold up so children can easily find their groups.
* If you have a large preschool enrollment, set up a different table for preschool registration.
* Enlist volunteers to serve as greeters to parents and children. Have greeters wear large name tags reading, "May I help you?" Choose one greeter to dress up as a VBS skit character, mascot or other theme-appropriate person.

Personnel

Make a good impression on first-time visitors to your church by choosing volunteers who are friendly and outgoing, knowledgeable about VBS procedures and well-organized. It also helps if they have readable handwriting and work well under stress. Also, make sure you provide your volunteers with all the pertinent information they will need beforehand, such as registration instructions (see p. 192), class or group rosters, teachers' names, class or group locations and pick up and drop off procedures. If your VBS charges a registration fee, keep a cash box handy with change. Volunteers should arrive thirty minutes before VBS will begin.

Each day at VBS there should be fewer and fewer newcomers. However, you will still need to have someone at the registration table each day. Don't forget to give volunteers updated rosters whenever changes are made.

The Week Before

While it would be nice to have everything completed far ahead of time, there are a few things that have to wait until the week before—such as decorating your facilities, dedicating your volunteers and having one final staff meeting.

Dedicating Volunteers

Plan ahead to designate a brief time slot in your church's worship service the Sunday before your VBS begins. Ask to use this time for a special dedication ceremony for all VBS volunteers. Inform VBS workers of what will take place ahead of time so they can attend and be prepared.

During the service, ask all volunteers, in general or by name, to stand up in front. Briefly explain what the children will be learning in VBS and acknowledge the investment your volunteers have made. Then have your pastor or other church leader pray that God will use these individuals to reach children's lives with His love during VBS.

Have a "Prep" Rally!

Make this last week before VBS a fun and meaningful time for your volunteers. Because everyone has been working so hard on their own the last few months, it's time to get together and share the excitement. A "prep" rally is a great way to do this. Send reminders by mail a week ahead of time. And remember to provide child care for those who will need it.

Start with Food and Fellowship

Depending on the time of day, plan to provide a light meal or dessert. While this is not necessary, it's another way of letting your volunteers know that they are appreciated. Plus, it gives them an opportunity to fellowship with one another, which builds unity.

Do not make this meal a potluck or an event planned by your volunteers. Ask a group of people not involved with VBS to help. Serve pizza, a giant submarine sandwich, Chinese food or a potato or salad bar. Set up chairs and tables with tablecloths. Use easy decorations or centerpieces that enhance your VBS theme.

Conduct a Final Staff Meeting

All of your VBS volunteers should attend the final meeting, no matter how small a role they have. In fact, of all the meetings you hold, this one should definitely be mandatory. If a volunteer cannot attend, make sure he or she knows what will be covered in your meeting. Try to make the agenda brief, but be sure to do the following:

* Review the overall goals of your VBS.
* Run through the daily schedule for students and staff, including staff devotions and registration.
* Distribute the following items to teachers/counselors/guides: a name tag, clipboard with attached pen (if possible), roster/attendance form, helpful hints and scratch paper.
* Explain to teachers/counselors/ guides the procedure for keeping attendance.
* Discuss any last-minute changes in staff, schedule, class locations, etc.
* Answer any general questions. (Answer specific questions after the meeting.)
* Remind volunteers of their impact. Have a pastor or other leader give a short devotional and close in prayer for the VBS staff and children.

Let the Decorating Begin!

A few simple decorations can transform any ordinary facility into a fun-loving adventure. After your meeting, allow volunteers to start decorating their rooms or designated areas. Enlist assistants and counselors who have no assigned areas to help other teachers. Set up a large working area for volunteers to create their decorations. Give a few brief instructions on where decorating supplies can be found and some helpful suggestions. Many publishers provide decorating ideas and sketches—share these with your volunteers. Play VBS or other inspirational music as your volunteers work and provide munchies for snacks.

Decorating Supplies

In addition to supplies from your curriculum and materials your church has on hand, you may need to purchase extra items for your prep rally. Here is a sample list of decorating items you can provide for your volunteers:

- ❑ butcher paper, white or brown
- ❑ construction paper
- ❑ pencils and marking pens
- ❑ tempera paints and various sizes of paintbrushes
- ❑ newspaper (to cover work areas)
- ❑ shallow containers
- ❑ masking tape or double-sided tape
- ❑ scissors
- ❑ cardboard boxes
- ❑ craft knives
- ❑ glue
- ❑ streamers
- ❑ stepladder(s)
- ❑ overhead projector(s)
- ❑ photocopies of clip art
- ❑ clip art on transparencies

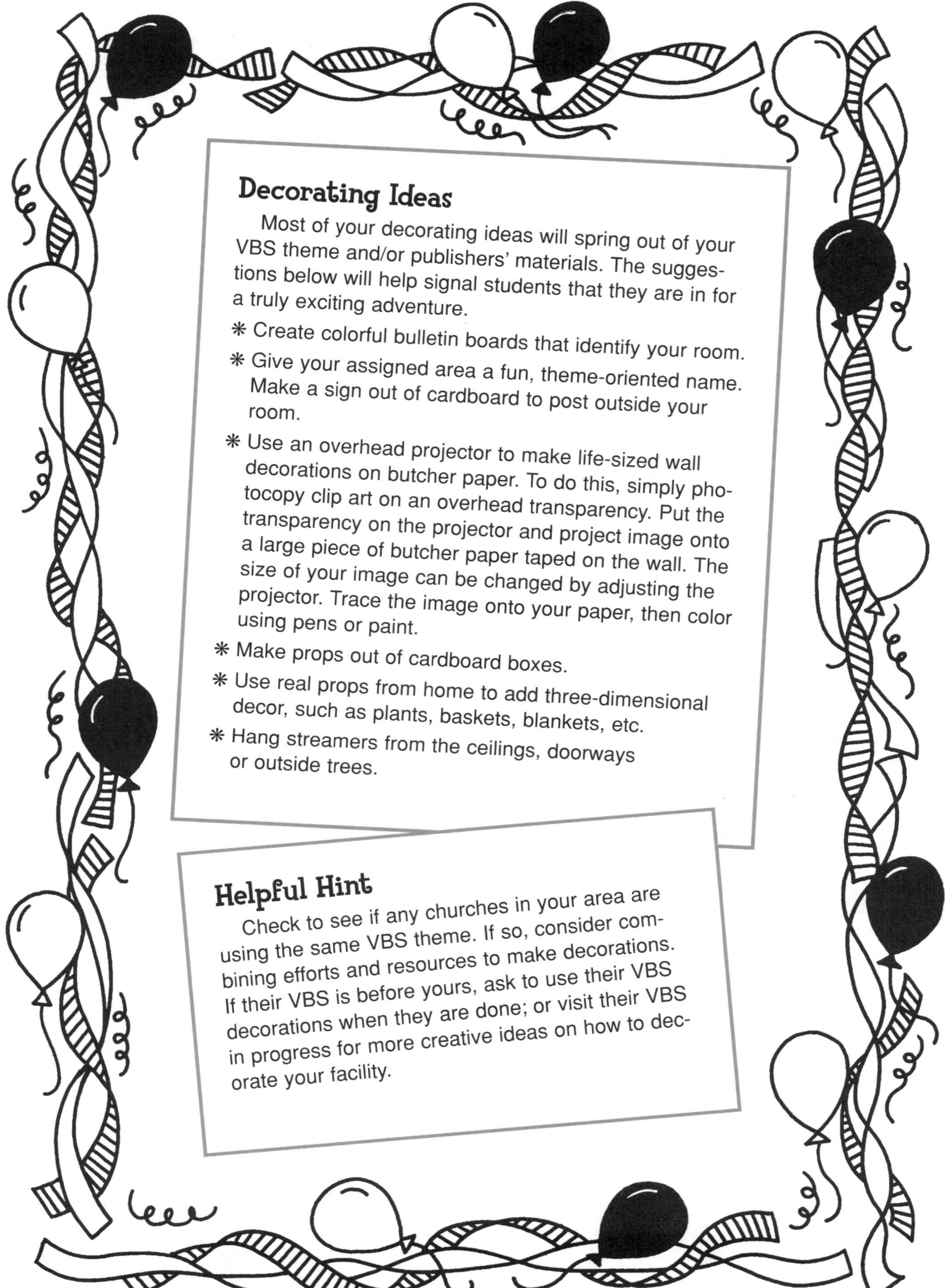

Decorating Ideas

Most of your decorating ideas will spring out of your VBS theme and/or publishers' materials. The suggestions below will help signal students that they are in for a truly exciting adventure.

* Create colorful bulletin boards that identify your room.
* Give your assigned area a fun, theme-oriented name. Make a sign out of cardboard to post outside your room.
* Use an overhead projector to make life-sized wall decorations on butcher paper. To do this, simply photocopy clip art on an overhead transparency. Put the transparency on the projector and project image onto a large piece of butcher paper taped on the wall. The size of your image can be changed by adjusting the projector. Trace the image onto your paper, then color using pens or paint.
* Make props out of cardboard boxes.
* Use real props from home to add three-dimensional decor, such as plants, baskets, blankets, etc.
* Hang streamers from the ceilings, doorways or outside trees.

Helpful Hint

Check to see if any churches in your area are using the same VBS theme. If so, consider combining efforts and resources to make decorations. If their VBS is before yours, ask to use their VBS decorations when they are done; or visit their VBS in progress for more creative ideas on how to decorate your facility.

Step 8

What to Do During VBS

By this time you should be feeling pretty excited! You've got registration under control. Your facilities are brightly decorated and fully stocked with all necessary supplies. You've prepared your volunteers for almost anything they may encounter. Everyone is in his or her assigned spot, ready to go. And then it hits you: "What exactly is my spot?"

Well, it isn't your office! And it isn't "filling in" or substituting in any one area. You may be the only one who is free to roam—and roaming is what you will need to be doing! Your presence is a key element to the smooth running of your VBS. So grab your assistant director, put on your walking shoes and get ready for one of the most exciting weeks of your life!

Your VBS-Week Responsibilities

In addition to being prepared for the unexpected, you will need to cover the following responsibilities. The rest of the chapter will explore some of them in more detail.

* Continue all staff support functions. Pray with and for them. Communicate with them and work at maintaining their spirit of enthusiasm.
* Conduct morning staff devotions.
* Lead all or a portion of the opening and closing assemblies. Present VBS awards and certificates to staff and children on last day of VBS.
* Make sure teachers are present and on schedule. If using the activity center method, signal appropriate times to rotate to the next center.
* Arrange for substitutes when needed.
* Visit departments; make any necessary adjustments.
* Be an "evangelism booster." Encourage all the children to bring new friends throughout the week. Pray for and remind your staff to prepare for the evangelism emphasis of your VBS.
* Secure additional supplies as needed.
* Assist with discipline problems and emergency situations as needed.
* Make sure registration and attendance records are being properly kept.
* Have someone available to run errands.
* Distribute any announcements and flyers for children to take home on the appropriate days.
* Supervise preparations and build enthusiasm for the closing program.
* Send home special invitations to your closing program.
* Supervise the ongoing photography/video taping of the VBS activities.
* Make sure all VBS volunteers clean up their areas on the last day of VBS.

Conducting the Assemblies

While most of the teaching at VBS occurs in the small class groups, much of the excitement is generated at the assembly times. (Early childhood groups are usually best provided for in their own rooms.) Assembly times can include the following features:

* Welcome and greetings (attenders and newcomers)
* Contests
* Announcements
* Missions projects
* Guest speakers
* Prayer
* VBS theme songs
* Skits that add humor with a point
* Backdrop scenery that sets a colorful setting

Choose an enthusiastic leader to conduct the opening and closing assembly times, coordinating activities with the music director, skit director and any other volunteers who will be participating. As director, don't remain totally in the background. Participate in the Opening Assembly as your comfort level allows. The children need to get to know you as the VBS Director. The following ideas should help.

Opening Assembly

Preparation

* Label rows identifying where each group shall sit—youngest children near the front.
* Cue VBS cassette or CD to pre-chosen songs.
* Set up song transparencies on overhead projector.
* If using a skit video, make sure video player is plugged in and ready to go.
* Have small prizes available.

Procedure

* Classes or groups assemble with their leaders outside the assembly area.
* VBS Director signals for children to enter one group at a time.
* As children enter, VBS music begins and music director starts leading the children and staff in one to three VBS songs (including theme song).
* VBS Director welcomes everyone, introduces the VBS theme, the lesson for the day and then the skit.
* Children watch the live skit or the skit video.
* VBS Director recaps what skit characters exemplified, asking for volunteers to answer questions. (Optional: Reward volunteers with VBS buttons or other small prizes.)
* VBS Director reads Bible memory verse for the day.
* Missions coordinator introduces or updates children on the VBS missions project.
* VBS Director closes assembly in prayer, then dismisses children in an orderly fashion to their classes.
* You may also want to incorporate a flag salute, offering, door prizes, contests, etc.

Closing Assembly

* Classes or groups assemble with their leaders inside the assembly area.
* As children enter, VBS music begins and music director starts leading the children and staff in one to three VBS songs (including theme song).
* VBS Director recaps the day, asking volunteers to tell what they learned in their own words, and reviews Bible memory verse.
* VBS Director makes announcements and updates children on the results of ongoing contests.
* VBS Director closes in prayer and dismisses children.

Maintaining Staff Support

Continuing the good communication you have established with your volunteers is critical to the success of your program. Finding extra time this week to meet together can be a difficult challenge. Most likely all of you will be anxious to go home by the end of each session. Consider these ways to keep communication going.

Conduct Morning Staff Devotions

Arrange for a place where staff will meet 15 minutes each day before your VBS begins, except for the first day. It's a good idea to make these meetings mandatory—otherwise you'll have poor attendance. (Allow some staff members to be available to assist with registering and greeting early arrivers.) Provide child care and refreshments such as coffee, iced tea and a treat. Make sure you begin on time and dismiss on schedule. Plan to conduct some or all of the following activities:

* **Sharing**—Ask one or two volunteers to share an encouraging story or special blessing he or she may have encountered the day before.
* **Short devotional—**Match the devotional to the lesson the children will be learning that day. (Some publishers provide short teacher devotionals for your convenience.) You may want to rotate the leading of the devotional among different volunteers.
* **Prayer**—Pray specifically for children and staff who have special needs. Pray that God's Spirit will enable you to fulfill the ministry He has entrusted to you.
* **Announcements**—Allow a few moments for any special announcements or last-minute organizational details.

Be Available

Plan on visiting each learning area at least once a day. Sit in on part of the session or simply poke your head in the class to let the teachers know you're there. If they have any questions, they can signal for your attention. Stay around for a while after each VBS day is over to allow volunteers to approach you with any problems or concerns. When they do, give them your full attention and try not to rush them. Follow through on all their concerns and pray with them.

Send Staff Memos or Newsletters

Foster regular communication with your workers by sending out a daily memo or newsletter (see p. 178 for sample newsletter). It can serve a "housekeeping" purpose—informing about the status of your VBS (enrollment, new friends, exciting highlights), announcing changes in schedule or classes, updating plans for the closing program, etc. Have the daily memo available for volunteers at the morning devotions. The following sample staff memo (next page) both reminds and encourages teachers/counselors to take three important steps during VBS.

Sample Staff Memo

Good Morning!

As you return to your busy classroom/center today, dreading repeats of yesterday's "mistakes" and anticipating multiplied moments of "success," keep in mind that the children in front of you don't just need your lesson—they need your love. Use these tips to build relationships with those wonderful little people God has placed in your circle of influence:

1. **Get to know your students personally.** Take advantage of informal times to become a friend by learning about the child's interests and concerns. Find out which children don't have a church home. Be sensitive to those who have special needs. Remember that children who regularly attend church have needs, too, and may benefit from your investment of time.
2. **Find a way to meet parents.** Talk to them as they bring or pick up their children. If this is not possible, make a phone call or a home visit to talk about their child's participation in VBS and to explain some of the goals of your VBS. Personally invite parents to the closing program or open house. Spend time at the closing program getting to know parents and making them feel welcome.
3. **Pray for your students and their families by name.** Ask God to help you find the most effective ways of sharing God's love with them.

Keeping Daily Records

Though not terribly exciting, this is one of your most important duties. Some of the work may be shared with a "record keeper" or other assistant. However, it is important that you know the daily status of enrollment, visitors, etc. Record keeping also involves jotting notes on the progress of your VBS—asking yourself what things work well and what things can be improved upon for next year. Regardless of whether you will be directing a subsequent VBS (and don't even think about that right now!), the notes you keep will be valuable information for your church. You will be glad you kept track of things as you follow up, evaluate and plan for next year's VBS. The following is a list of suggested records you will want to maintain:

- **Registration forms**—Make sure that all forms have complete information and that all newcomers have filled one out.
- **Roster forms**—Check to see that teachers/counselors are keeping accurate attendance records of the children under their care. Also, make sure that newcomers are listed on their rosters.
- **Total VBS attendance form**—Record the daily total number of students in each class and the sum total of attendance for each day (see p. 197).
- **Follow-up cards**—Record student's decisions for Christ (see p. 201).
- **VBS review**—Keep a summary of the progress of your VBS program. Highlight events that worked well and jot down ideas on how to improve your format (see p. 204).

Preparing for Evangelism

The apostle Paul wrote, "I pray that you may be active in sharing your faith" (Philemon 1:6, *NIV*). The entire VBS program is devoted to leading children to Christ. Most programs include one day with a special emphasis on evangelism. In addition to training your VBS staff on how to be a good testimony, think carefully on how you can prepare them for this important time (see pp. 97-99 and 114-115).

- Be sure staff members are familiar with the articles and lessons in the teacher manuals that focus on presenting the gospel.
- Instruct leaders and teachers to invite responses by saying, "If you're interested in knowing more about becoming a member of God's family, I'll be here after class to talk with you." Students sometimes feel hesitant to seek out busy adults, so schedule a quiet moment to talk informally with individual students.
- Give leaders and teachers a supply of evangelism booklets, "New Life Certificates" (see sample on p. 225) and follow-up cards (see sample on p. 201).
- Ask extra volunteers to be present during the invitation. Make sure volunteers are trained.
- Secure a supply of new Bibles to hand out to children who don't own one.

Encouraging Visitors

Don't limit your enrollment to the number of children you have on the first day. The children who are participating in your VBS program and are excited about it are your best publicity resources. Use the assembly times as well as your class visits to challenge kids to bring their friends to VBS. The following ideas have proven to be successful:

* **Offer incentives to classes or groups who have brought the most visitors.** While inviting their friends to VBS may come naturally for most children, you might consider promoting an incentive for bringing visitors. This gives children an extra boost of courage to invite neighbors or other children they may not know as well. If you have an ongoing point award system (e.g., points awarded for being on time, bringing a Bible, reciting Bible memory verse, etc.), offer extra points for bringing friends.
* **Make visitors, and those who invited them, feel special.** Each day during the opening assembly, ask children to stand with the visitor(s) they brought. Have each child (or teacher) introduce his or her guest(s). Lead children in a cheer or short welcome song after each guest is introduced. Hand a VBS button or other small treat to those who are standing.
* **Make a lasting impression.** Encourage teachers or counselors to emphasize the importance of telling others the good news. Suggest that one way to tell others about Jesus is by inviting them to VBS. Discuss with children possible friends or neighbors that they can invite. Then, make every effort to help visitors feel comfortable. Try to fill them in on important lessons that were learned on previous days. Give them extra assistance when completing ongoing projects. Present each visitor a "Thank You for Visiting" award or card.

Promoting the Closing Program

The closing event for your VBS is the culmination of your whole program. It will also be your best opportunity for forming relationships with the parents. Most of the planning and preparation for this event should already be coordinated by your music director (see p. 79). Step 9 includes helpful planning information for other elements of the program. When VBS is underway, use every opportunity to build excitement and enthusiasm among the staff and children for this event. Encourage children to take home and return the special invitations they will be given. When you see parents dropping off or picking up their children, invite them personally to come be a part of the excitement.

Recording Your VBS Memories

As with any memorable event, you will want to take lots of pictures and/or video tape of your VBS in progress. Plan to have someone available to capture both candid and action shots. Discuss with your photographer ahead of time the kind of media you would like to use in presenting the photos—slide show, video presentation or photo display. With today's technology, the possibilities of including images in your VBS program and using them afterwards are endless. Depending on the kind of camera and resources you have available, you may be able to do the following:

- **VBS highlight show**
  If you are using a video or digital camera, you will be able to show highlights from the previous day. Children love to see pictures of themselves in action. A videographer or a "reporter" can interview children about their activities. Set each day's show to exciting VBS or special music. Make sure that all necessary equipment is in working order beforehand and that the show has been previewed and cued and is ready to go.

- **Class pictures**
  Plan a time for a photographer to take a picture of each class, age group or entire VBS group. Have pictures developed and available for the last day of VBS.

- **Souvenir photos**
  Set up a fun, theme-oriented background at one of your learning centers for individual photos. Provide costumes and other props for children to use. With an instant camera or one-hour developing, you will be able to give each child a fun photo for a VBS souvenir by the end of the day.

- **Closing program slide presentation**
  Throughout the week, have your photographer periodically visit each classroom or learning center to take photos of the action with slide film. On the last day, take the film to be developed by a one-hour slide processing lab (call for locations beforehand). Photographer can then plan a slide show set to music for your closing program. Parents will enjoy seeing all the activities their children participated in at VBS.

- **Bulletin board display**
  Use regular print photographs to make a colorful VBS display on a bulletin board or poster. Choose photos that capture what your VBS was all about. Decorate the board according to your VBS theme. Display the finished product in a visible location in your church. Your congregation will enjoy seeing the exciting things that happened at your VBS.

The Final Days of Your VBS

The excitement will continue to build as your VBS program progresses. You'll probably notice that the children become more outgoing and energized while your volunteers grow weary! Encourage your staff to "hang in there," because the best is truly yet to come. Make sure teachers, counselors or leaders have all the information they need to finish the week well.

Preparing for Follow-up

Before the last day is over, your teachers/counselors will need to make sure they are ready to do follow-up. The following list will help you prepare your staff:

* Give each teacher/counselor a completed list of names, addresses and phone numbers for their particular class.
* Provide each teacher/counselor with an adequate number of postcards and stamps.
* Give each teacher/counselor a list of suggestions to help follow up on VBS (see p. 200).
* Challenge each teacher with the importance of personally following up students who have become members of God's family.
* Be sure that Sunday School teachers receive accurate information on all visitors so they, too, can begin to follow up.
* Give accurate information on all visitors to church's outreach leaders so families can be contacted quickly.
* Schedule one or more special events in the weeks following VBS. Invite students and/or their families to attend.

Preparing for Cleanup

On or before the last day of VBS you will need to let your staff know their responsibilities for cleaning up. This can be done at staff devotions and through a memo. Let volunteers know which areas will need to be cleaned, when they can start and where to put their materials. Some rooms can be cleaned up before the closing celebration. Others, such as the church sanctuary (or wherever you have your performance) and the hallways, should remain decorated until after the closing program. Here are some more helpful suggestions:

* Designate one room or area where all decorations and materials can be placed.
* Enlist a few strong individuals to help move large items.
* Have stepladders available for volunteers to use.
* Ask that all volunteers who do not have a designated area assist teachers in cleaning up.

Preparing Your Closing Program

The long-term impact of your Vacation Bible School will be determined in large part by how effectively you reach the parents of the children who attend. A well-publicized, well-planned closing program can touch entire families with the message of your VBS.

Programs can be presented in the afternoon or evening on the last day of VBS or on the Saturday or Sunday immediately following. Choose a time that works best for your church and community calendars. Be aware, however, that interest and attendance will decrease as you schedule your program farther from the last day of VBS.

Program Content

As with all elements of VBS, your closing program can be whatever you wish it to be. The possibilities are endless. Your program could include one or more of the following:

A musical presentation—This could be as simple as presenting the songs children learned during VBS with small script parts added to explain what children learned. Most published curriculums include a skit episode and music production for this final event. If so, the music director may be the logical person to coordinate the closing program. Step 5 contains specific guidelines for the music director regarding the actual program; however, the information from this chapter will be helpful if he or she is responsible for the entire closing program.

Food—People who would otherwise feel uncomfortable visiting a church will relax and enjoy themselves when there's good food at hand. Use some of the recipes from the VBS snacks and have children serve food to the parents. If you choose to do this, observe the following tips:

- Promote this event at the same time you promote VBS, encouraging reservations when people register.
- Send invitations home to the parents at midweek. Include a slip of paper for parents to indicate if they will be attending and how many will be coming. Have children return the slips at the next session.
- Make sure all publicity announcements clearly indicate a cut-off date and time for making reservations so that adequate preparations can be made.
- Be sure your menu includes something kids enjoy, even if it's hot dogs, fruit and ice cream.
- Provide comfortable places to sit. Set up tables and chairs or benches in close groups.
- Plan an efficient way for people to get their food. Have lines moving past both sides of the food table.
- Use music, either live or piped in through a sound system, to provide a background while people eat.
- Make the event free of charge so all families will want to attend.

Family photos— Arrange to have several skilled photographers take free family photos. These can be candid shots taken throughout the closing program or portraits posed with your VBS backdrop. Plan for the developed snapshots to be delivered personally to the homes of unchurched families or distributed at an upcoming all-church event to which they are invited.

Additional activities—

- Have skit characters repeat favorite VBS skits.
- Have children recite Bible memory verses.
- Make a slide show or video presentation showing the workers, children and various activities at VBS.
- Interview children live about their VBS experiences or play tape of recorded interviews as slides are shown.
- Present special awards to children and/or staff. (Do not use this time to hand out general participation awards to all VBS students—it will take too much time.)

* Invite visitors to classrooms.
* Record one of the Bible stories and have children pantomime the parts of the story.
* Use clip art to make bulletins for closing program. Children can color with crayons or markers.

Personnel

As noted above, your music director may be the logical choice to lead your closing program. However, since volunteers may be running low on time and energy by the last day of VBS, other people may need to carry some of this event's responsibilities. An event coordinator could organize the efforts of those handling publicity, food, photography and cleanup. Someone from your church's evangelism/outreach ministry would be an excellent choice, since it would provide a natural, effective way to build relationships with unchurched families.

All VBS staff members should be highly visible during this event. Teachers/counselors should sit with their classes during the program to help with control and cueing. They should wear large name tags identifying their roles and take the initiative in helping parents feel welcome.

General Guidelines

There are several things to keep in mind when planning an effective closing program.

* Plan ahead. Make sure all staff are aware of plans for closing program and the importance of attending.
* Have a written schedule of how the program should progress and who will be leading each section of the program. Be careful to start and end on time.
* Send invitations home two or three days before the event. (See sample invitation on p.191.)
* Make volunteer recognition an important element of the celebration. Ask them to stand or list each volunteer's name in a printed program.
* Ask your pastor or other church leader to close the program by thanking parents for sharing their children with you and inviting them to visit other events of your church family (give specific times and dates).
* Close with a brief prayer of gratitude.

Alternative Closing Programs

Open House

An open house is also an effective way to communicate to parents ways children have been learning of God and His love for them. Invite parents to come to VBS on the final morning of your school. (Let children make invitations as a craft project.)

Arrange chairs for parents around the edge of the room. Briefly explain how each part of the schedule helps children to accomplish that day's Bible aim. Parents may remain for part or all of the morning.

Another option is to hold an open house before or after the closing program. Serve refreshments to parents in the classrooms so they will have an opportunity to talk with teachers, see displays of children's work and view equipment and materials children enjoyed using during VBS.

Celebration Picnic

Some churches plan a celebration picnic with food and games for parents and children. This is usually scheduled right after the last day of VBS or on the weekend.

Hold your picnic on your church lawn or at a nearby park. Tell parents to bring blankets. Provide a simple lunch such as hot dogs, chips and lemonade; or elaborate on a VBS theme snack and serve a variety of finger-foods. Play familiar VBS games and set aside a time for awards and recognition.

VBS Fair

Use the event ideas on pages 60-66 to plan a VBS theme fair on the last day.

Your Guide to Effective Follow-up

One of the most exciting aspects of VBS is the opportunity to reach unchurched children with the good news of Jesus Christ. Some of the children may be learning about God for the first time. For them, the love and acceptance felt at VBS will be a new and welcome experience, leaving them wanting more.

Is your ministry over on the last day of Vacation Bible School? It doesn't have to be! You can be used by God to offer the children and volunteers from your VBS the opportunity to continue experiencing His love. Maximize the full potential of your VBS outreach by planning a proactive follow-up program. This chapter will give you ideas, suggestions and guidelines in several critical areas.

Follow Up on Children

By this time, your teachers/counselors should already have a list of students' names and suggestions on how to follow up (see p. 200). Here are a few things that you, as VBS Director, can do to assist in reaching unchurched students and families:

- **Reinforce the importance of follow-up with your teachers/counselors.** Make sure they have all the information and materials they need to get started.
- **Send a card from you or your pastor to each unchurched family**, thanking them for attending VBS and personally inviting them to visit your church services and Sunday School. (See p. 203.) Enclose a brochure describing church programs for all ages.
- **Ask church families to invite unchurched families to Sunday School and church.** Families can offer to provide transportation, meet visitors at the door, sit with them and introduce them to others.
- **Provide Sunday School leaders with a complete list of unchurched families whose children visited VBS.** Encourage Sunday School personnel to make contact with these families.
- **Create a mailing list of all unchurched families from VBS.** Give the ministry leaders within your church a copy of the mailing list to send promotions on other church events.
- **Two weeks after VBS is over, contact your teachers/counselors to see how their follow-up efforts are progressing.**
- **Consider planning a fall festival as a reunion for all participants of VBS and their families.** Have those attending dress according to the previous summer's VBS theme. Choose a lesson not used in VBS as the Bible emphasis. This is a tremendous time to present your various church ministries to those who are not regular attendees of your church.

Follow Up with Administrative Issues

In addition to following up on the children in your VBS program, you will also have to take care of a variety of "after-the-event" details. Responsibilities highlighted on your master checklist include the following, many of which will be developed more fully in this chapter:

* Thank the Lord for His blessing. (Pray for the follow-up efforts. These are the fruits of your Bible ministry.)
* Express appreciation to all workers.
* Have staff perform an evaluation of VBS program.
* See that supplies are packed, labeled and stored for future use.
* Compile and file all records, receipts and publications.
* Create a "debriefing file" complete with your checklists, communication records, personnel lists, etc.
* While the events of VBS are still fresh in your mind, fill out a VBS review sheet (see p. 204). Note how problems were solved and how to avoid similar ones in the future. Include notes of necessary adjustments in schedules, additional supplies needed, etc. Write down good ideas for next year. Make an extra copy and keep one for yourself and one for your church files.
* File names and addresses of workers to be contacted next year.

Dealing with Leftover Materials/Supplies

As teachers and staff begin to clean up their rooms, you will want to designate one area in which to store all the leftover materials and supplies. Once cleanup is completed, make sure all borrowed supplies are return to their owners. Then separate the materials into three categories:

1. **Items to be reused**—Keep all curriculum (teacher's books, visual resources, craft books, activity books, etc.) to use for future special events, emergency Sunday school lessons or other church programs. Collect, file and label lessons in a resource room where teachers can easily find them. Also, keep all leftover craft items, prizes, stickers and other general materials that are usable.
2. **Items to be passed on**—Call around to see if there are any churches in your area that are doing the same (or similar) VBS theme. Offer them any decorations that are still in good condition or any theme-specific items that cannot be returned to the publisher. You could also send materials to an inner-city church or a mission organization. Call ahead to see what items would be useful to them.
3. **Items to be trashed**—Throw away or recycle any decorations that are beyond repair, any used student papers and/or half-completed crafts. Do not throw away any attendance sheets or registration cards until you make sure you have all the information recorded.

Storing Records

When VBS is over you will want to gather all your records and then consolidate and file them. However tempting it may be to throw the mountain of papers away, don't neglect this important step in your follow-up activities. The records you keep will help in evaluating your VBS efforts and in planning for future children's programs.

* **Registration cards**—Hopefully, by the end of VBS, all of your cards carry all the pertinent information. If you are missing some information, try to obtain it from students' friends or local directories. Make sure that follow-up teachers/counselors have all the information

they need from the cards, such as addresses, phone numbers, parent's name and church affiliation. Computers are wonderful tools for collecting and maintaining these kinds of records. Printouts can be made as needed and the information is always available. However, it is still a good idea to save the registration cards and file them with your other VBS administrative records.

* **Roster/Attendance sheets**—Have teachers/counselors turn all attendance sheets back to you. Record total attendance for each day on a total attendance sheet (see p. 197). Once information is recorded you can throw these sheets away.
* **Other items**—In addition to your VBS records, you will also want to keep copies of the following: curriculum order receipts; VBS staff names, addresses and assignments; promotional mailings and brochures; purchase orders and receipts; missions and offering giving; staff memos; take-home announcements; and evaluations. These items will be invaluable for next year's VBS director.

Evaluating Your Program

Evaluating your VBS program will help reveal the strengths and weaknesses of your efforts. The end result will give both you and future VBS directors better insight when planning subsequent programs. Evaluations should be completed by all VBS staff, including you. Don't expect your VBS staff to fill out a long evaluation form on their own time. Have them complete it as a part of their last day's activities. Most VBS publishers provide an evaluation form in their curriculum. To develop your own, see sample on page 179.

Another effective way to get the feedback you need is to have volunteers briefly discuss a few questions at a volunteer appreciation event. Take written notes during this evaluation time as valuable information will most likely be discussed. Lead volunteers in brainstorming solutions to problems that may have been encountered.

You may also want to get feedback from a few of the students. Ask them questions rather than have them fill out a lengthy form.

Follow Up in Your Church

Don't let the efforts of your VBS vanish as soon as the program ends. There will be many people in your church who are interested in knowing the status of your VBS program. People who have been supporting the program through prayers and contributions deserve to know the results. There are many ways you can do this. Here is a list of suggestions:

* **Publish an encouraging announcement in your church bulletin.** Report on the average attendance, the number of unchurched children who attended, the number of volunteers, important decisions that were made, the status of your missions project and any other exciting information about your VBS program. You may also want to include a word of thanks to all who were involved and list their names.
* **Ask permission to have a few volunteers or students share their VBS experiences with the congregation during the next church services.**
* **Arrange to have a group of students sing one or two VBS songs at your next worship services.**
* **Leave decorations and samples of your crafts in the rooms for church members to see.** Visitors will feel more at ease returning to familiar surroundings.
* **Design a bulletin board showing photographs and samples of lessons that were taught at VBS.**
* **Publish a more in-depth report for your next church newsletter.** Include a thanks to all volunteers and list their names.

Follow Up with Your Staff

By now you realize the worth of your VBS staff. In addition to the impact VBS makes on the students, it also is quite an experience for the volunteer. Friendships are made. Gifts and talents are developed. And, hopefully, everyone involved will have had such a good time, they will be ready to do it again next year! So now that VBS is over, don't forget to follow up with your invaluable staff.

Appreciate Your Volunteers

One way to keep volunteers excited and geared up for the future is to take the time to recognize them for their efforts. Oftentimes volunteers feel unnoticed and quickly grow tired of giving their time and energy to the church. Let your volunteers know you appreciate them by:

- ✻ making or buying teacher certificates for every volunteer who has helped;
- ✻ honoring volunteers at the closing program with a certificate of appreciation and a small gift;
- ✻ inviting volunteers to a breakfast, brunch or lunch the day after the closing program;

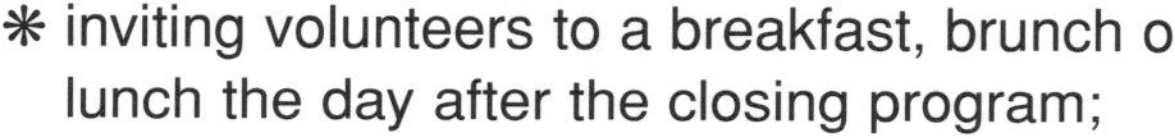

- ✻ asking for their opinions or comments on the success of your VBS;
- ✻ discussing with them ways to improve future VBS efforts;
- ✻ encouraging volunteers to participate in next year's VBS;
- ✻ including a general note of thanks and a list of VBS volunteers in the church newsletter or bulletin;
- ✻ mailing personal thank-you cards to every volunteer when VBS is over.

Fun Treats for Volunteer Appreciation

- ✻ A PayDay® candy bar—"You deserve a PayDay®, thanks for a wonderful job!"
- ✻ A pack of gum or roll of colorful tape—"Thanks for sticking in there! We're sure stuck on you!"
- ✻ A bag of Whoppers® candy—"Thanks for making our VBS a WHOPPING success!"
- ✻ A small candle or mini-flashlight— "Thanks for shining your light to the children of (name of community)."
- ✻ A can of soup—"You did a 'souper' job!"

Prepare Your Volunteers for Future Ministry

Your volunteers have been the backbone of your VBS ministry. In fact, VBS may have uncovered some talents and interests that are new even to the workers themselves. One of the most exciting aspects of your position is discovering individuals with the capacity to make a strong impact on the life of your church. Consider it a part of your job to ensure that volunteers get the training they need to continue on in service. Here are some ways you can guide your VBS staff into future effective ministries:

- ✻ Share the names of capable new volunteers with other ministry leaders in your church. Identify strengths and gifts that you observed through the VBS process.
- ✻ Encourage volunteers to serve by letting them know what you appreciated about their service.
- ✻ Ask church leaders to provide ongoing leadership training to interested volunteers.
- ✻ Help guide a new volunteer to a ministry that may be of interest to him or her.
- ✻ Keep volunteers informed on pertinent training opportunities.
- ✻ Make a list of possible candidates for next year's VBS director.

Follow Up with Prayer

When you think you've done all the follow-up you can possibly do, there is one final step—prayer. Prayer is *the* most important element in your follow-up efforts. These suggested requests should be a part of your daily prayer life:

- Praise God for giving you the strength and the opportunity to serve Him through VBS.
- Praise God for your faithful volunteers.
- Praise God for and continue to pray for the children who made decisions for Christ during VBS.
- Pray for continued spiritual growth in the lives of your VBS students.
- Pray for the follow-up efforts of your teachers/counselors.
- Pray that your church will continue to grow through your VBS outreach.
- Pray that volunteers will find a meaningful place of ministry with God's guidance.
- Pray that God would give you rest and the guidance needed to pursue future areas of ministry.
- Pray for the planning of next year's VBS.
- Pray for publishers who are preparing next year's VBS curriculum.

And Don't Forget Yourself!

Doctors, time-management experts and experienced ministry leaders agree—the best thing you can do after a period of stress or extreme busyness is to take time off to recuperate. Even the best VBS preparation and training in the world cannot prevent a director from feeling a little "fried" at times. Taking time off is good for your physical and mental well-being and can do much to strengthen your spiritual walk.

In Mark 1:35-39 Jesus Himself withdrew to a solitary place after a busy time of ministry. Retreating and allowing yourself to spend extra time with the Lord can "restore your soul." Plan on finding a solitary place to be alone or with your family to simply recuperate. You deserve it! And when you return, you will have the strength and insight to face your next challenge.

VBS Continues . . .

Imagine the impact on children's lives if you were to continue your VBS program beyond the normal five days! Rich benefits will result if you give your students special opportunities to build relationships and enhance what they are learning about God's love!

Below are lots of ideas you can use to add a day, a week or an entire summer of fun to your Vacation Bible School!

Field Trips

In Search of...

Pack a snack and walk or drive to a museum or library. Form groups of 6 to 8. Each group pretends to be a research team doing a study on a different creature, plant, object, painting, country, etc. Each research team must find out as much as they can about their item before time is called. Then each team reports on their topic to the other teams.

Zoo Trip

Pack a lunch and visit a nearby zoo. Invite parents to accompany the group and make a special effort to get to know parents of unchurched children. Arrange to have a tour of the zoo. Take photos of children with their favorite animals. When pictures have been developed, send to children as keepsakes of their time together at your VBS.

City Tour

Arrange to spend a day seeing highlights of your city or one nearby. Prepare children by discussing the many different kinds of people who live in cities and how these people need to work together to make their city a nice place to live. Places you might want to visit include city hall, library, art museum, fire station, police station, university, cultural center, hospital, rescue mission and soup kitchen. Have lunch or a snack at a city park.

City Tour "Plus"

Assign children to small groups and provide each group with a camera and film to use for the day. Leaders take small groups to different locations in the city. Children use cameras and film to chronicle the city tour. After the pictures have been developed, spend part of another day putting the photos in albums and talking about your experiences. (Optional: Use video camera and have volunteers take turns filming and narrating.)

Performing Arts Day

Arrange for children to see a professional play or musical. Discounts are often available for large groups.

Visit the "Other Side" of Town

Most people label a part of their own city as the "other side" of town. It's a place where people may seem different because of their customs or the color of their skin. Arrange for children to spend time on the "other side," learning about another culture and meeting people who seem different but with whom they probably have much in common. You might arrange such an exchange by contacting a church in the area.

Visit a Farm

Pack a lunch or a snack and travel to a nearby farm to experience country life firsthand. Arrange for a farmer to tell about the farm animals and crops. If possible, arrange for children to go on a hayride while at the farm.

Petting Zoo

Visit a local petting zoo. Take photos of children with animals. When pictures have been developed, send to children as a keepsake of your time together at your VBS.

Plant a Garden

Do you have an empty flower bed on your church property? Do you have a few seasoned gardeners willing to help out? If so, allow your students to start a flower or vegetable patch. You may be able to incorporate simple garden maintenance into your Sunday School routine.

Fruit Picking

Take your kids to an orchard to pick fruit. Allow time for picking as well as climbing and playing among the trees. Have older children compare a healthy tree and an unhealthy tree. Talk about what makes a plant healthy or unhealthy and how this relates to our spiritual lives.

Special Events

Sand Sculpting Contest

Just before school is out for the summer, post flyers around your town to advertise a sand sculpture event. Provide a large area of sand and have water available to give children an opportunity to work in groups sculpting giant sand castles or other creations. Provide snacks and information about your VBS program.

Pizza Bash

At an all-church gathering, form groups of five to six people. Provide a large pizza crust, pizza sauce, cheese and a variety of cut-up vegetable toppings for each group. While the pizzas are baking, have a slide show or video presentation showing VBS highlights.

Treasure Hunt

Collect small toys and items related to your VBS theme. List items on a sheet of paper, then hide them in a large outdoor area such as a park. In small groups, children search for the items, referring to list on paper. The team with the most objects wins.

Prayer Rally

At an all-church gathering, invite several people to share special prayer requests that God has answered and explain why prayer is important to them. Ask volunteers to suggest prayer requests. This is a wonderful opportunity to review your VBS missions project and pray for your missionary. Have several children and adults pray. End by singing "The Lord's Prayer."

Family Traditions Night

Many families have unique traditions. Invite several families in your church to share their family customs at a "Family Traditions Night" at your church. You may want to have families share information/traditions about each of the major holidays, as well as birthdays or other less common celebrations. Encourage families to use props, music, slides, videos, etc. Invite your pastor to share about church traditions that bring the church family closer together.

Crafts Workshop

Choose one of the more involved projects from your VBS craft book and set aside a day or evening to make the project. Break up your time by gathering for a few minutes of singing and a short message from the pastor. Your crafts workshop could be an evening for the whole family where parents and kids work together to complete projects, or it could be just for kids.

Funniest Home Videos

Invite families to come to a "home video" night at your church. Families submit video clips ahead of time. A panel selects a number of clips to be shown. (Each clip should be no more than two minutes.) Give prizes for the funniest, most unbelievable and most embarrassing.

Fun Olympics

Set up a variety of outdoor physical activities and games using your VBS theme. Make a torch out of tissue and construction paper. Pick a few teachers or children to pass the torch around your playing area. Divide group into teams to compete for fun. Have an awards ceremony at the end with toy medals.

Service Projects

Service projects allow a teacher to take a class beyond simply hearing about obeying God, talking about obeying God and even planning ways of obeying God. Acts of service done as part of a group are effective ways to help children actually begin obeying God by assisting others. Service projects that grow out of Bible lessons can help children:

* encourage one another to do what God's Word teaches;
* experience the joy of giving to others;
* accept responsibility to complete a task;
* learn to work together;
* recognize that God's Word leads His people to action.

Shopping Mall Outreach

Have some children rehearse playing rhythm instruments to Sunday School songs. Other children make or assemble VBS invitations or postcards. Take children to a shopping mall. Some children hand out invitations while others play rhythm instruments to VBS music.

Bake Sale

Using recipes from your VBS course or a cookbook, plan a bake sale or an after-church lunch. Participants form small groups. Each group prepares a different recipe, then packages it or helps to serve it. Children sell snacks or lunch tickets. The money earned can be used for a missions or charity project.

Love in Action

Your missions project during VBS may be to help a low-income child-care program. With the program director's consent, kids can help paint outdoor climbing equipment, paint over graffiti, or even design and paint a colorful scene on a wall behind the play area. Kids can also clean toys or do one-on-one storybook reading with the children in the program.

Faith in Action

Your mission project during VBS may be to help fix up or beautify a run-down area in your city. With city permission, kids can help paint benches, paint over graffiti, or even design and paint a colorful mural in an appropriate location. Kids can plant trees or decorative plants, pick up trash from a park or beach, or do gardening and simple paint jobs for elderly people in your church.

Balloon-O-Grams

Rent a helium tank. Help children fill balloons with helium, then tie strings to balloons. Attach Sunday School invitations or postcards to strings. Demonstrate how to hold and give out balloons without losing any. Take children to a shopping mall and let them hand out balloons to the children there.

Adopt a Family

Your mission project during VBS may be to raise money to help an individual family in your community. Contact your church's care ministry or your town's homeless shelter for ideas.

Canned Food Scavenger Hunt

In small groups with adult leaders, children canvass local neighborhoods collecting donations of canned food for a local mission or shelter. Prepare an information sheet about your church and the agency for which the food is intended for children to give to people they meet.

Prayer in Action

Arrange to take a small group of students to visit a person who is sick at home or in a hospital. Have students pray at the end of the visit. Ask students to write the person's name in their prayer journals and remember to pray for him or her during the next few weeks.

Sponsor a Child

Your mission project during VBS may be to raise money to help a group of needy children. Contact a representative of World Vision, Compassion, or other world relief organization for ideas on how to get your church involved.

Daily Bread

Arrange for children to visit a local mission or shelter and help serve a meal.

Thankful Kids

Children select city workers for whom they are thankful (such as police officers, fire fighters, teachers, librarians, nurses, doctors, trash collectors, etc.). They write thank-you notes to these workers and bake cookies or draw pictures for them as a way of expressing thanks. Arrange to have children deliver their gifts in person.

City Kids on the Streets

Large cities have their share of street kids and often there are special shelters that reach out to them. Contact your local shelter to find out the specific needs of street kids. Put together tote bags for these kids with items such as toiletries, socks, towels, an address book, stationery, stamps, pencils, pens and packaged snack foods.

Garden Help for Senior Citizens

Arrange to have small groups of students spend time doing yard work for senior citizens in your church or community.

Tips for Involving Children in Service Projects

Plan ahead to be sure your project is more than "busy work." Clearly explain to children how their work will benefit others. If possible, allow children time to brainstorm ideas to help others.

If the service project will last more than a week or two, consider making a chart or poster on which to record your progress.

Involve parents or responsible teens to supervise children as they work on their project.

Take pictures (photographs or videos) of children as they pull weeds, sort pictures, deliver canned goods, etc. Then display the photos in your classroom or show the video during a future class session.

Invite someone from the group that will benefit from the project to your class. Have children interview this person to learn about the needs they will be helping to meet.

- Schedules, Forms, Flyers and Handouts
- Awards and Certificates
- Clip Art

Director's Master Checklist by Categories

(NOTE: Fill in the months according to your VBS dates.)

ADMINISTRATION/LEADERSHIP DUTIES

24 WEEKS BEFORE:

- ❏ Begin regular prayer for VBS. Ask church groups to pray for VBS from now until the program is over.
- ❏ Determine type of VBS (mornings, evenings, camp format, Backyard Bible School, etc.).

20 WEEKS BEFORE:

- ❏ Meet with church leaders to discuss your role as VBS director.
- ❏ Decide on possible dates for VBS.

18 WEEKS BEFORE:

- ❏ Appoint VBS committee (assistant director, department leaders, publicity coordinator, etc.).
- ❏ Set goals and determine unique needs of your VBS.
- ❏ Choose setting and location for your VBS. Reserve area if needed.
- ❏ Meet with church leaders and secure a VBS budget.
- ❏ Establish and announce VBS dates in church bulletin/newsletter.

16 WEEKS BEFORE:

- ❏ Meet with VBS committee (including all department leaders) to:
  1. Pray for VBS.
  2. Outline time schedules for both self-contained classrooms and activity centers.
  3. Set deadline dates for all activities.
  4. Estimate VBS enrollment and determine staff needs (departmental and general).
  5. Compile lists of prospective workers.
  6. Schedule training workshop(s).
  7. Make a list of supplies to be purchased.

8 WEEKS BEFORE:

- ❏ Plan dedication service for workers; secure minister's approval and help.
- ❏ Plan closing program.
- ❏ Plan follow-up efforts with Sunday School leaders.

6 WEEKS BEFORE:

- ❏ Plan all activities for opening and closing assemblies and for any special mid-week events.

4 WEEKS BEFORE:

- ❏ Check and adjust time schedules if necessary.
- ❏ Plan for extra staff and special procedures needed for first-day registration.
- ❏ Finalize date, time and arrangements for closing program.
- ❏ Make arrangements for sound system and custodial support during and after VBS.
- ❏ Assign rooms and places for each class/center.

1 WEEK BEFORE:

- ❏ Plan for first-aid needs and disciplinary problems.
- ❏ Plan morning staff devotions.
- ❏ Hold an all-staff meeting to discuss any last-minute changes, announce room assignments and answer any questions.

DURING VBS:

- ❑ Conduct morning staff devotions.
- ❑ Lead all or a portion of the opening and closing assemblies. Present VBS awards and certificates to staff and children on last day of VBS.
- ❑ Make sure teachers are present and on schedule. If using the activity center method, signal appropriate time to rotate to next center.
- ❑ Visit departments; make any necessary adjustments.
- ❑ Be an "evangelism booster." Encourage all the children to bring new friends throughout the week. Plan for and remind your staff to prepare for the evangelism emphasis of your VBS.
- ❑ Assist with discipline problems and emergency situations as needed.
- ❑ Have someone available to run errands.
- ❑ Distribute any announcements and flyers for children to take home on appropriate days.
- ❑ Supervise preparations and build enthusiasm for the closing program.
- ❑ Supervise the ongoing photography/video taping of the VBS activities.

AFTER VBS:

- ❑ Begin follow-up efforts.
- ❑ Compile and file all records, receipts and publications.
- ❑ Create a "debriefing file" complete with your checklists, communication records, personnel lists, etc. Note how problems were solved and how to avoid similar ones in the future. Include notes of necessary adjustments in schedules, additional supplies needed, etc. Write down good ideas for next year.

PUBLICITY

16 WEEKS BEFORE:

- ❑ Plan publicity with publicity coordinator.
- ❑ Order publicity materials.

10 WEEKS BEFORE:

- ❑ Begin displaying banners and posters throughout church building and community.

8 WEEKS BEFORE:

- ❑ Make VBS flyers for church members to use for invitations.

4 WEEKS BEFORE:

- ❑ Distribute theme buttons and/or T-shirts to all staff members to wear to church from now through the end of VBS.
- ❑ Mail postcard invitations to invite prospects to attend and/or deliver flyers/door hangers throughout neighborhood.
- ❑ Make and photocopy any flyers or announcements that will be going home with the children each day.

DURING VBS:

- ❑ Distribute any announcements and flyers for children to take home on the appropriate days.
- ❑ Send home special invitations to your closing program.

AFTER VBS:

- ❑ Prepare slide show or video presentation showing VBS highlights.
- ❑ Publish outcome of VBS successes in church bulletin or post on bulletin boards.

VOLUNTEER RECRUITMENT/TRAINING

16 WEEKS BEFORE:

❏ Meet with VBS committee to estimate enrollment and determine staff needs (departmental and general), compile lists of prospective workers and schedule training workshop(s).

❏ Send letter and response postcards to veteran VBS volunteers you want to return.

❏ Begin personal contacts to recruit rest of staff.

12 WEEKS BEFORE:

❏ Publicize in the church bulletin the need for workers. Give names of department leaders as "persons to see."

10 WEEKS BEFORE:

❏ Meet with department leaders to work out training workshop procedures. Discuss the overall goals and aims for VBS and the individual lesson aims.

❏ Outline and prepare for training workshop(s).

❏ List all VBS staff in church bulletin, asking prayer for them and for any remaining vacancies.

❏ Contact all recruits, confirming preliminary assignments, notifying them of training workshop(s).

8 WEEKS BEFORE:

❏ Publicize training workshop(s) in church bulletin. Identify new staff additions and remaining vacancies.

❏ Enlist qualified crew of child-care workers for volunteers' children.

6 WEEKS BEFORE:

❏ Meet with the leaders (missions, publicity, finance, crafts, snacks, transportation, etc.) for prayer and to determine if they are accomplishing their assignments. Use the checklists from this section for evaluations.

❏ Plan for and enlist substitutes.

4 WEEKS BEFORE:

❏ Conduct training workshop(s).

1 WEEK BEFORE:

❏ Hold dedication service for volunteers.

❏ Distribute class rosters/attendance sheets to teachers or counselors.

❏ Assist leaders or teachers in last-minute preparations.

DURING VBS:

❏ Continue staff support functions. Pray with and for them. Communicate with them and work at maintaining their spirit of enthusiasm.

❏ Arrange for substitutes when needed.

❏ Visit departments; make any necessary adjustments.

❏ Present VBS awards and certificates to staff and children on the last day of VBS.

AFTER VBS:

❏ Express appreciation to all workers.

❏ Have staff perform an evaluation of your VBS program.

❏ File names/addresses of workers to be contacted next year.

PREREGISTRATION/ REGISTRATION

8 WEEKS BEFORE:

❏ Plan and prepare preregistration activities.

6 WEEKS BEFORE:

❏ Begin preregistration.

4 WEEKS BEFORE:

❏ Plan for extra staff and special procedures needed for first-day registration.

1 WEEK BEFORE:

❏ Assign preregistered children to classes or groups.

❏ Distribute class rosters/attendance sheets to teachers or counselors.

❏ Assign volunteer(s) to purchase or make name tags for each class.

DURING VBS:

❏ Make sure registration and attendance records are being properly kept.

AFTER VBS:

❏ Compile and file all records, receipts and publications.

CURRICULUM

20 WEEKS BEFORE:

❏ Compare and evaluate VBS curriculum choices.

18 WEEKS BEFORE:

❏ Decide on a VBS curriculum and return all unused kits to publisher.

❏ Order basic VBS curriculum (such as a Starter Kit).

16 WEEKS BEFORE:

❏ Order curriculum materials.

12 WEEKS BEFORE:

❏ Distribute curriculum materials to department leaders.

4 WEEKS BEFORE:

❏ Order any extra materials needed based on preregistration indicators.

SUPPLIES

16 WEEKS BEFORE:

❏ Publish bulletin insert listing craft supply needs, refreshment donations and other materials needed.

10 WEEKS BEFORE:

❏ Distribute second notice regarding supplies.

❏ Distribute supplies to department leaders.

8 WEEKS BEFORE:

❏ Purchase remaining craft supplies.

4 WEEKS BEFORE:

❏ Make sure all leaders and teachers have last-minute supplies.

❏ Check and adjust supplies as needed.

❏ Update bulletin insert to provide final request for items still needed.

DURING VBS:

❏ Secure additional supplies as needed.

AFTER VBS:

❏ See that supplies are packed, labeled and stored for future use.

FACILITIES

18 WEEKS BEFORE:

❏ Choose setting and location for your VBS.

6 WEEKS BEFORE:

❏ Plan theme-decorating ideas. This may include having backdrops painted.

4 WEEKS BEFORE:

❏ Make arrangements for sound system and custodial support during and after VBS.

1 WEEK BEFORE:

❏ Hold a preparation day for staff to decorate and arrange indoor rooms (if possible).

DURING VBS:

❏ Make sure all VBS volunteers clean up their areas on the last day of VBS.

AFTER VBS:

❏ Make sure facility is cleaned up and returned to original condition.

Director's Master CheckList by Date

(NOTE: Fill in the months according to your VBS dates.)

24 WEEKS BEFORE:

- ❏ Begin regular prayer for VBS. Ask church groups to pray for VBS from now until the program is over.
- ❏ Determine type of VBS (mornings, evenings, camp format, Backyard Bible School, etc.).

20 WEEKS BEFORE:

- ❏ If you are a first-time director, meet with former VBS directors and/or leaders to glean pertinent information and suggestions.
- ❏ Meet with church leaders to discuss your role as VBS director.
- ❏ Decide on possible dates for VBS.
- ❏ Compare and evaluate VBS curriculum choices.

18 WEEKS BEFORE:

- ❏ Appoint VBS committee (assistant director, department leaders, publicity coordinator, etc.).
- ❏ Set goals and determine unique needs of your VBS.
- ❏ Choose setting and location for your VBS. Reserve area if needed.
- ❏ Meet with church leaders and secure a VBS budget.
- ❏ Decide on a VBS curriculum and return all unused kits to publisher.
- ❏ Order basic VBS curriculum (such as a Starter Kit).
- ❏ Establish and announce VBS dates in church bulletin/newsletter.

16 WEEKS BEFORE:

- ❏ Meet with VBS committee (including all department leaders) to:
  1. Pray for VBS.
  2. Outline time schedules for both self-contained classrooms and activity centers.
  3. Set deadline dates for all activities.
  4. Estimate VBS enrollment and determine staff needs (departmental and general).
  5. Compile lists of prospective workers.
  6. Schedule training workshop(s).
  7. Make a list of supplies to be purchased.

- ❑ Plan publicity with publicity coordinator.
- ❑ Order publicity and curriculum materials.
- ❑ Send letter and response postcards to veteran VBS volunteers you want to return.
- ❑ Begin personal contacts to recruit rest of staff.
- ❑ Publish bulletin insert listing craft supply needs, refreshment donations and other materials needed.

12 WEEKS BEFORE:

- ❑ Distribute curriculum materials to department leaders.
- ❑ Publicize in the church bulletin the need for workers. Give names of department leaders as "persons to see."
- ❑ Choose and plan missions project.

10 WEEKS BEFORE:

- ❑ Distribute second notice regarding supplies.
- ❑ Distribute supplies to department leaders.
- ❑ Meet with department leaders to work out training workshop procedures. Discuss the overall goals and aims for VBS and the individual lesson aims.
- ❑ Outline and prepare for training workshop(s).
- ❑ List all VBS staff in church bulletin, asking prayer for them and for any remaining vacancies.
- ❑ Contact all recruits, confirming preliminary assignments, notifying them of training workshop(s).
- ❑ Begin displaying banners and posters throughout church building and community.

8 WEEKS BEFORE:

- ❑ Purchase remaining craft supplies.
- ❑ Plan and prepare preregistration activities.
- ❑ Make VBS flyers for church members to use for invitations.
- ❑ Publicize training workshop(s) in church bulletin. Identify any new staff additions and remaining vacancies.
- ❑ Plan dedication service for workers; secure minister's approval and help.
- ❑ Plan closing program.
- ❑ Plan follow-up efforts with Sunday School leaders.
- ❑ Enlist qualified crew of child-care workers for volunteers' children.

6 WEEKS BEFORE:

- ❏ Meet with the leaders (missions, publicity, finance, crafts, snacks, transportation, etc.) for prayer and to determine if they are accomplishing their assignments. Use the checklists from this section for evaluations.
- ❏ Begin preregistration.
- ❏ Plan all activities for opening and closing assemblies and for any special mid-week events.
- ❏ Plan theme-decorating ideas. This may include having backdrops painted.
- ❏ Plan for and enlist substitutes.

4 WEEKS BEFORE:

- ❏ Make sure all leaders and teachers have last-minute supplies.
- ❏ Conduct training workshop(s).
- ❏ Distribute theme buttons and/or T-shirts to all staff members to wear to church from now through the end of VBS.
- ❏ Mail postcard invitations to invite prospects to attend and/or deliver flyers/door hangers throughout neighborhood.
- ❏ Check and adjust time schedules and supplies.
- ❏ Plan for extra staff and special procedures needed for first-day registration.
- ❏ Update bulletin insert to provide final request for items still needed.
- ❏ Make and photocopy any flyers or announcements that will be going home with the children each day.
- ❏ Finalize date, time and arrangements for closing program.
- ❏ Make arrangements for sound system and custodial support during and after VBS.
- ❏ Order any extra materials needed based on preregistration indicators.
- ❏ Assign rooms and places for each class/center.

1 WEEK BEFORE:

- ❏ Hold dedication service for volunteers.
- ❏ Hold a preparation day for staff to decorate and arrange indoor rooms (if possible).
- ❏ Plan for first-aid needs and disciplinary problems.
- ❏ Assign preregistered children to classes or groups.
- ❏ Distribute class rosters/attendance sheets to teachers or counselors.
- ❏ Assign volunteer(s) to make or purchase name tags for each class.
- ❏ Assist leaders or teachers in last-minute preparations.
- ❏ Plan morning staff devotions.
- ❏ Hold an all-staff meeting to discuss any last-minute changes, announce room assignments and answer any questions.

DURING VBS:

- ❏ Continue all staff support functions. Pray with and for them. Communicate with them and work at maintaining their spirit of enthusiasm.
- ❏ Conduct morning staff devotions.
- ❏ Lead all or a portion of the opening and closing assemblies. Present VBS awards and certificates to staff and children on last day of VBS.
- ❏ Make sure teachers are present and on schedule. If using the activity center method, signal appropriate times to rotate to the next center.
- ❏ Arrange for substitutes when needed.
- ❏ Visit departments; make any necessary adjustments.
- ❏ Be an "evangelism booster." Encourage all the children to bring new friends throughout the week. Pray for and remind your staff to prepare for the evangelism emphasis of your VBS.
- ❏ Secure additional supplies as needed.
- ❏ Assist with discipline problems and emergency situations as needed.
- ❏ Make sure registration and attendance records are being properly kept.
- ❏ Have someone available to run errands.
- ❏ Distribute any announcements and flyers for children to take home on the appropriate days.
- ❏ Supervise preparations and build enthusiasm for the closing program.
- ❏ Send home special invitations to your closing program.
- ❏ Supervise the ongoing photography/video taping of the VBS activities.
- ❏ Make sure all VBS volunteers clean up their areas on the last day of VBS.

AFTER VBS:

- ❏ Thank the Lord for His blessing. (Pray for the follow-up efforts. These are the fruits of your Bible ministry.)
- ❏ Make sure facility is cleaned up and returned to original condition.
- ❏ Express appreciation to all workers.
- ❏ Have staff perform an evaluation of your VBS program.
- ❏ Prepare slide show or video presentation showing VBS highlights.
- ❏ Publish outcome of VBS successes in church bulletin or post on bulletin boards.
- ❏ Begin follow-up efforts.
- ❏ See that supplies are packed, labeled and stored for future use.
- ❏ Compile and file all records, receipts and publications.
- ❏ Create a "debriefing file" complete with your checklists, communication records, personnel lists, etc. Note how problems were solved and how to avoid similar ones in the future. Include notes of necessary adjustments in schedules, additional supplies needed, etc. Write down good ideas for next year.
- ❏ File names/addresses of workers to be contacted next year.

Sample Activity Center Flow Chart and Schedule

Sample Three-Hour Schedule

	1ST GRADE (group a)	**1ST GRADE** (group b)	**2ND GRADE**	**3RD GRADE**	**4TH GRADE**	**5TH/6TH GRADE**
9:00–9:15	Opening Assembly	Opening Assembly	Opening Assembly	Opening Assembly	Opening Assembly	Opening Assembly
9:20–9:45	Bible Story/App. A	Craft Center A	Snack Center	Bible Story/App. B	Music Center	Craft Center B
9:50–10:15	Bible Learning Activity Center A	Bible Story/ App. A	Craft Center A	Bible Learning Activity Center B	Bible Story/ App. B	Snack Center
10:20–10:45	Snack Center	Bible Learning Activity Center A	Bible Story/ App. A	Craft Center B	Bible Learning Activity Center B	Music Center
10:50–11:15	Music Center	Music Center	Bible Learning Activity Center A	Snack Center	Snack Center	Bible Story/ App. A
11:20–11:45	Craft Center A	Snack Center	Music Center	Music Center	Craft Center B	Bible Learning Activity Center B
11:50–12:00	Closing Assembly	Closing Assembly	Closing Assembly	Closing Assembly	Closing Assembly	Closing Assembly

Activity Center Schedule Worksheet

(Create your own schedule by filling in times, classes and activities.)

Self-Contained Classroom Schedule Worksheet

Class						
Opening Assembly						
Bible Story/ Application						
Recreation/ Snacks						
Crafts						
Other						

Recruitment Planning Worksheet

VBS Dates ______________________ VBS Director ________________________________

VBS Committee Members	Oversee Following Areas	Phone Number

Names of Staff Prospects	Phone Number	Requested Job

Vacation Bible School Volunteers

Date_______________Time_______________

BEFORE VBS, I WOULD LIKE TO HELP BY:

❑ Praying for teachers and students
❑ Providing craft materials
❑ Distributing publicity materials
❑ Preparing craft materials
❑ Painting banners, backdrops, sets, etc.
❑ Preregistering students

DURING VBS, I WOULD LIKE TO HELP IN ONE OR MORE OF THE FOLLOWING AREAS:

❑ Department Leader ❑ Teacher ❑ Assistant
❑ Prekindergarten (3–4 yrs)
❑ Kindergarten (5 yrs)
❑ Primary (1st & 2nd grade)
❑ Middler (3rd & 4th grade)
❑ Junior (5th & 6th grade)
❑ Youth (7th & 8th grade)
❑ Missions Coordinator
❑ Photographer

Promotion Day: ❑ Coordinator ❑ Helper
Registration: ❑ Coordinator ❑ Helper
Transportation: ❑ Coordinator ❑ Helper
Skit: ❑ Director ❑ Helper
Craft: ❑ Coordinator ❑ Helper
Music: ❑ Director ❑ Teacher ❑ Pianist ❑ Guitarist
Snacks: ❑ Coordinator ❑ Helper ❑ Providing Snacks

AFTER VBS, I WOULD LIKE TO HELP IN FOLLOW-UP BY:

❑ Praying for follow-up program
❑ Calling on prospective families for congregation
❑ Writing postcards to children who attended VBS

Name ______________________________

Phone ______________________________

If you have any questions about Vacation Bible School or your involvement in it, please call

____
(name and phone number)

PLEASE RETURN THIS FLYER IN THE OFFERING PLATE OR TO THE CHURCH OFFICE.

Vacation Bible School Volunteers

Date_______________Time_______________

BEFORE VBS, I WOULD LIKE TO HELP BY:

❑ Praying for teachers and students
❑ Providing craft materials
❑ Distributing publicity materials
❑ Preparing craft materials
❑ Painting banners, backdrops, sets, etc.
❑ Preregistering students

DURING VBS, I WOULD LIKE TO HELP IN ONE OR MORE OF THE FOLLOWING AREAS:

❑ Department Leader ❑ Teacher ❑ Assistant
❑ Prekindergarten (3–4 yrs)
❑ Kindergarten (5 yrs)
❑ Primary (1st & 2nd grade)
❑ Middler (3rd & 4th grade)
❑ Junior (5th & 6th grade)
❑ Youth (7th & 8th grade)
❑ Missions Coordinator
❑ Photographer

Promotion Day: ❑ Coordinator ❑ Helper
Registration: ❑ Coordinator ❑ Helper
Transportation: ❑ Coordinator ❑ Helper
Skit: ❑ Director ❑ Helper
Craft: ❑ Coordinator ❑ Helper
Music: ❑ Director ❑ Teacher ❑ Pianist ❑ Guitarist
Snacks: ❑ Coordinator ❑ Helper ❑ Providing Snacks

AFTER VBS, I WOULD LIKE TO HELP IN FOLLOW-UP BY:

❑ Praying for follow-up program
❑ Calling on prospective families for congregation
❑ Writing postcards to children who attended VBS

Name ______________________________

Phone ______________________________

If you have any questions about Vacation Bible School or your involvement in it, please call

____
(name and phone number)

PLEASE RETURN THIS FLYER IN THE OFFERING PLATE OR TO THE CHURCH OFFICE.

Join us for fun in the Son at Vacation Bible School.

Be a part of our Vacation Bible School program.
Put a check in the box next to the area(s) that interest(s) you the most.

Name ______________________________

Phone number ______________________

❏ Music Director
❏ Skit Director
❏ Bible Story Teacher
❏ Publicity Coordinator
❏ Craft Coordinator
❏ Counselor/Guide
❏ Snack Coordinator
❏ Bible Learning Activities Coordinator

❏ ______________________________

Return this form to ______________________________

Join us for fun in the Son at Vacation Bible School.

Be a part of our Vacation Bible School program.
Put a check in the box next to the area(s) that interest(s) you the most.

Name ______________________________

Phone number ______________________

❏ Music Director
❏ Skit Director
❏ Bible Story Teacher
❏ Publicity Coordinator
❏ Craft Coordinator
❏ Counselor/Guide
❏ Snack Coordinator
❏ Bible Learning Activities Coordinator

❏ ______________________________

Return this form to ______________________________

VBS Staff Record

Name ______________________________ Phone ______________

❏ Adult ❏ Middle School ❏ High School

Address ______________________________ City/Zip ______________

Job Placement ______________________________

Screening Info: ❏ Already on file ❏ New App. screened on ______________ (date)

Communication: ❏ In person ________ (date) ❏ Called ________ (date) ❏ Wrote ________ (date)

Response ______________________________

____

____

____

____

Name ______________________________

VBS Staff Record

Name ______________________________ Phone ______________

❏ Adult ❏ Middle School ❏ High School

Address ______________________________ City/Zip ______________

Job Placement ______________________________

Screening Info: ❏ Already on file ❏ New App. screened on ______________ (date)

Communication: ❏ In person ________ (date) ❏ Called ________ (date) ❏ Wrote ________ (date)

Response ______________________________

____

____

____

____

Name ______________________________

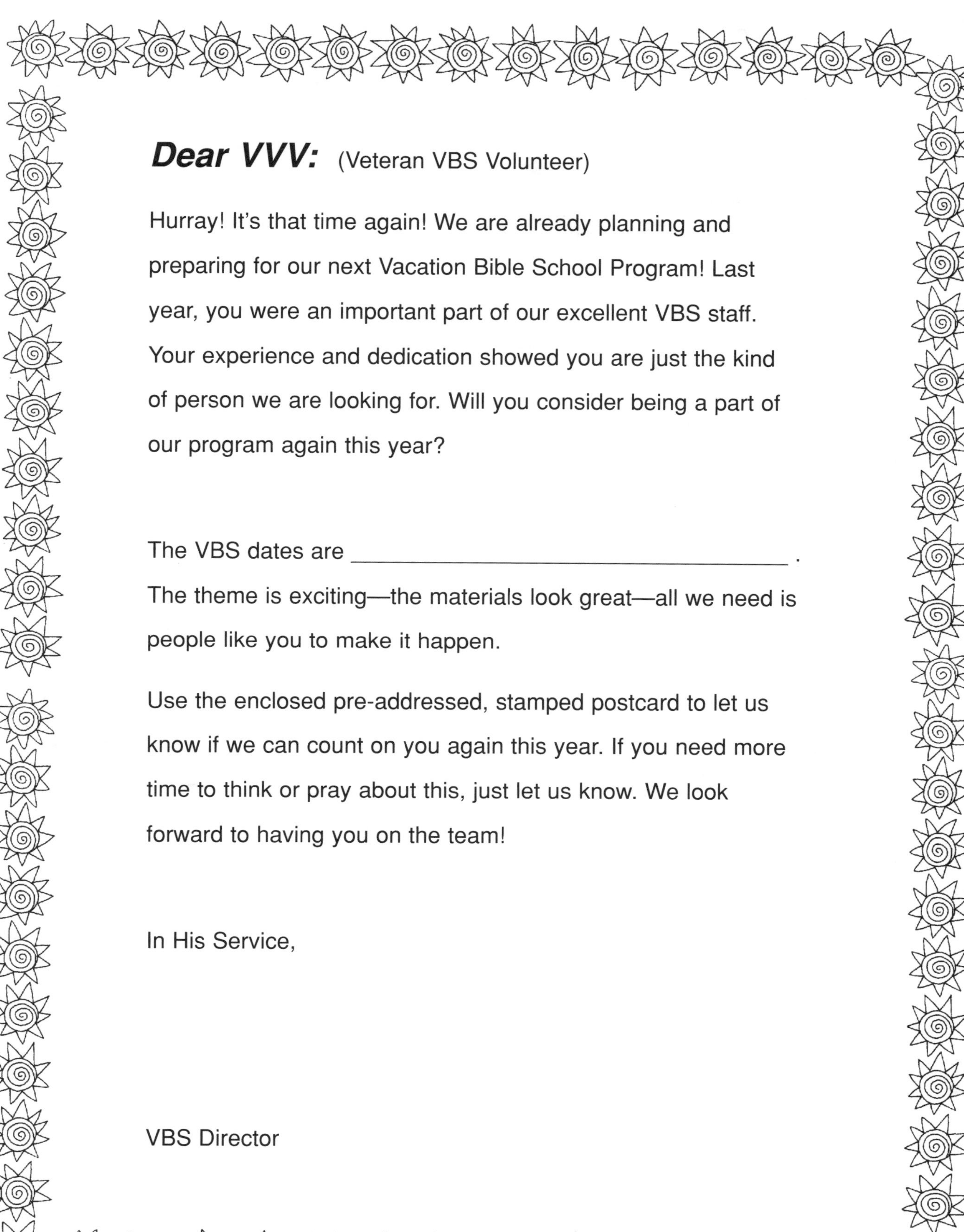

Dear VVV: (Veteran VBS Volunteer)

Hurray! It's that time again! We are already planning and preparing for our next Vacation Bible School Program! Last year, you were an important part of our excellent VBS staff. Your experience and dedication showed you are just the kind of person we are looking for. Will you consider being a part of our program again this year?

The VBS dates are ________________________________.
The theme is exciting—the materials look great—all we need is people like you to make it happen.

Use the enclosed pre-addressed, stamped postcard to let us know if we can count on you again this year. If you need more time to think or pray about this, just let us know. We look forward to having you on the team!

In His Service,

VBS Director

Dear VBS Director,

❑ YES,
I would like to serve at VBS.
The area I would like to serve in is

____

❑ NO,
I will not be able to serve in VBS this year, but I will be praying for you.

Name ____________________________________

Dear VBS Director,

❑ YES,
I would like to serve at VBS.
The area I would like to serve in is

____

❑ NO,
I will not be able to serve in VBS this year, but I will be praying for you.

Name ____________________________________

Adult VBS Volunteer Application Form

Name ______________________________

Address ______________________________

Phone (home) ______________________ (work) ______________________

How long have you been at that address? ______________________

Are you a member of ______________________? ( ) Yes ( ) No
(name of church)

How long have you been attending? ______________________

If not, what is your home church? ______________________

Please list other churches where you have regularly attended in the last five years.

____

Have you ever been charged with or convicted of child abuse or a crime involving actual or attempted sexual molestation of a minor? ( ) Yes ( ) No

If yes, please explain. ______________________

Have you ever worked at a church before in a ministry or other work involving either children or youth? ( ) Yes ( ) No

If yes, where did you work and what did you do? ______________________

____

PERSONAL REFERENCES:

Name ______________	Name ______________
Address ______________	Address ______________
______________	______________
Phone ______________	Phone ______________
Years Known ______________	Years Known ______________

APPLICANT'S STATEMENT

The information contained in this application is true and correct to the best of my knowledge. I authorize any of the above references or churches to give you any information that they may have regarding my character and fitness to work with youth or children.

Signature ______________________ Date ______________

Driver Application Form

(Each time participants are transported by private vehicle as part of a church-sponsored out-of-town event or activity, the driver is required to complete all statements on this form. The minimum age for all drivers is twenty-five years; maximum age is sixty-five years. In order to protect the interests of both the driver and our church the following information needs to be on file before any trip takes place. **A driver may transport participants only after the driver has completed and signed this form.)**

Driver's name ____

Driver's license number ______________________ Expiration date _____________

Do you have any physical condition or are you
taking any medication which would affect driving safety? ( ) yes ( ) no

If yes, explain. ____

Have you been cited for a moving violation and/or accident within the past year? ( ) yes ( ) no

If yes, explain. ____

Has your license ever been suspended or revoked? ( ) yes ( ) no

If yes, explain. ____

Registered owner of vehicle ______________________

Year of vehicle _______ Make of vehicle __________ Vehicle license _____________

How many working seat belts are in your vehicle? _______ Seating capacity of vehicle? _______

Does your vehicle have any known mechanical or safety deficiencies? ( ) yes ( ) no

Do you have liability insurance? ( ) yes ( ) no

Name of liability carrier ____

Policy number ____________________ Policy expiration date ________________

Is this an assigned risk policy? ( ) yes ( ) no

NOTE: In case of accident or claim with a private vehicle, your insurance listed above may provide your only coverage.

I certify that the answers provided are true and correct to the best of my knowledge.

Signature of driver ________________________________ Date ___________

Address ____________________________________ Phone _____________

The above driver has been APPROVED for trips or activities.

Pastor or Children's Director ____________________________ Date ___________

VBS Teen Helper Application Form

Name ______________________________

Address ______________________________ Phone ______________

Are you a member of our church? ❑ Yes ❑ No
How long have you been attending our church? ____________

Have you ever worked with a ministry involving children? ❑ Yes ❑ No

If so, what did you do? ______________________________

____

Who was your adult supervisor? ______________________________

What did you enjoy most about the experience? ______________________________

____

With which age group are you most comfortable?
❑ Preschool ❑ Kindergarten ❑ Primary ❑ Middler ❑ Junior

With which activities are you most comfortable?
❑ Bible Story/Application ❑ Crafts ❑ Music ❑ Games ❑ Bible Learning Activities

Are you available to work every day during VBS? ❑ Yes ❑ No

If not, which days are you available? ______________________________

Please give two adult references.

Name ____________________ Name ____________________

Address ____________________ Address ____________________

____________________ ____________________

Phone ____________ Years Known ____ Phone ____________ Years Known ____

This information is true and correct to the best of my knowledge. I authorize everyone named above to give you information they may have regarding my character and ability to work with children.

Signature ______________________________ Date ____________

Teen Helper Commitment Form

Name ____

Address ____

City ______________________________ Zip ________________

Phone ________________________ Grade in fall ______________

PLEASE READ AND SIGN.

REALIZING THAT BEING A YOUTH VOLUNTEER FOR VBS IS AN HONOR AND A PRIVILEGED PLACE OF SERVICE FOR THE LORD, I COMMIT THE FOLLOWING:

My time

I will attend all general VBS meetings and any department training sessions (dates will be announced at the orientation meeting).

I will prepare for my VBS responsibilities and arrive Monday through Friday,

____________________________ (dates), at ____________ (AM) ____________ (PM).

I will participate in the closing program/open house on ____________________.

My energies

I will exhibit responsibility, dependability and integrity. I understand VBS to be a children's program. My leadership will be for the children. Their safety and enjoyment will be my primary focus.

My accountability

I understand that if my leadership comes into question I will be spoken to and, if continue concern occurs, I may be asked to step out of VBS.

Signature ____

PARENT—PLEASE READ AND SIGN.

I have read the above commitment and stand in support of ____________________ to serve in Vacation Bible School. I understand the time and date commitments for this VBS ministry.

Signature ____

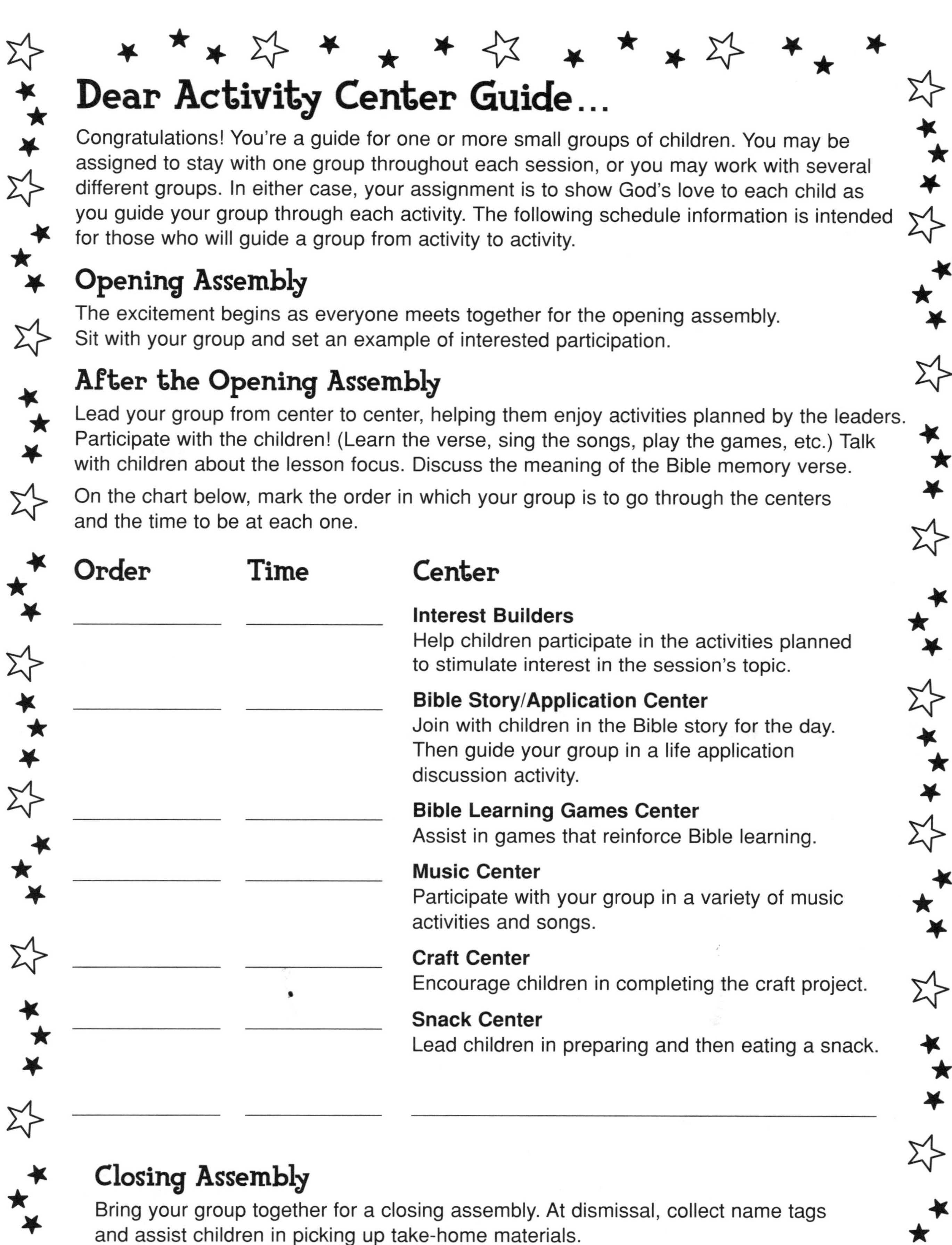

Dear Activity Center Guide...

Congratulations! You're a guide for one or more small groups of children. You may be assigned to stay with one group throughout each session, or you may work with several different groups. In either case, your assignment is to show God's love to each child as you guide your group through each activity. The following schedule information is intended for those who will guide a group from activity to activity.

Opening Assembly

The excitement begins as everyone meets together for the opening assembly. Sit with your group and set an example of interested participation.

After the Opening Assembly

Lead your group from center to center, helping them enjoy activities planned by the leaders. Participate with the children! (Learn the verse, sing the songs, play the games, etc.) Talk with children about the lesson focus. Discuss the meaning of the Bible memory verse.

On the chart below, mark the order in which your group is to go through the centers and the time to be at each one.

Order	Time	Center
____________	____________	**Interest Builders** Help children participate in the activities planned to stimulate interest in the session's topic.
____________	____________	**Bible Story/Application Center** Join with children in the Bible story for the day. Then guide your group in a life application discussion activity.
____________	____________	**Bible Learning Games Center** Assist in games that reinforce Bible learning.
____________	____________	**Music Center** Participate with your group in a variety of music activities and songs.
____________	____________	**Craft Center** Encourage children in completing the craft project.
____________	____________	**Snack Center** Lead children in preparing and then eating a snack.
____________	____________	______________________________

Closing Assembly

Bring your group together for a closing assembly. At dismissal, collect name tags and assist children in picking up take-home materials.

Helpful Hints for Activity Center Guides

- ❑ Pray for each child in your group, asking for God's help in guiding them.
- ❑ Ahead of time, walk the route your group will take. Check entrances and exits as well as locations of restrooms and drinking fountains.
- ❑ Check with leaders about a signal telling when it's time for your group to move to the next center.
- ❑ When you arrive at a center, be prepared with a quick game in case the leader at that center is not quite ready.
- ❑ Learn each child's name, and use it often. To get a child's attention, say the child's name first. ("Allison, it's time to sit together on the floor.")
- ❑ Sit with your group: on the floor, at a table, etc.
- ❑ Give your attention to the children, not another guide. Treat each child as a favorite. Children who are new to the church and children who are "left out" will need your special attention.
- ❑ Focus your attention on what children are doing right. ("I like the way Erin asked Jake for the glue. Good work, Erin!") Avoid mostly noticing problems.
- ❑ When a child causes a problem, tell the child what to do rather than what to stop doing. ("Mariano, work only on your own paper. Let Keith finish his own work.") Positive guidance is better than negative.
- ❑ Help a child who is having problems getting along or following directions. Sit by the child; separate children who don't work well together.
- ❑ If a problem behavior continues, talk with the activity leader about how to deal with that child.

Helpful Hints for Activity Center Guides

- ❑ Pray for each child in your group, asking for God's help in guiding them.
- ❑ Ahead of time, walk the route your group will take. Check entrances and exits as well as locations of restrooms and drinking fountains.
- ❑ Check with leaders about a signal telling when it's time for your group to move to the next center.
- ❑ When you arrive at a center, be prepared with a quick game in case the leader at that center is not quite ready.
- ❑ Learn each child's name, and use it often. To get a child's attention, say the child's name first. ("Allison, it's time to sit together on the floor.")
- ❑ Sit with your group: on the floor, at a table, etc.
- ❑ Give your attention to the children, not another guide. Treat each child as a favorite. Children who are new to the church and children who are "left out" will need your special attention.
- ❑ Focus your attention on what children are doing right. ("I like the way Erin asked Jake for the glue. Good work, Erin!") Avoid mostly noticing problems.
- ❑ When a child causes a problem, tell the child what to do rather than what to stop doing. ("Mariano, work only on your own paper. Let Keith finish his own work.") Positive guidance is better than negative.
- ❑ Help a child who is having problems getting along or following directions. Sit by the child; separate children who don't work well together.
- ❑ If a problem behavior continues, talk with the activity leader about how to deal with that child.

Working Successfully with Teen Helpers

Having a young person assist you will bring some added responsibilities as well as benefits. Here are a few tips to make this a positive experience for you, the young person, and the children:

- ❑ Begin praying for your young helper that he or she will enjoy positive growth through this ministry opportunity.
- ❑ Talk to your youth guide before VBS. Tell him or her several reasons why you are glad you'll be working together (e.g., "I've been told you're a very caring person," etc.).
- ❑ Find out the type of activities the young person enjoys and any experience he or she has had working with children.
- ❑ Plan each session's tasks for the young person to do. Seek to avoid "dead time" when the young person feels unneeded.
- ❑ Do not limit young people to "flunky" jobs, but be alert to assigning jobs the young person will view as being meaningful.
- ❑ Emphasize the importance of learning each child's name and building friendships with each one. Encourage the young person to look for moments to sit next to a child and become better friends.
- ❑ Give lots of praise and encouragement. Feelings of nervousness and uncertainty probably will not show under a teenager's facade of being "cool." However, the young person's confidence and satisfaction depend to a great extent on your affirmation of things done well.
- ❑ Take a few minutes at the end of the session to review how things went and to prepare the young person for the next session.

Working Successfully with Teen Helpers

Having a young person assist you will bring some added responsibilities as well as benefits. Here are a few tips to make this a positive experience for you, the young person, and the children:

- ❑ Begin praying for your young helper that he or she will enjoy positive growth through this ministry opportunity.
- ❑ Talk to your youth guide before VBS. Tell him or her several reasons why you are glad you'll be working together (e.g., "I've been told you're a very caring person," etc.).
- ❑ Find out the type of activities the young person enjoys and any experience he or she has had working with children.
- ❑ Plan each session's tasks for the young person to do. Seek to avoid "dead time" when the young person feels unneeded.
- ❑ Do not limit young people to "flunky" jobs, but be alert to assigning jobs the young person will view as being meaningful.
- ❑ Emphasize the importance of learning each child's name and building friendships with each one. Encourage the young person to look for moments to sit next to a child and become better friends.
- ❑ Give lots of praise and encouragement. Feelings of nervousness and uncertainty probably will not show under a teenager's facade of being "cool." However, the young person's confidence and satisfaction depend to a great extent on your affirmation of things done well.
- ❑ Take a few minutes at the end of the session to review how things went and to prepare the young person for the next session.

Departmental Personnel

	Early Childhood	Primary	Middler	Junior	Youth
Department Leader(s)					
Craft Leader(s)					
Teacher(s)					
Assistant(s)					
Skit Characters					

General Personnel

Missions	Music	Follow-Up
Publicity	Recreation	Bible Learning Activities
Finance	Prayer	Snacks
Crafts	Skits	Registration

Craft Personnel

Coordinator ______________________ Assistant(s) ______________________

Department	Craft Leader(s)	Teacher(s)
Early Childhood		
Primary		
Middler		
Junior		

Craft Personnel

Coordinator ______________________ Assistant(s) ______________________

Department	Craft Leader(s)	Teacher(s)
Early Childhood		
Primary		
Middler		
Junior		

VBS Staff Training and Fellowship

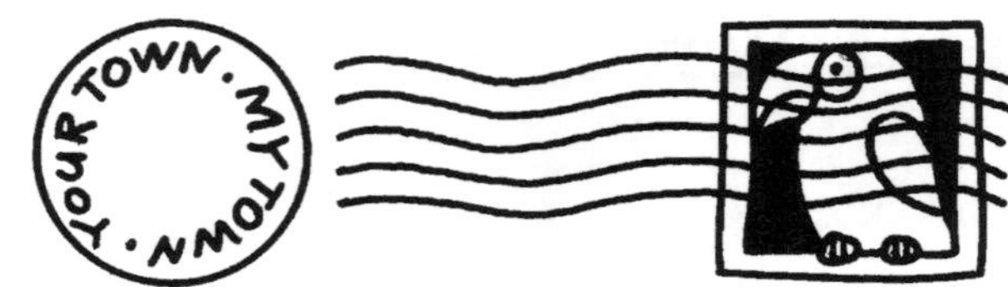

VBS is approaching and it's time to get geared up. We will be introducing our exciting program and have lots to show you! We will also have a fun time of fellowship as we begin to build our team. Don't miss this very important meeting!

____
(Name of VBS Director)

Date ____________________ Time ____________________

Place ______________________________________

If you cannot attend, please let me know.

VBS Staff Training and Fellowship

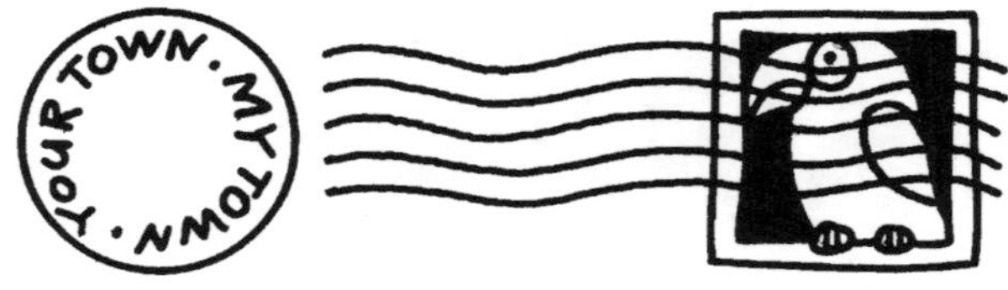

VBS is approaching and it's time to get geared up. We will be introducing our exciting program and have lots to show you! We will also have a fun time of fellowship as we begin to build our team. Don't miss this very important meeting!

____
(Name of VBS Director)

Date ____________________ Time ____________________

Place ______________________________________

If you cannot attend, please let me know.

VBS Staff Meeting Planning Sheet

VBS Materials Needed

- ❑ ____________________
- ❑ ____________________
- ❑ ____________________
- ❑ ____________________
- ❑ ____________________
- ❑ ____________________
- ❑ ____________________
- ❑ ____________________

Equipment Needed (audio-visual, tables, chairs)

- ❑ ____________________
- ❑ ____________________
- ❑ ____________________
- ❑ ____________________
- ❑ ____________________
- ❑ ____________________
- ❑ ____________________
- ❑ ____________________

Room Preparation Ideas ____________________

____

____

Refreshments ____________________

____

____

Announcements to be made ____________________

____

____

Agenda ____________________

____

____

____

____

DON'T FORGET

❑ Send flyers ❑ Make reminder calls ❑ Make name tags ❑ ____________________

VBS DAILY GAZETTE
VBS STAFF NEWS
REMINDERS
ANNOUNCEMENTS
THINGS TO DO TODAY
LAST SESSION'S ATTENDANCE

VBS Staff Evaluation

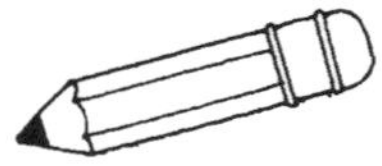

Thanks for being part of our Vacation Bible School!
Please complete the following evaluation form to help us plan for next year's program.

My job at VBS was ______________________________

1. My preparation for VBS was: (circle one)

   easy   manageable   time-consuming   overwhelming

   Comments:

2. Were the printed materials you received easy to understand and follow? Explain.

3. What, if any, instructions, materials or guides could have better prepared you for your assignment?

4. How well did the VBS time schedule work for you?

5. What aspects of VBS did you enjoy most?

6. What aspects of VBS did your students enjoy most?

7. Did you sense God's presence in this ministry? Was it an effective outreach?

8. What areas of VBS could be improved?

9. Would you consider being involved in VBS again? _____Yes _____No _____Same Job

   Different Job ______________________________

Letter to the Pastor

Dear (Name of Pastor),

This letter is to let you know how you can be a part of our very special Vacation Bible School. You are an important part of our church and greatly admired by our children. We would like you to see Vacation Bible School as a special opportunity to relate with the children in our church and community. I have listed several suggestions on how you can be involved before, during and after our VBS program. Please take the time to read this, and let me know what works best for you! Thanks!

In His Service,

(VBS Director's Signature)
VBS Director

Before VBS

- ❏ **Communicate with me!** I need to know I have your support as I embark on this responsibility. Your interest and input in our plans is so important to me. I would love to meet briefly with you on a regular basis so I can keep you up-to-date.
- ❏ **Promote VBS to the congregation.** Your positive comments have a big impact on our congregation. I need your help in promoting VBS in order to recruit and communicate our VBS vision. Please keep us in mind when making announcements, in your newsletters, etc.
- ❏ **Pray for us.** Please keep me, our volunteers and the children who will be attending VBS in your prayers.
- ❏ **Help with our dedication service.** I would like to use the Sunday before VBS as a time for dedicating our volunteers. Let me know if this can be done and how you would like to do it.

During VBS

- ❏ **Be visible.** I will give you the schedule of VBS classes and their locations. Choose different locations to visit briefly each day. I know our volunteers would love to see your support and be able to talk with you.
- ❏ **Come to our assemblies.** I would like to introduce all the children to you on one of the days. Also, we would love to have you be a part of our assemblies in any way you can.
- ❏ **Greet parents.** Several unchurched parents will be dropping their children off near our registration table. It would be great to have you present so that newcomers can meet you.
- ❏ **Talk to the kids.** Do you know how special it is to a child to have the pastor acknowledge them? Even just a "hello" or smile can mean a lot! This is a great time to let the children get to know you better.
- ❏ **Come to our closing celebration.** On (date of closing celebration) we will be having a closing celebration for the families of our students. I would love to have you at this program to share something with the families, to invite them to our church and to close in prayer. Your involvement will mean a great deal to visitors.

After VBS

- ❏ **Inform our congregation.** I would like our congregation to know the results of our VBS and any comments you had about it. Also, a general appreciation for all our volunteers would make them feel special.
- ❏ **Reach out to visitors.** Assist in planning effective ways to reach our unchurched VBS families. Our teachers will follow up individually, but they will need help in making these families feel welcomed and getting them plugged in.

Pastor's Daily Schedule

Day/Date ____

Time	Age-Group	Room	Assignment

(NOTE: Make a copy for each day of VBS.)

Record of VBS Expenses

DATE	DESCRIPTION	QUANTITY	COST (Enter in proper column)					
			Curriculum	Supplies	Crafts	Snacks	Misc.	Purchaser

VBS General Receipt Ledger

Use this ledger to keep track of money spent. Attach receipts to corner and submit to ______________________

Item	Used For	$ Amount	Date
	Total $		

Submitted by ______________________ Approved by ______________________

VBS General Receipt Ledger

Use this ledger to keep track of money spent. Attach receipts to corner and submit to ______________________

Item	Used For	$ Amount	Date
	Total $		

Submitted by ______________________ Approved by ______________________

List of Supplies Needed

Please make a list of all the VBS supplies you will need and submit list to

____

Item	Quantity	Color	Size	Date Needed By
1.				
2.				
3.				
4.				
5.				
6.				
7.				
8.				
9.				
10.				
11.				
12.				
13.				
14.				

Submitted by ____

Supply Checklist

Department ________________________ Date of Request ____________________

Teacher Requesting ____

SUPPLY	QUANTITY NEEDED
Pencils	
Crayons	
Child's scissors (right-handed and left-handed)	
Teacher scissors	
Glue (bottles)	
Glue sticks	
Clear cellophane tape	
1-inch masking tape roll	
Water-based markers (wide)	
Water-based markers (narrow)	
Ruler	
Measuring stick	
9"x12" construction paper (multi-color)	
12"x18" construction paper (multi-color)	
White poster board	
Other:	

Snack Supplies List

Snack Coordinator ___________________________________

	Name of Snack	Ingredients Needed	Kitchen Supplies Needed	Items Purchased By
Session 1				
Session 2				
Session 3				
Session 4				
Session 5				

Recreation Schedule

Recreation Coordinator ______________________________

	Game and Brief Instructions	Supplies Needed
Session 1		
Session 2		
Session 3		
Session 4		
Session 5		

Publicity & Announcements

VBS BANNER

Where Posted? ______________________ When Posted? ______________________

______________________ ______________________

VBS POSTERS

______________________ ______________________

______________________ ______________________

______________________ ______________________

VBS FLYERS

Where Distributed? ______________________ When Distributed? ______________________

______________________ ______________________

______________________ ______________________

______________________ ______________________

______________________ ______________________

VBS ANNOUNCEMENTS

Script ____

____

____

____

____

Dates for announcement ____

Person making announcement ____

Contact for questions ______________________________ Phone ______________

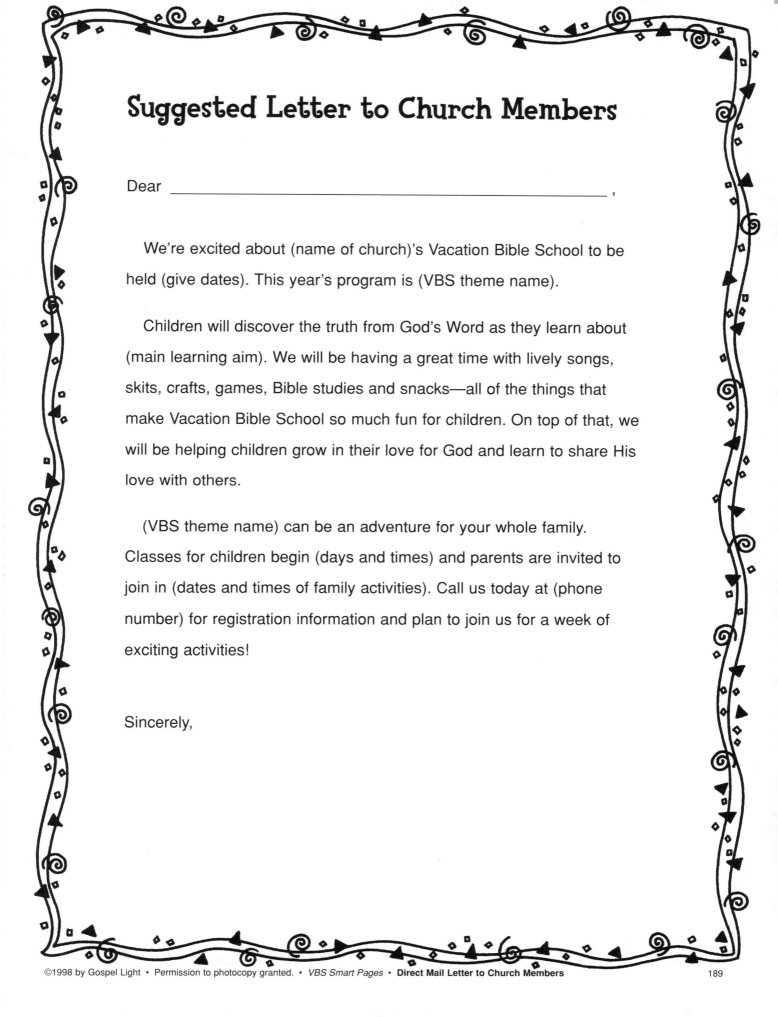

Suggested Letter to Church Members

Dear ____,

We're excited about (name of church)'s Vacation Bible School to be held (give dates). This year's program is (VBS theme name).

Children will discover the truth from God's Word as they learn about (main learning aim). We will be having a great time with lively songs, skits, crafts, games, Bible studies and snacks—all of the things that make Vacation Bible School so much fun for children. On top of that, we will be helping children grow in their love for God and learn to share His love with others.

(VBS theme name) can be an adventure for your whole family. Classes for children begin (days and times) and parents are invited to join in (dates and times of family activities). Call us today at (phone number) for registration information and plan to join us for a week of exciting activities!

Sincerely,

Suggested Letter to Community

Dear ____,

I'd (We'd) like to invite your children and their friends to join us for a fun-filled, exciting program that will add a new dimension to their lives. (VBS theme name) is this year's Vacation Bible School to be held (give dates) at (name of church). Children will have a great time with lively songs, skits, crafts, games, Bible stories and snacks—all of the things that make Vacation Bible School so much fun. On top of that, children will be encouraged to grow in their love for God as they learn about (main learning aim).

Enroll your children now in (name of church)'s Vacation Bible School by calling us at (church phone number). Have them join their friends for a week of fun activities!

Sincerely,

Invitation

(name of family or person[s] you're inviting)

You are invited to join the fun at the

(name of closing program)

starring

(child's name)

and other special friends.

(place)

(date/time)

Registration will begin at ______________________ each day.
(time)

Please arrive prepared and on time.

1. Give a warm welcome to parents, caregivers and children.

2. Ask for each child's full name and greet each child by his or her first name.

3. Hand parents or caregivers all appropriate registration forms and a pen. Ask him or her to fill out all the information on the forms.

4. While caregiver is filling out the forms, add the child's name to the appropriate roster. Then, make a name tag for the child.

5. After forms have been completed, briefly check to see that all pertinent information is filled out.

6. Give child name tag, VBS button, etc. Tell child the name of his or her teacher, where to find the class and thank child by name for being a part of your VBS.

7. Tell caregiver when, where and how to pick up his or her child. Hand out any information about your program.

8. Check "Day One" square next to the child's name for attendance purposes.

VBS Registration

Name ______________________________

Street Address ______________________________

City ____________________ State __________ Zip __________

Home phone (__________) ______________________________

Parent(s) name(s) ______________________________

Parent(s) work phone ______________________________

In case of emergency, contact ______________________________

Allergies or other medical conditions ______________________________

Doctor's name ______________________________

Doctor's phone ______________________________

Date of Birth ____________________ School grade just completed __________

School child attends ______________________________

Name of home church, if any ______________________________

Nursery/Toddler VBS Registration Card

(FOR VOLUNTEERS' CHILDREN ONLY)

Child's Name ______________________ Date of Birth ____________

Volunteer Parent's Name ______________________ VBS Duty ____________

Location during VBS ______________________

Feeding Times ______________________

List any allergies ______________________

What comforts your child (pacifier, favorite toys, blanket, singing, etc.)?

____

Nap schedule for your child? ______________________ Toilet trained? ❑ No ❑ Yes

Other helpful information ______________________

Nursery/Toddler VBS Registration Card

(FOR VOLUNTEERS' CHILDREN ONLY)

Child's Name ______________________ Date of Birth ____________

Volunteer Parent's Name ______________________ VBS Duty ____________

Location during VBS ______________________

Feeding Times ______________________

List any allergies ______________________

What comforts your child (pacifier, favorite toys, blanket, singing, etc.)?

____

Nap schedule for your child? ______________________ Toilet trained? ❑ No ❑ Yes

Other helpful information ______________________

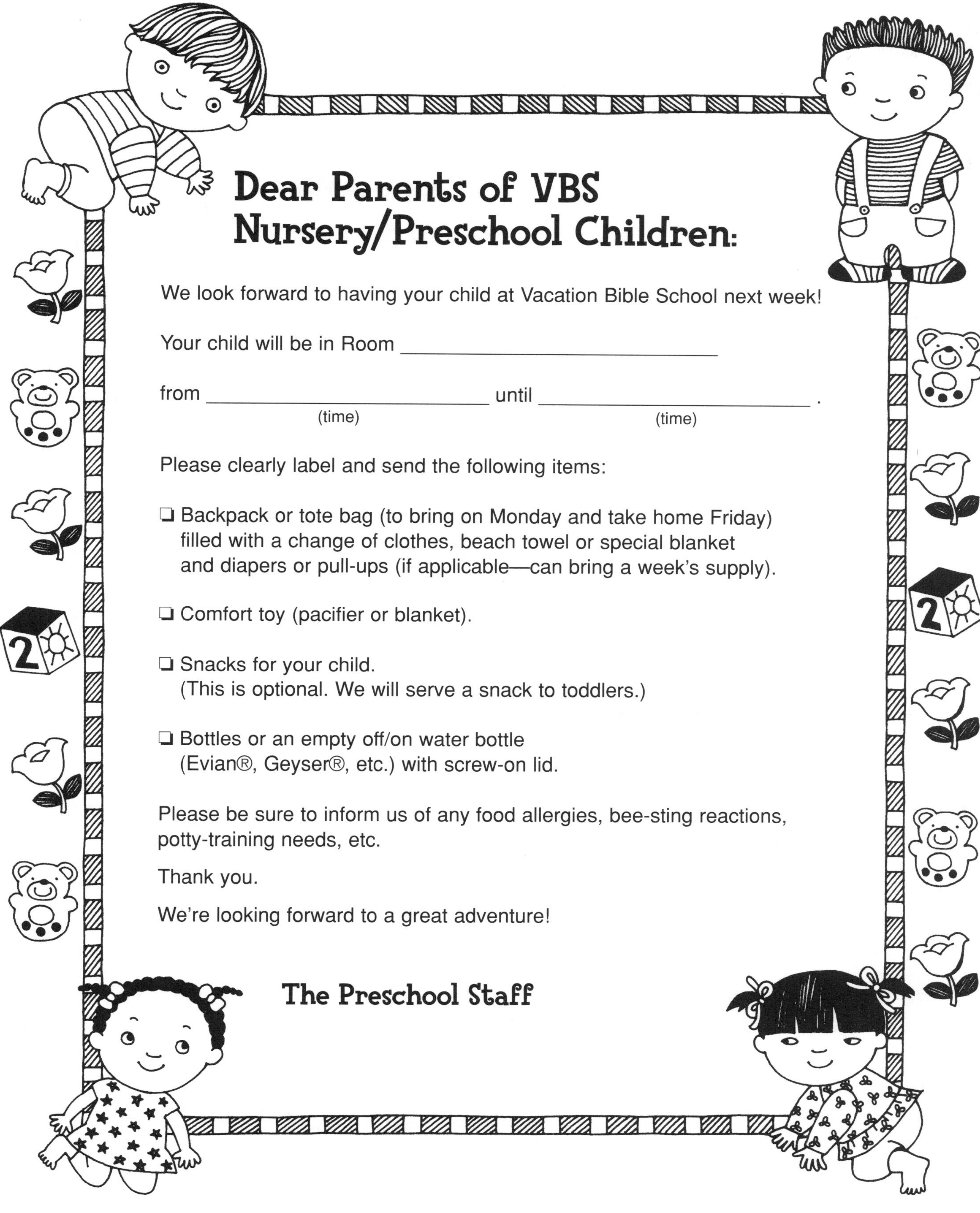

Dear Parents of VBS Nursery/Preschool Children:

We look forward to having your child at Vacation Bible School next week!

Your child will be in Room ______________________________

from ___________________________ until __________________________ .
(time) (time)

Please clearly label and send the following items:

- ❑ Backpack or tote bag (to bring on Monday and take home Friday) filled with a change of clothes, beach towel or special blanket and diapers or pull-ups (if applicable—can bring a week's supply).
- ❑ Comfort toy (pacifier or blanket).
- ❑ Snacks for your child. (This is optional. We will serve a snack to toddlers.)
- ❑ Bottles or an empty off/on water bottle (Evian®, Geyser®, etc.) with screw-on lid.

Please be sure to inform us of any food allergies, bee-sting reactions, potty-training needs, etc.

Thank you.

We're looking forward to a great adventure!

The Preschool Staff

VBS Roster/Attendance Form

Grade ______ **Teacher's Name** ____________________ **Class/Group** ____________

Child's Name / Phone Number	DAY 1		DAY 2		DAY 3		DAY 4		DAY 5	
	Here	Brought visitor	Here	Brought visitor	Here	Brought visitor	Here	Brought visitor	Here	Brought visitor
1.										
2.										
3.										
4.										
5.										
6.										
7.										
8.										
9.										
10.										
11.										
12.										
13.										
14.										
15.										
16.										
17.										
18.										

VBS Total Attendance Tally

Class/Group	Session 1	Session 2	Session 3	Session 4	Session 5
Total Student Attendance					
VBS Staff					

Average Student Attendance ____________

Vacation Bible School

Date ______________________________

Department ________________________

Children ________________________

Staff ___________________________

Total Attendance ____________________

Missions Offering $ _______________

Vacation Bible School

Date ______________________________

Department ________________________

Children ________________________

Staff ___________________________

Total Attendance ____________________

Missions Offering $ _______________

Vacation Bible School

Date ______________________________

Department ________________________

Children ________________________

Staff ___________________________

Total Attendance ____________________

Missions Offering $ _______________

Vacation Bible School

Date ______________________________

Department ________________________

Children ________________________

Staff ___________________________

Total Attendance ____________________

Missions Offering $ _______________

Vacation Bible School

Counselor/Guide Name:____________________

	Monday	Tuesday	Wednesday	Thursday	Friday
# Kids					
$ Offering					

Vacation Bible School

Counselor/Guide Name:____________________

	Monday	Tuesday	Wednesday	Thursday	Friday
# Kids					
$ Offering					

Vacation Bible School

Counselor/Guide Name:____________________

	Monday	Tuesday	Wednesday	Thursday	Friday
# Kids					
$ Offering					

Vacation Bible School

Counselor/Guide Name:____________________

	Monday	Tuesday	Wednesday	Thursday	Friday
# Kids					
$ Offering					

Suggestions for Follow-up

Dear Teacher/Counselor,

Well, VBS is over, right? Wrong. Following up on our students is a crucial part of our VBS outreach ministry. VBS has planted many seeds in many lives. But many of these seeds need to be cared for by someone like you in order to grow and be nurtured. Follow-up is the essential process that must happen between planting and harvesting. Don't neglect this important step!

As a teacher/counselor, you have gotten to know your students well during VBS and are the best person to invite an unchurched child to Sunday School and church. I have enclosed a list of your students' names, addresses, phone numbers, parent's name and church affiliation. Here are some suggestions on practical ways that you can make a difference in the life of a child:

- ❏ Send a postcard or greeting card to each child. Write a personal note thanking the child for attending and adding any other special messages.
- ❏ Pray regularly for each student.
- ❏ Seek to become a friend by visiting their homes. Stop by a child's house and deliver a special gift package—homemade cookies, children's Bible or storybook, etc.
- ❏ Invite an unchurched family to church. Arrange transportation if needed.
- ❏ Introduce students to Sunday School teachers.
- ❏ Remember birthdays with cards or phone calls.
- ❏ Keep in touch throughout the year by sending cards and inviting them to special church events.
- ❏ Plan a family picnic or outing to help parents get acquainted in a comfortable setting.
- ❏ Share your own relationship with Christ as you talk with them about the significance of becoming a Christian.
- ❏ Plan a VBS reunion with your group. For example, host a pool party, a picnic at the park or a slumber party. (Ask a church family for assistance.)

Please let me know if I can assist you with any of these suggestions. Thanks again for your commitment to our VBS program and the children.

In His Service,

(VBS Director's Name)
VBS Director

Follow-up Card

Child's name ______________________________

Address ______________________________

______________________ Phone ____________

Parent's name(s) ______________________________

Decision made ________________ Date ____________

Other info. ______________ Teacher's name ____________

Review decision ❑ yes ❑ no   Present certificate ❑ yes ❑ no

Need a Bible ❑ yes ❑ no   Talk w/ Parent ❑ yes ❑ no

Follow-up Card

Child's name ______________________________

Address ______________________________

______________________ Phone ____________

Parent's name(s) ______________________________

Decision made ________________ Date ____________

Other info. ______________ Teacher's name ____________

Review decision ❑ yes ❑ no   Present certificate ❑ yes ❑ no

Need a Bible ❑ yes ❑ no   Talk w/ Parent ❑ yes ❑ no

Follow-up Card

Child's name ______________________________

Address ______________________________

______________________ Phone ____________

Parent's name(s) ______________________________

Decision made ________________ Date ____________

Other info. ______________ Teacher's name ____________

Review decision ❑ yes ❑ no   Present certificate ❑ yes ❑ no

Need a Bible ❑ yes ❑ no   Talk w/ Parent ❑ yes ❑ no

Follow-up Card

Child's name ______________________________

Address ______________________________

______________________ Phone ____________

Parent's name(s) ______________________________

Decision made ________________ Date ____________

Other info. ______________ Teacher's name ____________

Review decision ❑ yes ❑ no   Present certificate ❑ yes ❑ no

Need a Bible ❑ yes ❑ no   Talk w/ Parent ❑ yes ❑ no

Dear ______________________________,

(Name of VBS student)

Didn't we have a great time at Vacation Bible School? I enjoyed getting to know you and making new friends! Thanks for making it special! We would love to see you again at Sunday School and church. Hope to see you soon!

____

(Church)

Sunday School starts at ______________________

Children's Church starts at ______________________

Midweek Program starts at ______________________

Love, ______________________________

(VBS Teacher/Counselor)

(P.S. If you need a ride or have any questions, please call me. I would be happy to help you. We can't do the VBS week all over again, but we can get together and have fun all year! I'll be looking forward to seeing you!)

Dear ______________________________,

(Name of VBS student)

Didn't we have a great time at Vacation Bible School? I enjoyed getting to know you and making new friends! Thanks for making it special! We would love to see you again at Sunday School and church. Hope to see you soon!

____

(Church)

Sunday School starts at ______________________

Children's Church starts at ______________________

Midweek Program starts at ______________________

Love, ______________________________

(VBS Teacher/Counselor)

(P.S. If you need a ride or have any questions, please call me. I would be happy to help you. We can't do the VBS week all over again, but we can get together and have fun all year! I'll be looking forward to seeing you!)

Come ✓ Us Out!

We enjoyed having your child at Vacation Bible School and would like to invite you and your family to join us for regular services.

Sunday church services begin at ______________________________

Midweek Program held ______________________________

For other information, please call ______________________________

We'd love to see you!

____

(VBS Director or Pastor)

Come ✓ Us Out!

We enjoyed having your child at Vacation Bible School and would like to invite you and your family to join us for regular services.

Sunday church services begin at ______________________________

Midweek Program held ______________________________

For other information, please call ______________________________

We'd love to see you!

____

(VBS Director or Pastor)

Director's VBS Review

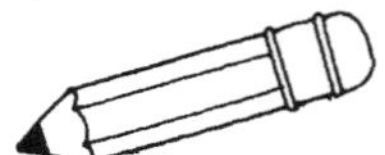

Name of VBS Program ______________________________

Date ______________________ Time ______________________

Name of VBS Director ______________________________

Number of Volunteers __________ Average Number of Students who Attended __________

Summary of Events ______________________________

____

____

____

____

____

____

____

____

____

Benefits ______________________________

____

____

Recommendations ______________________________

____

____

Awards and Certificates

The awards and certificates on the following pages may be personalized for various uses. Just follow these simple procedures:

1. Tear out certificate and letter the name of your program on the appropriate line.
2. Make as many copies of certificate as needed.
3. Letter each child's certificate with his or her name (and achievement when appropriate).

Thanks Sew Much
for Doing Your Part at

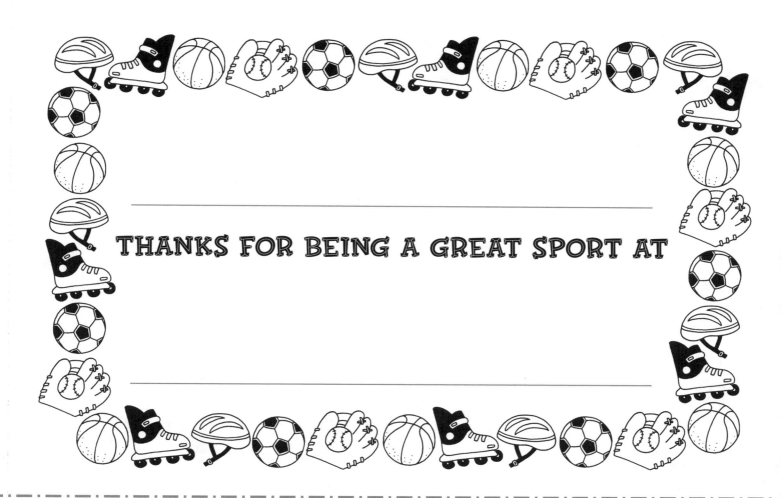

THANKS FOR BEING A GREAT SPORT AT

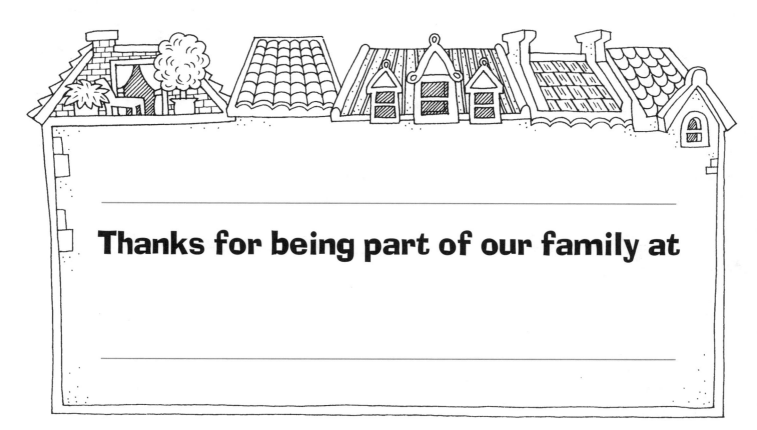

Thanks for being part of our family at

Thanks so much for

Thanks for playing your part at

Good Friend Award

____

was a good friend at

____

Good
Neighbor Award
was a good friend at

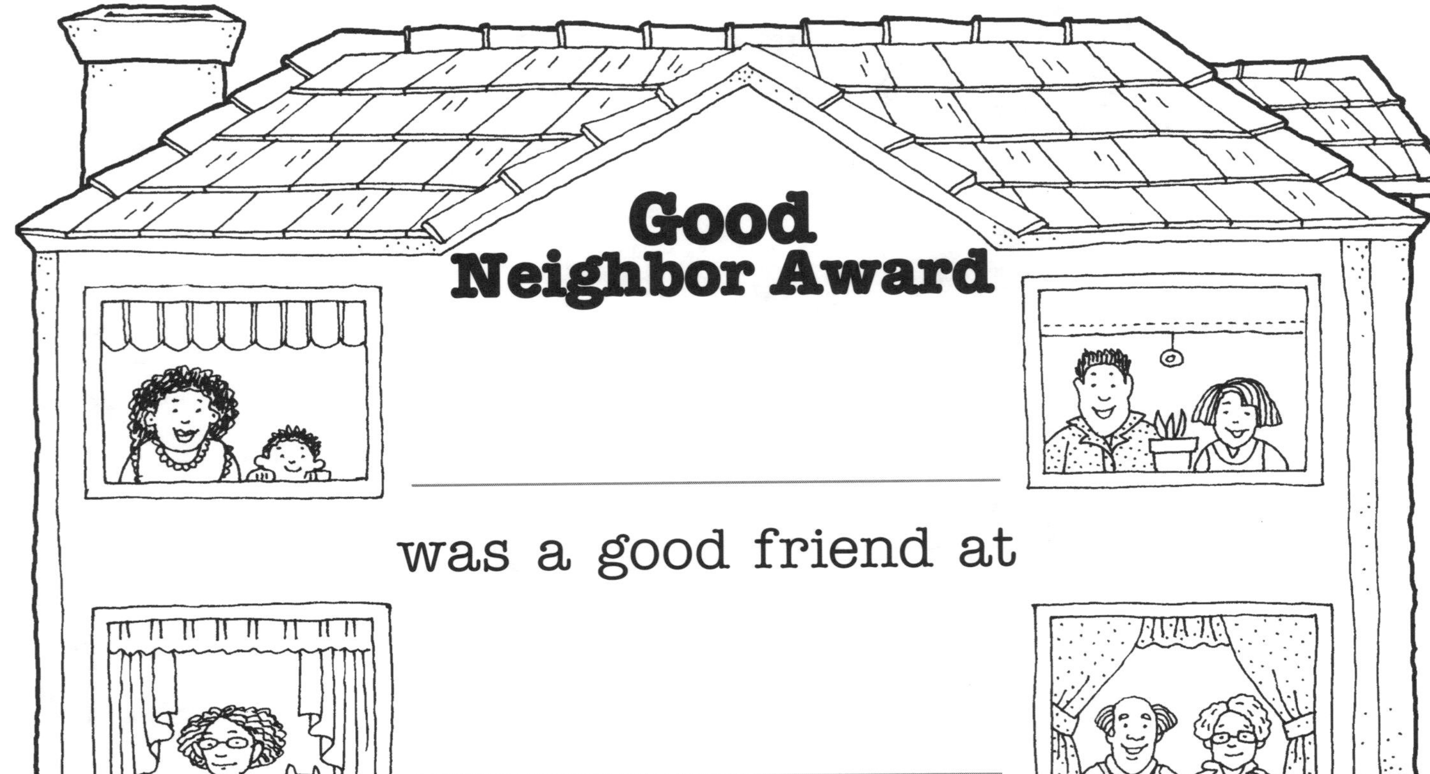

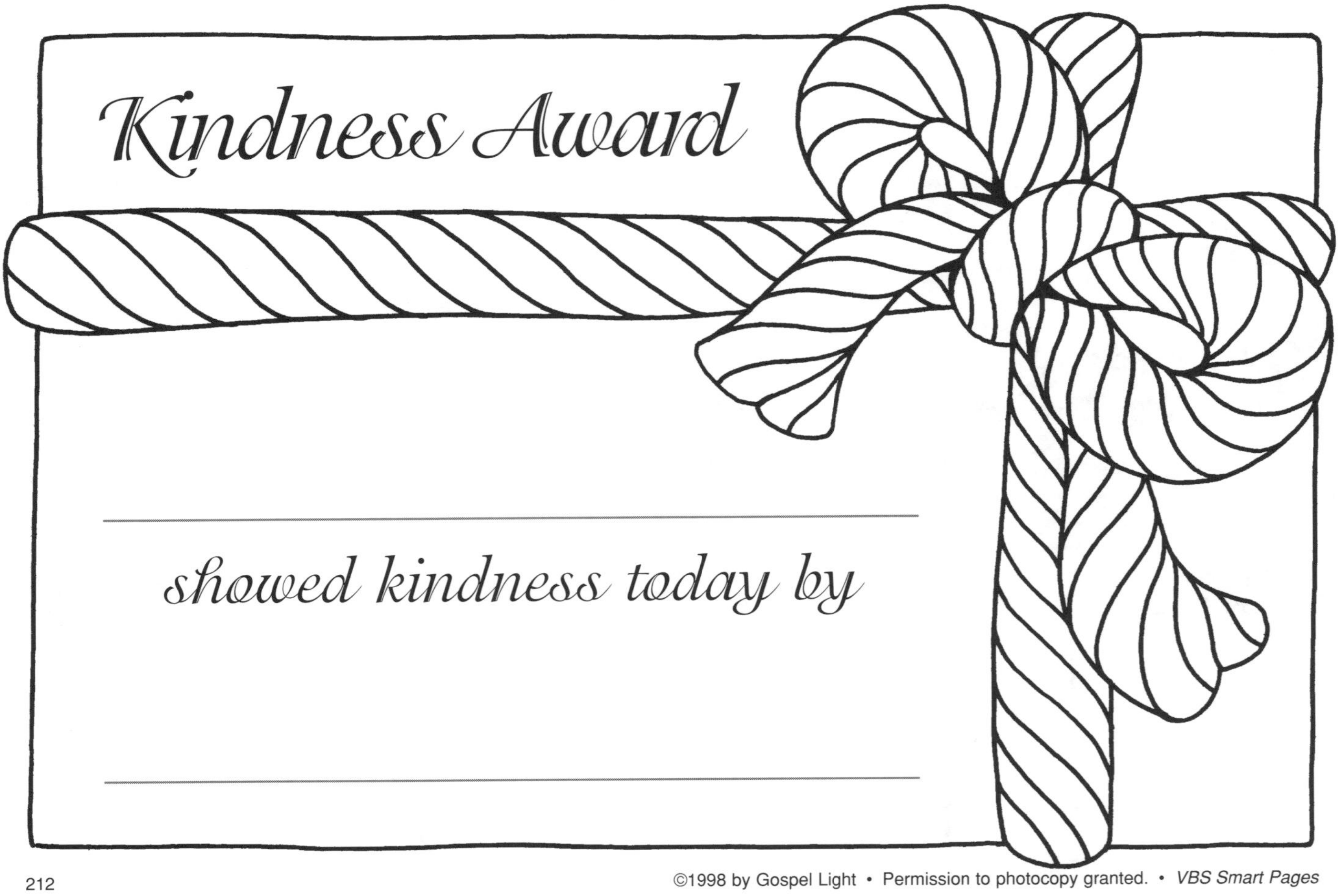

Kindness Award
showed kindness today by

Visitor Award

____

We're glad you came to

____

Visitor Award

We're glad you came to

Visitor Award

we're glad you came to

You are appreciated for

YOU ARE SPECIAL BECAUSE

You are appreciated for

YOU ARE SPECIAL BECAUSE

This special award
is given to
for

This special award
is given to
for

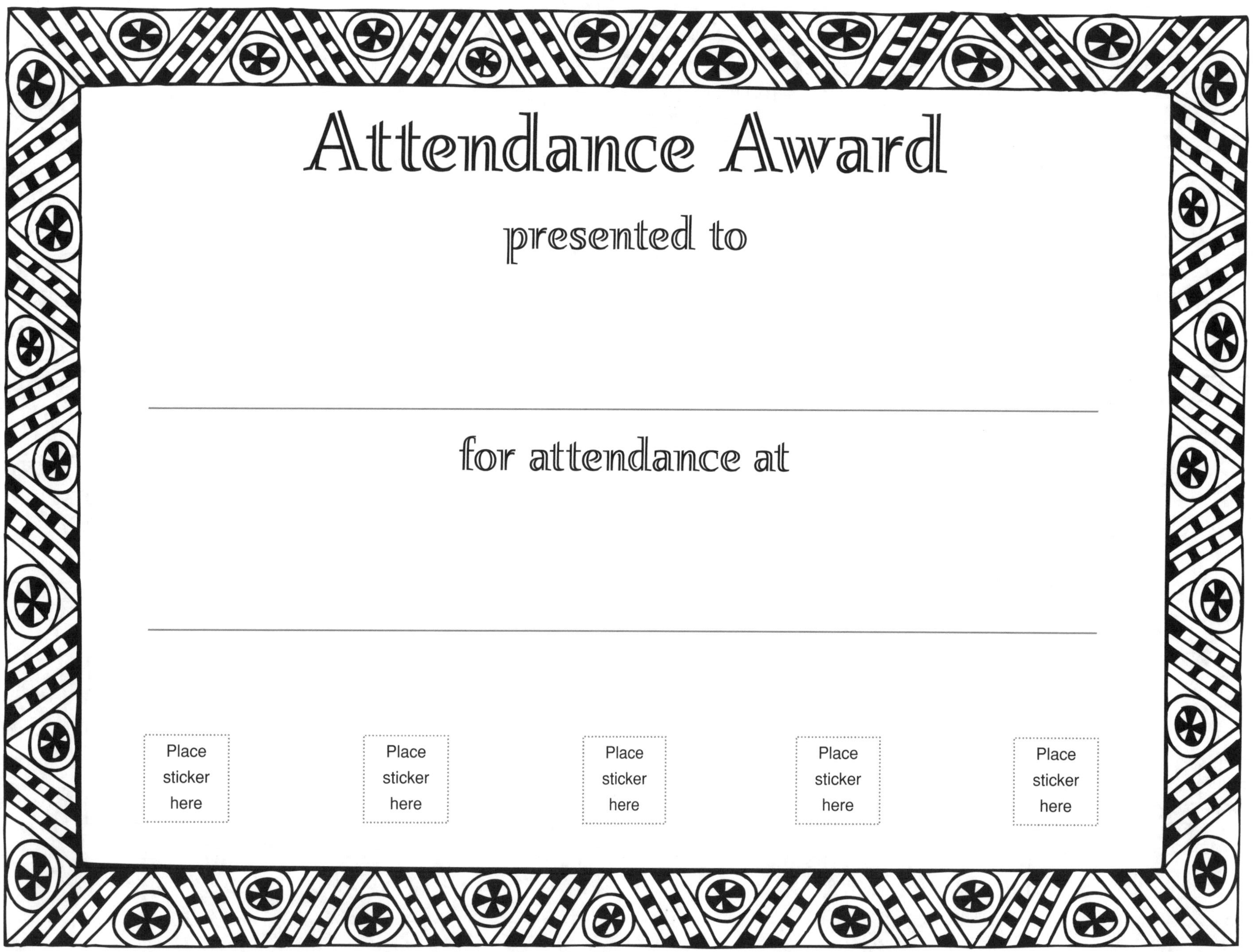
Attendance Award
presented to
for attendance at
Place sticker here
Place sticker here
Place sticker here
Place sticker here
Place sticker here

ATTENDANCE AWARD

PRESENTED TO

FOR ATTENDANCE AT

Place sticker here	Place sticker here	Place sticker here	Place sticker here	Place sticker here

When
What
Where
Come along

We need your
HELPING
HANDS

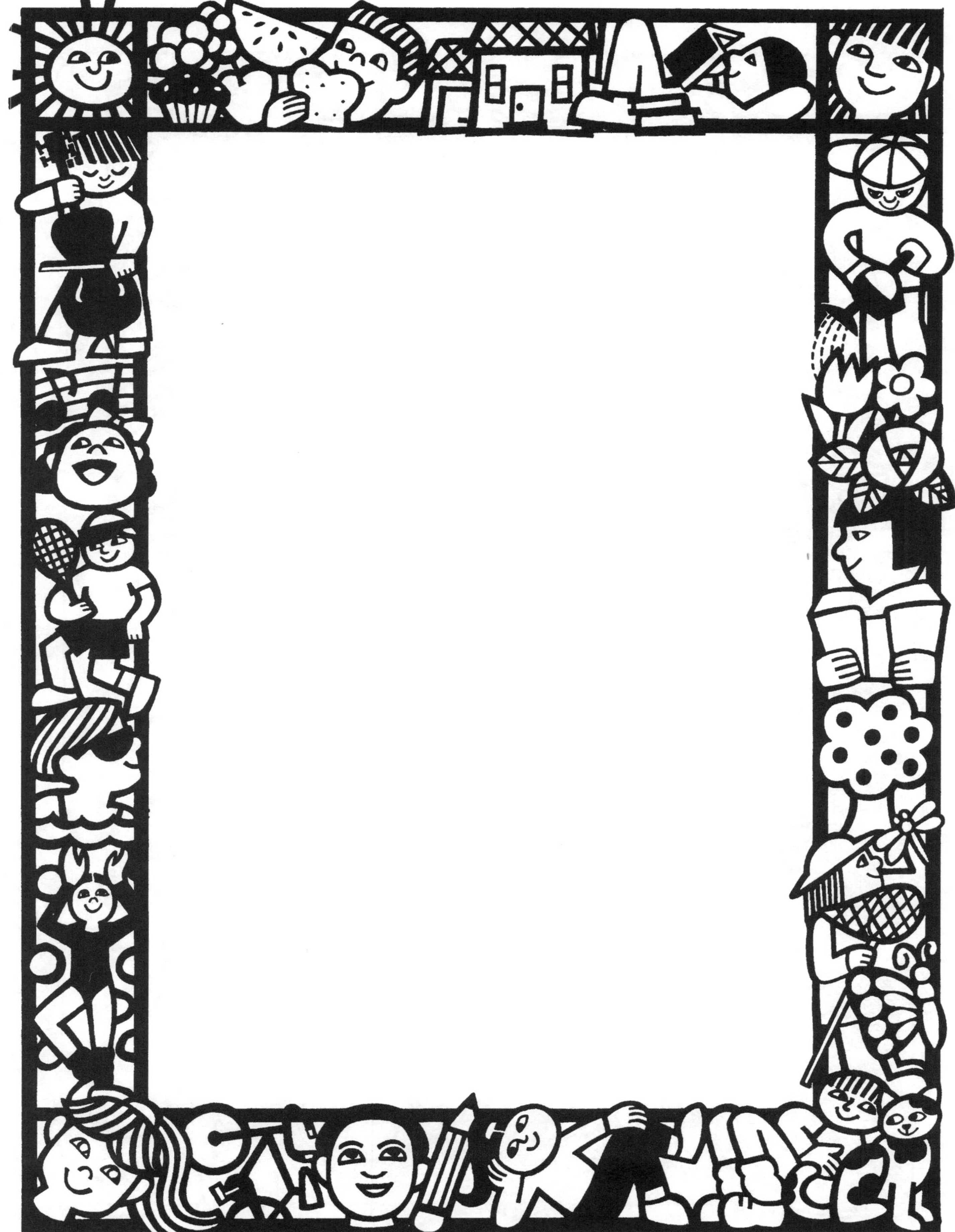

Bring a Friend!

You Just Made a Life-Changing Decision! You Are Now a Member of God's Family!

Notes:

If you have any questions
or concerns or just want to talk,
please call

____

____
(counselor's name)

at

____
(phone number)

"God loved us and sent his son."
1 John 4:10

CONGRATULATIONS!

Let's Review...

I became a child of God by:

* Knowing God loves me and wants me to have eternal life in Heaven with Him.
* Knowing I have done wrong things.
* Believing that Jesus died on the cross to take the punishment for my sins. Three days later He rose from the dead and is now my living Savior.
* Asking Jesus to forgive my sins.
* Wanting to spend time with God and do what is right.

New Life Certificate

I want everyone to know that

on ______________________
(month/day)

of ______________________
(year)

I, ______________________

______________________,
(name)

became a Christian (child of God).

Now What Do I Do?...

1. Spend time with God by reading His letter to me, the Bible. (Psalm 119:11)
2. Obey what God tells me to do in the Bible. (James 1:22)
3. Spend time with God by praying to Him. I can talk to Him about anything and share my feelings with Him, just like a best friend. (Colossians 4:2,3)
4. Pray and ask God for forgiveness when I sin. (1 John 1:9)
5. Spend time with other Christians at church, Sunday School or Bible clubs. (Hebrews 10:25)
6. Tell others about God and how I accepted Jesus Christ. (Mark 16:15b)

Clip Art
Summer!
Summer!
JULY
AUGUST
JUNE
JUNE
JULY
AUGUST

DAYCARE NURSERY PROVIDED

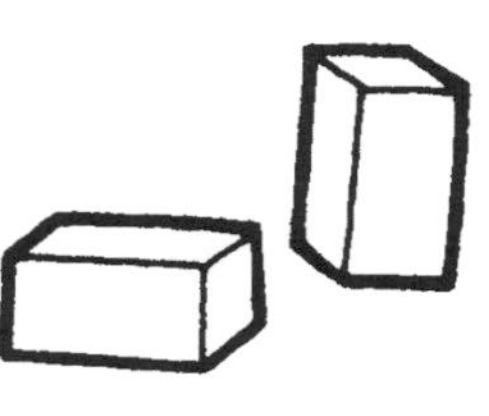

BIBLE

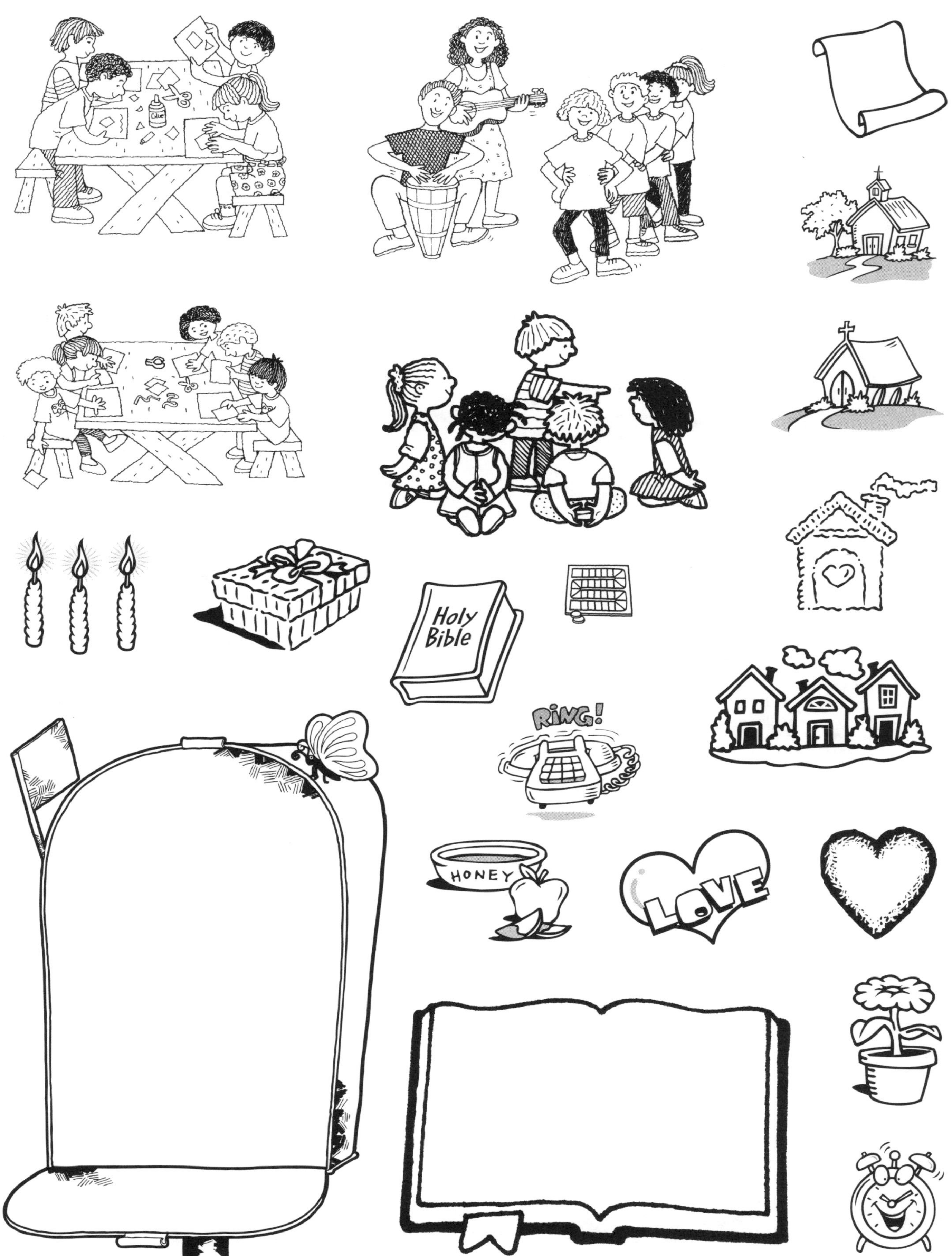
Glue
Holy Bible
RING!
HONEY
LOVE

TEACHERS NEEDED
FOR ALL AGES

TEACHERS NEEDED
FOR ALL AGES

Missions
The World

SIGN
UP!

Helping
Hands

Missions

Sign
Up!

MissionS

Our Mission:
Mission

Volunteers
Needed

Vacation Bible School

Vacation Bible School

Vacation Bible School

Thank You!

Note of Thanks...

NOTE OF Thanks...

BIBLE
MILK

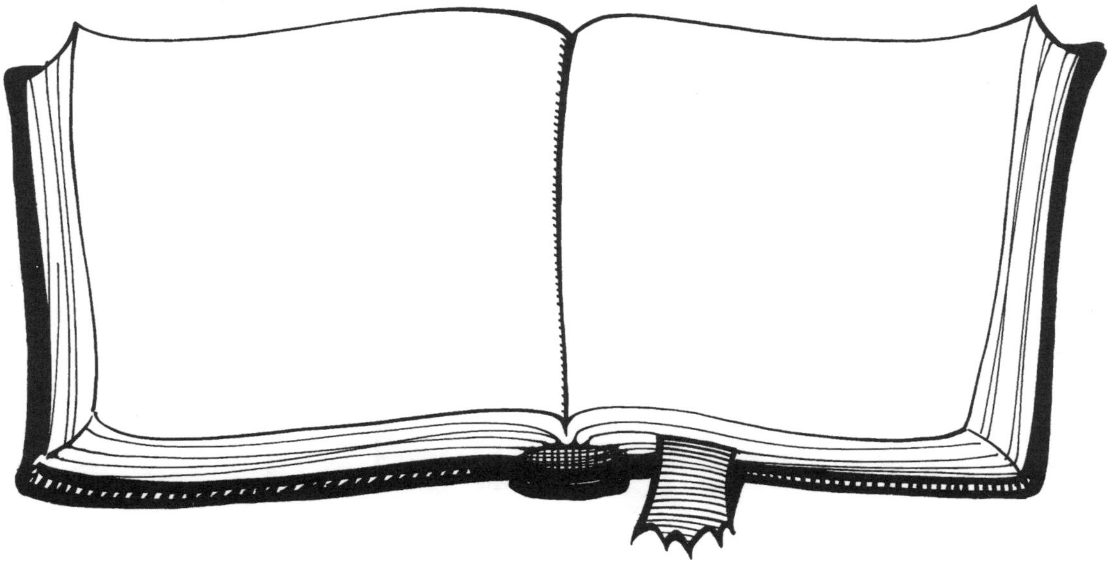

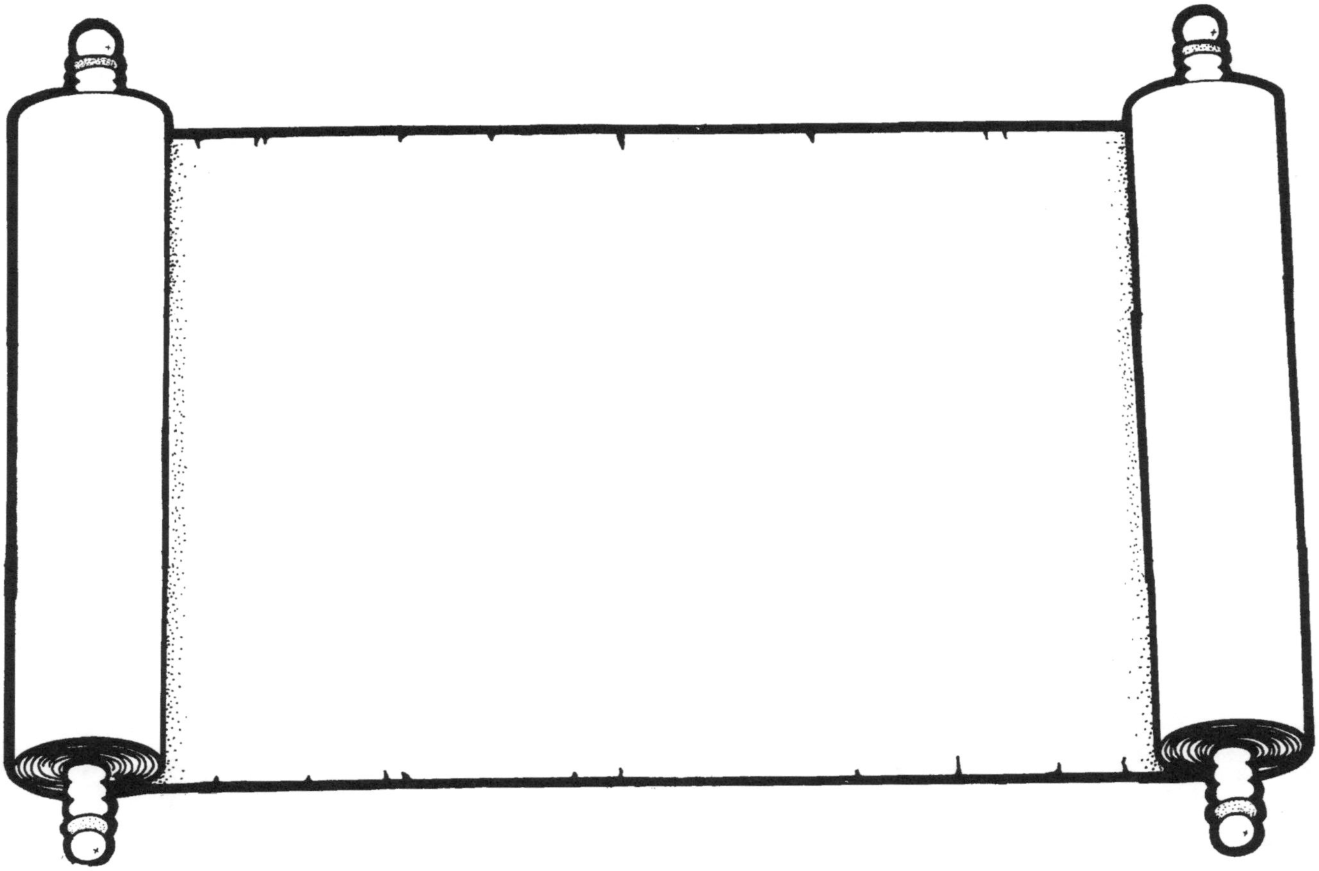

A

B

C

D

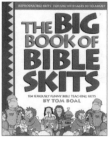

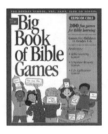

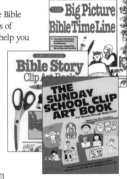